CAMBRIDGE STUDIES IN EARLY MODERN HISTORY

The Cost of Empire

The Cost of Empire is a study of early modern government finance in the kingdom of Naples, one of the most important European dominions of the Spanish Empire. Professor Calabria focuses on the period from the mid-sixteenth century to the time of the Thirty Years' War. He connects fiscal developments to larger issues, such as the seventeenth-century crisis, the decline of Italy and Spain, and the economic and social significance of investments in government securities markets in early modern Europe.

The Cost of Empire blends quantitative data on economic, fiscal and financial affairs with non-quantitative material detailing attitudes, economic behavior and administrative practices. The quantitative material includes analyses of government budgets from 1550 to 1638 and a computer study of about 4,500 investors and their investments in state securities in the later sixteenth century. The work is unrivalled in the breadth, comprehensiveness and sophistication of its analysis of an early modern fiscal system.

CAMBRIDGE STUDIES IN EARLY MODERN HISTORY

Edited by Professor J.H. Elliott, Oxford University, Professor Olwen Hufton, Harvard University and Professor H.G. Koenigsberger

The idea of an "early modern" period of European history from the fifteenth to the late eighteenth century is now widely accepted among historians. The purpose of Cambridge Studies in Early Modern History is to publish monographs and studies which illuminate the character of the period as a whole, and in particular focus attention on a dominant theme within it, the interplay of continuity and change as they are presented by the continuity of medieval ideas, political and social organization, and by the impact of new ideas, new methods and new demands on the traditional structures.

For a list of titles published in the series, please see end of book

The Cost of Empire

The Finances of the Kingdom of Naples in the Time of Spanish Rule

Antonio Calabria

Associate Professor of History, University of Texas, San Antonio

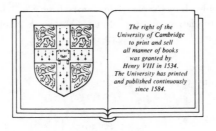

The right of the
University of Cambridge
to print and sell
all manner of books
was granted by
Henry VIII in 1534.
The University has printed
and published continuously
since 1584.

CAMBRIDGE UNIVERSITY PRESS

Cambridge
New York   Port Chester
Melbourne   Sydney

Published by the Press Syndicate of the University of Cambridge
The Pitt Building, Trumpington Street, Cambridge CB2 1RP
40 West 20th Street, New York, NY 10011, USA
10 Stamford Road, Oakleigh, Melbourne 3166, Australia

First published 1991

Printed in Great Britain at the University Press, Cambridge

British Library cataloguing in publication data

Calabria, Antonio
The cost of empire: the finances of the Kingdom of Naples
in the time of Spanish rule. – (Cambridge studies in early
modern history)
1. Italy. Naples (Kingdom). Finance, history
I. Title
332.094573

ISBN 0–521–39176–8

Library of Congress cataloguing in publication data

Calabria, Antonio
    The cost of empire: the finances of the kingdom of Naples in the
time of Spanish rule/Antonio Calabria.
    p.   cm. – (Cambridge studies in early modern history)
Includes bibliographical references.
ISBN 0-521-39176-8
    1. Finance, Public–Italy–Naples (Kingdom)–History. 2. Naples
(Kingdom)–Appropriations and expenditures–History. 3. Naples
(Kingdom)–History–Spanish rule, 1442–1707.   I. Title.
II. Series.
HJ1188.N36C35   1990
336.45′7–dc20   90-1503   CIP

ISBN 0 521 39176 8

SE

iv

Contents

Figures

List of figures

Appendix I

Acknowledgments

This book is the revised version of a doctoral dissertation written at the University of California, Berkeley. In the course of the years which this project has taken, I have accumulated many debts, which I would like here to acknowledge.

The dissertation research received funding from several organizations, and I express my gratitude to them in this more public forum than the thesis: the University of California, Berkeley; the Mabelle McCloud Lewis Memorial Fund, Stanford University; the Istituto Italiano per gli Studi Storici in Naples, and the Fondazione Einaudi in Turin.

But the book would never have seen the light without the generous Fulbright Senior Research Grant I received in 1983. That grant allowed me to return to the archives and to bring back a large quantity of microfilm, some of which I have put to use in this work. The task of securing microfilm was made easier also by a faculty research grant from the University of Texas, San Antonio.

Needless to say, I thank the personnel of all the archives and libraries I visited in my search for documents. I take special pleasure, however, in remembering the great Archivo General de Simancas, that jewel among archives, and the many archivists who make it such a pleasure to work there, in particular Doña Ascensión de la Plaza Santiago, the director, and Doña Adela González Vega. At the Archivio di Stato in Naples, I thank especially the director and *dottori* Biagio Ferrante and Sergio Masella.

I would like to express my gratitude also to a number of people whose help has been important in various ways over the years. First and foremost are my teachers at Berkeley, Gene Brucker and Randolph Starn, who were my mentors and who became my models. I was very much inspired also by Giorgio Spini, whom I was fortunate enough to meet at a formative point in my development as a historian, while still at Berkeley. To Giuseppe Galasso, who revitalized the writing of the history of Naples, I owe a greater debt than I can say. He supported my work from the very beginning, and he has been more than generous with his time and his help, both of which have been decisive on many occasions. Salvo Mastellone and the late Ernesto Sestan encouraged my research at an early stage; Engel Sluiter first introduced me to the field of early modern public finance in a seminar I took from him at Berkeley a long time ago.

In Naples, I profited from conversations with the many good friends I made while at the Istituto Italiano per gli Studi Storici: Gian Mario Anselmi, Nicola Auciello, Anna Bozzo, Gérard Delille, Eluggero Pii, Anna Maria Rao. Over the years, they have provided me with friendship, hospitality, and good cheer in Naples and other cities in Italy, as have Giovanni Vitale, Eugenio and Dede Alacevich and all the "amici del Castello." I have enjoyed a good friendship also with three other specialists of the history of Naples, Roberto Mantelli, John Marino and Giovanni Muto, whom I thank for their helpful suggestions and criticisms.

Several people read earlier versions of this work, or helped in various ways to improve it. I thank Woodrow Borah, Helmut Koenigsberger, Geoffrey Parker, Robert Patch, I.A.A. Thompson, James Tracy, Modesto Ulloa, Jan de Vries, Claudia Vultaggio and, in particular, Domenico Sella. I am grateful to Richard Fisher for handling my manuscript at Cambridge University Press with great courtesy and efficiency and to Margaret Jull Costa for her expert and invaluable editorial suggestions.

My gratitude goes also to some friends and colleagues closer to home for their support. First among them, ever since my first year at Berkeley, has been David LoRomér, more a brother than a friend. John Martin has shared his impressive knowledge of Italian history with me and helped make up for the relative isolation of the last few years. Woodruff Smith has been more than generous with his time and expertise, and he has helped greatly to strengthen this book, which he read and commented upon at every stage.

I thank also Gilberto Miguel Hinojosa, who has added a sparkle to everyday life, and Skip Gosling, who encouraged me to computerize the data I have used in the last chapter of this work and who helped me take my first steps into computer literacy. Ray Gay designed and perfected the format for entering the data on investors on a mainframe computer and was unstinting in his aid. Neil Helgeson and Gary Pinnell put their vast knowledge of hardware and software at my disposal and were prodigal with help and advice. Mary Elizabeth Lennon did the intricate computer work for chapter 5 of this work with patience and skill. Elisa Valderas Jiménez, Martha LaRoque and Juana Smith have been of great help over the years, with typing and computer advice, with cheerfulness and great efficiency.

My dear wife, Dian Degnan, a historian in her own right, has borne the enterprise of Naples with patience and good humor, and she has been constant in her devotion, encouragement, and good advice. She has also saved me from committing many errors in this book, best left unmentioned. Silverio and Maria Loreta, Dean and Cynthia Anthony and Stephen Degnan all have contributed to the outcome of this venture. I remember, too, "the boys," Pucci and Polly, and the late Joseph Pandolfo for the affection and good cheer they have provided. My mother, Concetta Alibrandi Calabria, has helped in countless ways over many years, and it is to her and to the dear memory of my father, Salvatore Calabria, that I dedicate this work.

Abbreviations

ADPR	Archivio Doria Pamphilj, Rome
AGS	Archivo General, Simancas
ASN	Archivio di Stato, Naples
BCR	Biblioteca Casanatense, Rome
BNM	Biblioteca Nacional, Madrid
BNN	Biblioteca Nazionale, Naples
BPUG	Bibliothèque Publique et Universitaire, Geneva
BSNSP	Biblioteca della Società Napoletana di Storia Patria, Naples
HHStA	Haus-, Hof-, und Staatsarchiv, Vienna
IVdDJ	Instituto de Valencia de Don Juan, Madrid

ASI	*Archivio Storico Italiano*
ASPN	*Archivio Storico per le Province Napoletane*
NRS	*Nuova Rivista Storica*
RSI	*Rivista Storica Italiana*

c., cc.	carta, carte
F., Ff.	fascio, fasci
f., ff.	folio, folios
leg.	legajo
n.d.	no date

Weights and measures[1]

$acino = \frac{1}{20}$ *trappese* = 0.045 grams
botte = 12 *barili* = 523.5 liters
cantaro = 100 *rotoli* = 89.10 kilograms
carro = 36 or 48 *tomoli*
libbra = 12 *oncie* = 320.76 grams
oncia = 30 *trappesi* = 26.73 grams
rotolo = 1,000 *trappesi* = 0.891 kilograms
salma = 16 *staia* = 147.31 kilograms
staio = 10.333 *rotoli* = 9.207 kilograms
$sterlino = \frac{1}{20}$ *oncia* $= \frac{1}{360}$ *libbra* = 0.891 grams
tomolo = 30 to 40 *rotoli* = 26.73 to 35.64 kilograms (for bread)[2]; 55.3 liters

---

[1] For the following units and their metric equivalents, cf. Carlo Afan de Rivera, *Tavole di riduzione dei pesi e delle misure delle Due Sicilie* (Naples, 1840), pp. 21–22; Ronald E. Zupko, *Italian Weights and Measures from the Middle Ages to the Nineteenth Century* (Philadelphia, 1981); Catello Salvati, *Misure e pesi nella documentazione storica dell'Italia del Mezzogiorno* (Naples, 1970); Renato Urga, "La privativa del tabacco nel Napoletano durante il Viceregno," *Studi in onore di R. Filangieri* (Naples, 1959), vol. 2, pp. 551–72; Luigi De Rosa, *Studi sugli arrendamenti del Regno di Napoli. Aspetti della distribuzione della ricchezza mobiliare nel Mezzogiorno continentale (1649–1806)* (Naples, 1958), p. 2; p. 33, n 1.
[2] ASN. *Sommaria. Consulte*, vol. 11, f. 54v and vol. 13/1, f. 268v.

Monetary units and exchange rates

MONETARY UNITS

The basis of the Neapolitan monetary system was the ducat, a gold coin whose content is reported to have been 66 *acini* of fine gold, the equivalent of 10 Italian *lire* of 1914.[1] The ducat was used as money of account: apparently, it was always rated at 10 *carlini*, even when its official exchange value was set at a higher rate.[2] The *scudo*, a gold coin struck in 1538 and weighing 3.3858 grains of gold was also used as money of account; it too was rated at 10 *carlini* even though its legal exchange value was 11 *carlini* until 1542, 11.5 *carlini* from 1543 and 13 *carlini* in 1583.[3]

The most important subdivision of the ducat was the *carlino*, a silver coin used as money of account and serving as an intermediary between large-scale or international payments and daily transactions.[4] In its silver subdivisions, the *carlino* was rated as ½ *tarì* = 10 *grana* = 20 *tornesi*.[5] In the second half of the fifteenth century, 86.55 *carlini* were struck per *libbra* (Neapolitan pound) of silver; from 1510 to 1554, the coin was devalued in weight by 23.89 percent, in the following manner:[6]

Year	*Carlini* per *libbra* of silver
1510	87.35
1516	92.35
1542	100.00
1552	105.00
1554	107.23

From 1554 to 1610, the *carlino* underwent no apparent alteration; in 1582 and 1583, however, half- and quarter-*carlini* were struck on the basis of 116.13 *carlini*

---

[1] Renato Urga, "La privativa del tabacco," p. 552, n. 2.

[2] Giuseppe Coniglio, *Il Regno di Napoli al tempo di Carlo V* (Naples, 1951), p. v. On the whole question of Neapolitan coinage, especially from a numismatic point of view, cf. L. Dell'Erba, "La riforma monetaria angioina e il suo sviluppo storico nel Reame di Napoli" in *ASPN*, 1932, pp. 195–206; 1933, pp. 5–66; 1934, pp. 39–136; 1935, pp. 46–153.

[3] Ginseppe Galasso, *Economia e società nella Calabria del Cinquecento* (Naples, 1967), pp. 217–218.

[4] *Ibid.*

[5] Coniglio (*Il Regno*, p. v) reports that the *grano* was struck in silver in 1572 and in copper in 1630. Before 1630, Coniglio writes, the *grano* was indicated in accounts but it was not correlated to specie. In small payments, the copper subdivisions of the *grano* were used (1 *sestino* = 2 *cavalli* = ⅙ *tornese* = 1/12 *grano*; the *doppio cavallo* [= 2 *cavalli*] and the *tre cavalli* [= 3 *cavalli*] were also used).

[6] Galasso, *Economia e società*, p. 218.

xiii

per *libbra*. This maneuver amounted to an effective devaluation of the *carlino* of 34.18 percent with respect to the second half of the fifteenth century.[7] It involved a reduction in fineness of the *carlino* from 67.5 to 62 *acini* of silver.[8]

No official devaluation affected Neapolitan coinage from 1591 to 1611 and from 1622 to 1691. Yet of all the currencies on the foreign exchange markets with which the Kingdom had relations over the period 1591–1707, Naples' was the only one to undergo serious alterations.[9] In 1611, the Mint struck silver coins of 3 *cinquine* or (1½ *carlini*) on the basis of the weight of the half-*carlino* issued in 1583.[10] The next devaluation, in July 1617, was more serious: the Mint issued coins of 4, 6, and 12 *carlini* on the basis of the weight of the half-*carlino* struck in 1583, but with a decrease in fineness of 15½ *sterlini* per *libbra*.[11] With respect to the *carlino* current before 1611, the decrease in weight imported a devaluation of 8.4 percent; the decrease in fineness, a devaluation of 7.5 percent. In 1611, then, the currency had been devalued by 15.9 percent.[12] In July 1618, the coins of 3 *cinquine* were decreased in weight from 62 to 56 *acini* of silver, so that with respect to the 3 *cinquine* of 1611, a devaluation of 11.91 percent obtained, despite the fact that the 1618 coins showed an improvement in fineness of 3.5 *sterlini* per *libbra*. In 1620, the currency was again devalued, so that by that year the cumulative devaluation, with respect to the pre-1611 rate, amounted to 33.1 percent.[13] The cumulative devaluations can be expressed as in the following table:

Year	Cumulative Devaluation (%)
1611	8.40
1617	15.90
1618	20.31
1620	33.10

EXCHANGE RATES FOR THE NEAPOLITAN DUCAT[14]

Spain

1 ducat = 0.8333333 Castilian ducat (1563; 1575)[15]
0.824242 Castilian ducat (1575)[16]

[7] *Ibid.*, p. 218.
[8] Luigi De Rosa, *I cambi esteri del Regno di Napoli dal 1591 al 1707* (Naples, 1955), p. 33, n. 1.
[9] *Ibid.*, p. 26. Sicily had a devaluation of 9.432 percent in 1609 and Rome one of 4.7 percent in 1648. Florence witnessed no variation in the title or weight of its currency in that period, and Spain saw no reduction in the *peso* of 8 *reales*, that basis of foreign exchanges (*ibid.*, pp. 34–35).
[10] *Ibid.*, p. 332.   [11] *Ibid.*, p. 333.   [12] *Ibid.*, p. 333.   [13] *Ibid.*, p. 34.
[14] The following exchange rates are reported or worked out from different types of transactions, descriptions and valuations. That variety is one of the factors in the fluctuations in the value of the Neapolitan ducat.
[15] ASN. *Sommaria. Consulte*, vol. 2, f. 25r (25 October 1563); vol. 4, f. 47v (27 May 1575), vol. 5, ff. 119r–121r (27 July 1575). The ducat at Barcelona was worth the same amount (1561; *ibid.*, vol. 1, f. 254v, 24 May 1561).
[16] AGS. *Estado*, leg. 1068, f. 4, 10 January 1575: "A razon que por cada ducado que paga en napoles de a

0.8264462 Castilian ducat (1576)[17]
0.824242 Castilian ducat (1582)[18]
0.7675486 Castilian ducat (1592)[19]
0.8356313 Castilian ducat (1607–08)[20]
0.6926406 Castilian ducat (1618–20)[21]

Italy

1 ducat =	2.7	Sicilian *once* (1586)[22]
	1	Venetian ducat (1563)[23]
	0.9090909	Florentine florin (1575)[24]
	9.5238095	Roman *giuli* (1593)[25]
	10	Roman *giuli* (1594)[26]
	60–66.67	Genoese *soldi* (1617–18)[27]

Germany

1 ducat = 1.3333333 florins (1582)[28]

---

diez carlines y de a diez granos por carlin se haze pagar en sicilia diez Reales castellanos que cada real vale onze de los dhos granos. . .").

[17] AGS. *Secretarías Provinciales*, leg. 3, unfol. ("Su Mag.d ha hecho mrd" [30 October 1576; a grant of 800 Castilian ducats to the Genoese merchant banker Stefano de Mari]), and leg. 3, unfol. ("Nos que aqui bajo firmamos" [5 November 1576; affidavit signed in Madrid by the financiers Niccolò Grimaldi, Baldassar Cattaneo, Ettore Piccamiglio, Agostino Spinola, Antonio Serra and Bernabò Centurione, which calculated the value of De Mari's pension at 968 Neapolitan ducats]).

[18] BPUG. Collection Favre, vol. 33, f. 45r ("cada carlin de moneda de Napoles vale diez granos cada onze granas hazen un Real Cast.no." If 1 *real* = 34 *maravedís* and 1 Castilian ducat = 375 *maravedís*, 1 Neapolitan ducat, or 100 *grana*, = 9.0909 *reales*, or 309.0909 *maravedís*, or 0.824242 Castilian ducats).

[19] ASN. *Sommaria. Consulte*, vol. 4, f. 143v (29 October 1592); 20,053 Castilian *reales* = 2,368.76 Neapolitan ducats.

[20] *Ibid.*, vol. 30, f. 206r (*consulta* dated 13 July 1623).

[21] AGS. *Estado*, leg. 1884, f. 105, c. 13r on (cf. Antonio Calabria, *State Finance in the Kingdom of Naples in the Age of Philip II* (Ph.D. dissertation, University of California, Berkeley, 1978), pp. 369–73). It may be that the Sommaria did not take into account the devaluations effective from 1611 on (cf. Antonio Calabria, *State Finance in the Kingdom of Naples in the Age of Philip II* (Ph.D. dissertation, University of California, Berkeley, 1978), pp. 369–73).

[22] ASN. *Sommaria. Consulte*, vol. 9, ff. 33r–v (17 February 1586). On Sicilian coins, cf. Koenigsberger, p. 200.

[23] ASN. *Sommaria. Consulte.*, vol. 2, f. 16r (18 May 1563): "quali ducati de moneta venetiana comonementi se valutano al pari con li ducati correnti di questo Regno," and f. 29v (20 December 1563).

[24] *Ibid.*, vol. 5, ff. 124r–126v (31 October 1575): "perche ogni nove reali florentini valeno per dieci reali del Regno").

[25] But 11.11111 – 12.5 *giuli* from localities in the Papal States such as Bologna, Urbino and the Marche (*ibid.*, vol. 1, f. 298r [15 December 1593]).

[26] Ten *giuli* also from Fano, Macerata, Ancona and Urbino but 11.764705 *giuli* from Bologna; 3.2786885 *testoni* of 3 *giuli* from Rome, Ancona, Fano, Macerata, Urbino and Florence, but 3.8461538 Bologna *testoni* "if new" and 3.4482758 "if old." (*ibid.*, vol. 13/1, ff. 298r–299v and vol. 14, ff. 95r–97r; 27 May 1594).

[27] *Ibid.*, vol. 27, ff. 49r–v (30 June 1618). According to this document, in November 1617 the ducat had traded variously at 63 Genoese *soldi* in "moneta cartularia" and at 66.667 *soldi*, apparently in specie. After that date, however, it traded "at less than 60 *soldi*."

[28] BPUG. Collection Favre, vol. 33, f. 52r.

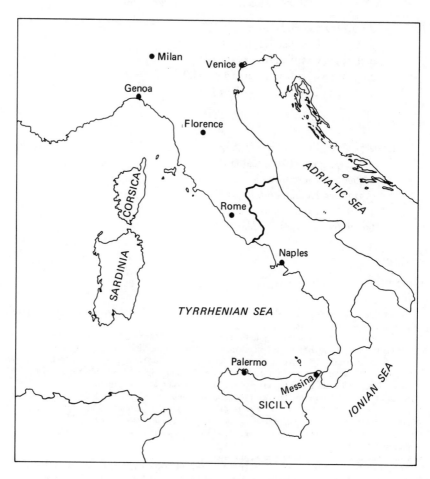

Map 1 General map of Italy

Map 2 The twelve provinces of the Kingdom of Naples, adapted from *Italia*, Giovanni Antonio Magini (Bologna, 1620)

Introduction

In the fifteenth century, the winds of change that were transforming kingdoms and principalities in Western Europe swept also over the Kingdom of Naples. Under the leadership of King Alfonso the Great, the Aragonese dynasty wrested control of the Kingdom from the Angevins in 1442 and embarked on a remarkable course of state-building that strengthened and renewed the power of the Monarchy. The Aragonese rulers succeeded in abating the force of an adventurous and unruly nobility and in refurbishing the Kingdom's institutions. Like many states in the North, Naples thus acquired the rudiments of a state army, a viable fiscal organization and a relatively effective bureaucracy. The royal reforms served also to stimulate productive activities, not least because of the social truce they assured. Partly as a consequence, the Kingdom came to witness economic expansion and demographic growth. Its capital, the city of Naples, was rapidly transformed into a full-scale administrative center; it came to serve as well as a magnet for growing numbers of immigrants from areas nearby and far afield alike. Overly rapid growth, to be sure, brought its own problems, but the tears in the fabric of the Kingdom, heritage of the preceding turbulent century, mended, and by the later fifteenth century Naples was one of the most important and populous members of the Renaissance state system.

A century and a half later, that process of construction, and reconstruction, had run its course. A new, difficult chapter had begun for the Kingdom; "crisis" and "decline" were to be important themes in it.

Despite recurrent famine and plague, the city of Naples was the most populous urban center in Europe, but its growth had long since grown cancerous, marked by runaway parasitism and pauperization. Economic activities still showed resiliency, in part no doubt because of the prevailing localism and particularism. Even so, however, the signs of crisis were everywhere. Ever since the 1580s, bad harvests and the attendant famines had become a fixture in the Kingdom and had led to a contraction in the production of grain. Sicilian wheat had to be imported to provision the capital at more frequent intervals and in greater quantities than ever before. At the same time, thousands of hectares of land were transferred from agriculture to stock-farming. Though many a fortune was made in transhumance, that transfer highlighted a shift in the Neapolitan economy, one borne out by all other economic indicators. The silk trade in Calabria, the primary silk-growing

I

province in the Kingdom, for example, had been buoyed for most of the later sixteenth century by a steady demand and by many a boom year. At peak times, about 500,000 pounds of silk passed every year through the dry-customs port of Cosenza, the hub of Calabria's silk trade, and it reached not only Naples and the provinces in the Kingdom but Northern Italy as well. By 1655, however, only 116,000 pounds of silk were shipped through Cosenza, and it went only as far as Naples and regional centers in Southern Italy. Some ports did bear witness to adaptation in the face of generalized adversity. The city of Monteleone, for example, saw its silk shipments rise from 22,000 pounds in 1572 to about 330,000 pounds in 1603 and 220,000 pounds in 1655. In the balance, however, the seventeenth century brought about a net loss, a real decline in the silk industry in the Kingdom, as it did in Southern agriculture and economic activities generally.

By 1600, too, public authority in Naples had been heavily compromised, and in the next fifty years it was to yield decisively, once again, to private preserve. Under the Aragonese dynasty, lands in the royal domain had amounted to nearly 7 percent of all properties in the Kingdom. At the end of the sixteenth century, they had shrunk to less than 4 percent. In 1609, Philip III had wanted to grant the Genoese banker Battista Serra the right to send his own agents into the Kingdom, so as to levy the direct taxes that were to repay Serra for his loans to the Crown. In the name of reason of state, the Council of Italy had objected strenuously to the proposed concession, warning that such a measure might touch off a revolt on the part of the venal officeholders. As the 1647–48 uprising was to show, the Council's warning had been prophetic, but it went unheeded before what was soon to become a new policy. By the 1620s, in fact, the bankers' agents themselves collected many of the direct taxes, and in 1648 private receivers were granted all but a few of the royal gabelles, in return for the relatively paltry yearly sum of 300,000 ducats. Thus by the mid-seventeenth century the state apparatus which had been revolutionized in the fifteenth century and consolidated in the sixteenth lay in disarray or in shambles.

Why did the process of state building in Naples come full circle? Why were the modernizing energies tapped by the Aragonese dynasty in the 1450s already spent by the early 1600s? These are important questions, and they invest many of the crucial themes of early modern history – state building or "absolutism," and its limits; the crisis of the seventeenth century; the connection between economic conjunctures and the political process; the decline of Italy and of Spain.

Despite their resonance, though, those questions have not attracted the attention they deserve. In the United States and Britain, students of Italian history have, by and large, restricted their focus to North-Central Italy and the great republics of Florence and Venice, even though the experience of the sixteenth century cut those republics down to size.[1] Students of the Spanish Empire, for their part, have looked

---

[1] Notable recent exceptions are the remarkable books by Domenico Sella, *Crisis and Continuity: The Economy of Spanish Lombardy in the Seventeenth Century* (Cambridge, Mass., 1979), and John Marino, *Pastoral Economics in the Kingdom of Naples* (Baltimore, 1988).

westward from Spain to the Habsburg possessions in the New World. In Italy, ever since the seventeenth century, the question of Spanish rule in Naples has inspired a vast body of literature. For a long time, however, most of it served to fuel a dispute whose vehemence and bitterness has been exceeded only by its sterility, on the "corruptive" effect of Spanish administration.[2] From the lofty vantage point of his idealism, Benedetto Croce was able to view Spanish Naples with some perspective.[3] Not surprisingly, though, Croce's revisionism did not lead to a reformulation of the problems of Imperial history, and his serenity lent itself easily to complacency. Thus, in 1951, Giuseppe Coniglio could hark back to Croce and attempt to exculpate Spain and Spanish rule for the "maladministration" and for the growing fiscal burden that came to weigh upon the Kingdom.[4]

More recent research in Neapolitan history, however, has struck a more promising note. Giuseppe Galasso has made a most notable contribution to the history of the Kingdom in the early modern period with his magisterial publications on economy and society in sixteenth-century Calabria, on Habsburg ideology and statecraft during the rule of Charles V, on the reform attempts of Viceroy Count Lemos in the early seventeenth century.[5] For a long time, Luigi De Rosa has been contributing studies on economic and banking affairs in the Kingdom that have been as distinguished as they have been numerous.[6] Rosario Villari and Vittor Ivo Comparato have greatly increased our understanding of social tensions in town and country before the revolt of 1648,[7] while Gérard Delille has focused with great profit on economic, social, demographic and familial structures in the Kingdom.[8]

---

[2] That literature is reviewed and essentially adopted by Gabriele Pepe in his bristlingly polemical *Il Mezzogiorno d'Italia sotto gli Spagnoli. La tradizione storiografica* (Florence, 1952). For a more balanced discussion, cf. Ernesto Pontieri's essays in *Nei tempi grigi della storia d'Italia* (Naples, 1966).

[3] In *La Spagna nella vita italiana durante la Rinascenza* (Bari, 1917) and *Storia del Regno di Napoli* (Bari, 1925).

[4] Giuseppe Coniglio, *Il Regno di Napoli al tempo di Carlo V* (Naples, 1951). Despite this criticism, it must be stressed that with that book, and his many other publications, Coniglio has made a very useful contribution to the history of the Kingdom of Naples in the sixteenth and seventeenth centuries. Among other things, Coniglio was among the first Italian scholars to make use of the vast riches of the Archivo General de Simancas.

[5] Giuseppe Galasso, "Momenti e problemi di storia napoletana nell'età di Carlo V," and "Le riforme del conte di Lemos e le finanze napoletane nella prima metà del Seicento," both originally published in *Archivio storico per le province napoletane* and reprinted, with other essays on the history of Naples from the Middle Ages to modern times, in *Mezzogiorno medievale e moderno* (Turin, 1965); *Economia e società nella Calabria del Cinquecento* (Naples, 1967); *Dal Comune medievale all' Unità. Linee di storia meridionale* (Bari, 1971); *Intervista sulla storia di Napoli* (edited by Percy Allum; Bari, 1978).

[6] See in particular *I cambi esteri del Regno di Napoli dal 1591 al 1707* (Naples, 1955) and *Studi sugli arrendamenti del Regno di Napoli. Aspetti della distribuzione della ricchezza mobiliare nel Mezzogiorno continentale (1649–1806)* (Naples, 1958).

[7] Rosario Villari, *La rivolta antispagnola a Napoli. Le origini (1585–1647)* (Bari, 1967) and *Mezzogiorno e contadini nell'età moderna* (Bari, 1961); Vittor Ivo Comparato, *Uffici e società a Napoli (1600–1647). Aspetti dell'ideologia del magistrato nell'età moderna* (Florence, 1974).

[8] Gérard Delille, *Croissance d'une société. Montesarchio et la Vallée Caudine aux XVIIe et XVIIIe siècles* (Naples, 1973); *Agricoltura e demografia nel regno di Napoli nei secoli XVIII e XIXe* (Naples, 1978); *Famille et propriété dans le Royaume de Naples (XVe–XIXe siècle)*, (Rome, 1985).

Giovanni Muto has illuminated the political and institutional aspects of early modern Neapolitan financial life,[9] while Roberto Mantelli has brought to light important institutional, financial and administrative mechanisms in the Kingdom.[10]

Despite studies of such breadth and obvious interest, though, a history of the Kingdom of Naples which addresses the questions posed above and which seeks to account for change by exploring the connections between the economy, politics and society was yet to be written.

This book attempts to fill that gap by showing that from the late sixteenth century onwards, economic, political and social factors worked together to undermine the basis of Naples' great fifteenth-century achievements. As in Lombardy, plagues, famines and population decline figured prominently in the story of seventeenth-century Naples. The vagaries of international demand took a heavy toll on Naples, as they did, again, on Lombardy. In fact, as Northern Italy saw its overseas export outlets shrink and its industrial base become dislocated, it fell back on its own agriculture, thus reducing or closing its markets for wine, oil, silk, grain and wool to its traditional supplier, the Kingdom of Naples. That drop in demand for Southern agricultural products was as distinctive a feature of Southern Italy as the severe plagues, epidemics and population fall.

In all that, the two Italies shared the same fate. But they parted company in that political, and especially fiscal, pressures in the South were much heavier than in the North. As Domenico Sella has shown, the fiscal pressure imposed on Lombardy did not play a crucial role in restructuring that region's economy. Spanish fiscalism, Sella has cogently argued, did not help matters, but it was neither as intense and sustained nor as deleterious as other writers have insisted.

Naples' story, however, was different. Taxation played at best a secondary role in Lombardy's involution *because* the Kingdom of Naples bore its own weight and Lombardy's as well. In the seventeenth century, as in the sixteenth, Spanish policy deliberately and understandably shifted the costs of war in Italy and, to some extent in Central Europe, from the North to the South, in great part because Lombardy was too near the war theaters and too important a transit point for Imperial troops to be imperiled by harsh taxation. Naples, however, was a different case. Ever since the Spanish conquest, in 1504, it had played a role consonant with its position in the Imperial system and in Spanish strategy. When it was no longer a beachhead for action "against the common enemy of Christendom," it became, and it remained, a vital supply base of money, men and arms for "the defense and security of my Kingdoms and states," as successive rulers from Charles V to Philip IV called their far-flung ventures. War and war finance thus came to loom large over the Kingdom, as over Castile, from the early sixteenth century to the end of the Thirty Years' War.

---

[9] Giovanni Muto, *Le finanze pubbliche napoletane tra riforme e restaurazione (1520–1634)* (Naples, 1980).

[10] Roberto Mantelli, *Burocrazia e finanze pubbliche nel Regno di Napoli* (Naples, 1981) and *Il pubblico impiego nell'economia del Regno di Napoli: retribuzioni, reclutamento e ricambio sociale nell'epoca spagnuola (secc. XVI–XVII)* (Naples, 1986).

Ironically, then, the very forces that in an earlier age had strengthened the Crown's authority and abetted its state building came to serve as a prime motor of dissolution in the sixteenth and seventeenth centuries. As Alan Ryder has shown, in fact, in the fifteenth century warfare had served as a catalyst for much of Alfonso's restructuring of the Neapolitan state, and it had enabled the Aragonese king to break or to loosen the nobility's grip on power in the Kingdom.[11] But the changed nature of warfare in the sixteenth and seventeenth centuries worked mightily to unravel the webs spun by fifteenth-century kings.[12]

War, indeed, imposed many and severe strains on Naples, as it did on Castile. Ever since the 1520s its cost had proved much too burdensome, and from the 1550s it outstripped even the Kingdom's burgeoning tax base and its productive capacities. The Monarchy came thus to be ever pressed for ready cash, squeezed at the same time by rising prices and ever greater commitments. The fiscal screws were turned harshly and repeatedly, but state income was regularly outstripped by expenditure. The Crown was thus forced to resort to deficit financing in a massive and systematic way. In that dizzying process of expense and indebtedness, the Crown came increasingly to rely on obliging but exacting bankers, "whence [Ambassador Bernardo Navagero told the Venetian Senate] has come much wealth for Germans and Genoese and other merchants."[13]

The cost of all that was hard to calculate, for it went beyond the swollen budget deficits to invest the economy, the society and the very structure of state authority in Naples. Genoese bankers came to acquire a stranglehold on finances in Naples, as in Castile, and they added profit to profiteering as they dominated the shipping industry, the export trade, the provisioning of the city of Naples and the fiscal machinery of the state. For their services in Naples and abroad, they were further rewarded with pensions and prebends, with lands, fiscal concessions, and titles of nobility. They passed on to others, whose savings they had "invested," the cost of the Crown's bankruptcies, and by the end of the sixteenth century they held apanages in Naples and Spain.[14]

Loans by merchant bankers, however, were only part of the system through which the Crown raised funds for its war efforts. In the 1540s and 1550s, the Crown was eminently successful in creating in Naples a dynamic market for its securities. It guaranteed those securities by mortgaging its future revenues, and it stimulated a veritable rush onto the government bond market by the relatively high interest rates

---

[11] Alan Ryder, *The Kingdom of Naples under Alfonso the Magnanimous: The Making of a Modern State* (Oxford, 1976).

[12] Cf. Michael Roberts, *The Military Revolution, 1560–1660* (Belfast, 1956); Geoffrey Parker, *The Army of Flanders and the Spanish Road, 1567–1659: The Logistics of Spanish Victory and Defeat in the Low Countries' War* (Cambridge, 1972); I.A.A. Thompson, *War and Government in Habsburg Spain 1560–1620* (London, 1976).

[13] Eugenio Albèri, ed., *Relazioni degli ambasciatori veneti al Senato*, series 1, vol. 1, p. 301 (1546) (Florence, 1839). Cf. also Raffaele Ciasca, ed., *Istruzioni e relazioni degli ambasciatori genovesi*, (Rome, 1951) vol. 1, p. 202.

[14] Cf. Antonio Calabria, "Finanzieri genovesi nel Regno di Napoli nel Cinquecento," *RSI*, 1989, pp. 578–613, and the works there cited.

it paid. In the Netherlands, as James Tracy has shown, the same system was a source of strength, at least in part because of the progressively lower interest the securities bore.[15] But Naples, again, was another story. Credit conditions there, and the Crown's unending need for money, made it so that even at the end of the century, after repeated forced conversions of the debt, redeemable bonds could pay as much as 10 percent interest. Lifeterm annuities were no less than a windfall, for they paid on the average 13 and sometimes as much as 20 percent!

The effects of such policies were clear even before 1600. State securities syphoned off massive amounts of capital from growing numbers of investors – Neapolitans and foreigners, nobles and merchants, state officials and religious institutions. By the 1590s, investment in state securities worked like a magnet in Neapolitan society. It attracted several times the capital than even a generation earlier and a broader range of investors – a very wealthy few, with perhaps hundreds of thousands of ducats in capital investments; a sizable middle group, with several thousand ducats; and a growing mass of small fry, with 100, 50 or even less than one ducat. At the same time, cash-crop farmers could obtain credit only under the harsh *alla voce* system. In the 1580s and 1590s, they were being driven into bankruptcy or peonage-like indebtedness by high interest rates and non-existent profits, and land was taken out of cultivation and given over to grazing.[16]

Because of its financial straits, then, the Crown came in part to compete with enterprise in the Kingdom. The state and enterprise alike in the later sixteenth century were caught in a much wider movement which ran like a fever through society and of which investment in state securities, the flight from risk-taking and the rush to land and titles were clear symptoms. Then, in the 1620s and 1630s, as the flames of war raged anew over Central Europe and consumed ever growing amounts of money from the Kingdom, as the economy faltered and society stagnated, the forces that in an earlier age had impelled or abetted modernization spent themselves or were even reversed.

This book discusses such themes in five chapters. The first sketches economic trends in the Kingdom in the sixteenth and the seventeenth centuries. It examines productive structures, with their strengths and their liabilities over the long term. It focuses on the "Indian summer" buoyancy of the sixteenth-century economy and assesses the impact of the seventeenth-century crisis, using a variety of indicators, the silk trade in Calabria in particular.[17] Thus the first chapter sets the economic context for the rest of the volume, and subsequent chapters show whether or to what

[15] James Tracy, *A Financial Revolution in the Habsburg Netherlands* (Berkeley, 1985).
[16] Silvio Zotta, "Momenti e problemi di una crisi agraria in uno 'stato' feudale napoletano (1585–1615)," *Mélanges de l'Ecole Française de Rome*, 1978, pp. 715–96.
[17] The Calabrian silk trade is approached through a sample series of twenty-three registers by fiscal officials (*credenzieri*), which record the day-by-day movement of silk through dry-customs ports in the sixteenth and seventeenth centuries (ASN. *Sommaria. Arrendamenti*, F. 161/II ff.). Additional summary registers provide yearly figures, with some gaps, until 1759. That material makes up a data base of over 7,000 cases for computer analysis, and it will be the object of a forthcoming study.

degree those realities were reflected or ignored by fiscal developments in the sixteenth and seventeenth centuries.

Chapter 2 then presents an analysis of the fiscal system in the Kingdom in the early modern period. It focuses on elements of continuity and change in taxation and fiscal administration, and it examines the innovations that Spanish rule brought to Naples. Thus in addition to the several sources of tax revenue which Spain found and kept unchanged in the Kingdom, the chapter treats the loan system and the introduction of a market for securities in the Kingdom in the 1540s and 1550s.

Chapters 3 and 4 analyze government income and government expense in the Kingdom from 1550 to 1638. Those chapters are heavily quantitative, and they place the data for both income and expenses in the context of the price movement in the Kingdom. Both are based on a remarkable series of budgets and of fiscal reports, spaced at intervals of five to thirteen years. Such sources are eminently suited to measure both continuity and change in receipts and outlay for a period that, until now, has been approached by historians in a descriptive or fragmentary fashion.

Chapter 5 focuses on the establishment of a government bond market in the Kingdom and on its fortunes from the 1540s to the late 1590s. It summarizes some of the conclusions of a larger forthcoming study on investors and investments in the public debt in the Kingdom, generalizing on the basis of a computer analysis of a very large body of data, over 8,000 transactions for the sale of securities to about 4,500 investors.

A conclusion and two appendices follow the body of the work. The conclusion summarizes some of the results of this book, while the first Appendix presents tables for the figures in the text and graphs for some economic indicators and for the finances of the city of Naples in the late sixteenth and early seventeenth centuries. The second Appendix, intended for specialists, discusses in some detail the intricate problems presented by the quantitative sources for the core chapters.[18]

This study, however, is not simply based on quantitative sources. It has profited also from a wide range of other materials from several archives. Of great usefulness have been manuscripts from the National Libraries in Madrid and Naples, the Archivio Doria Pamphilj in Rome and the Haus-, Hof-, und Staatsarchiv in Vienna, and the Collection Favre at the Bibliothèque Publique et Universitaire in Geneva. Especially important have been the proverbially rich series of papers from *Estado, Visitas de Italia* and *Secretarías Provinciales* at the great Archivo General in Simancas and some equally fruitful but (at least in the United States) largely unknown series in the State Archive in Naples.

An invaluable source has been the great collection of documents drafted by the Sommaria, Naples' counterpart to the Castilian Consejo de Hacienda. The

---

[18] In the event that even more explanations about the sources should be required, the reader can consult Calabria, *State Finance.* Also useful, for methodological purposes and for a sense of the difficulties the sources can present to the unwary, is Antonio Calabria, "Per la storia della dominazione austriaca a Napoli, 1707–1734," *ASI,* 1981, pp. 459–77.

Introduction

Sommaria's output is as informative as it was prolific – its *Notamenti, Partium, Arrendamenti* and *Dipendenze* sections alone could provide significant materials to teams of scholars for several lifetimes. This book has made particular use of the Sommaria's *Consulte*, the series of synthetic reports which that magistracy's indefatigable personnel prepared for the Viceroys and which Professor Galasso, starting almost thirty years ago, first brought to the attention and the benefit of historians.

The early modern Southern Italian economy

The Kingdom of Naples [Ambassador Paolo Tiepolo told the Venetian Senate in 1563] is a rather large and reasonably inhabited country; fruitful and abundant in many crops, especially in wheat, not only for its own use but also for many other areas. . .[1]

Ambassador Tiepolo's sanguine description of the Neapolitan Kingdom attested to the lively expansion of Southern Italian agriculture, to the "Indian summer" buoyancy of the Italian economy after the 1550s.[2] Even more, though, the Venetian ambassador's statement echoed a theme – that of the unbounded fertility of the Southern Kingdom – that was as common as it was to prove durable in early modern descriptions of the Kingdom of Naples.

Some time after Tiepolo's report to the Venetian Senate, in fact, when the signs of economic difficulty in Southern Italy were becoming ever more apparent, a "Delectable and Useful Discourse of the Things that are in the Kingdom of Naples" could still wax rhapsodic about Naples' riches:

This Kingdom produces. . .all things needed not only to sustain the life of men, but also to bring them ease and pleasure – truly a rare thing [the author of the "Discourse" proclaimed] and one which I think is not to be found in any other Kingdom of which we have news. For it produces grain, barley, legumes, oil, wine, almonds. . .saffron. . .and silk not only for its own needs but also to give to other countries in great quantity, as it does in abundance, for a million in gold, with much utility for the people of the Kingdom and for the King. . .[3]

Naples, the "Discourse" continued,

has. . .great quantity of livestock of every sort, for its own use, and to give to others. . .[as well as] beautiful and good horses, which are deemed more apt for war than whatsoever other horses of whatsoever other country, and most beautiful mules.[4]

---

[1] Albèri, ed., *Le relazioni degli ambasciatori veneti al Senato*, series, 1, vol. 5, p. 10 (Florence, 1861).

[2] The phrase "Indian summer" to characterize the Italian economy in the 1550s is Carlo M. Cipolla's (cf. his *Storia dell'economia italiana. Saggi di storia economica* [Turin, 1959], vol. 1, p. 17. It is also used by Galasso in his "Momenti e problemi," in *Mezzogiorno medievale e moderno*, pp. 172–173.

[3] AGS. *Visitas de Italia*, leg. 23/3, f. 98r. The discourse is undated. Internal evidence (ff. 113v–114r) suggests that it may have been composed in the 1570s. A version of the text (BNM. Ms. 2659, ff. 14r–40v) is to be found just before a summary State of the Royal Patrimony for 1571–72 (*ibid.*, ff. 41r–47v; on States of the Royal Patrimony, cf. Appendix II, below). Parts of the 1575 report to the Venetian Senate by Ambassador Girolamo Lippomano bear striking similarity to the "Discourse" (cf. Albèri, ed., *Relazioni degli ambasciatori veneti al Senato*, series 2, vol. 2, pp. 265–311 [Florence, 1841]).

[4] AGS. *Visitas de Italia*, leg. 23/3, f. 98r.

Because of its "beautiful woods, mountains, valleys and plains," furthermore, the Kingdom

produces most excellent wines. . .and a great quantity of fruit of every kind in every season, and every sort of game, and since it is surrounded by the sea it has great quantity of very good fish.[5]

Besides such commodities "necessary to sustain man's life," and others as well, the Kingdom sported also "things to acquire and to preserve [men's] health," that is to say "baths, geysers and hot sands, which are better and in greater number than in whatsoever other country."[6] And "for the devotion and salvation of the souls of the people," Naples could boast of no less than "three bodies of the twelve Apostles, that is to say, St. Andrew's, St. Bartholomew's and St. Matthew's. . ."[7]

The pride which exudes from the "Delectable and Useful Discourse. . ." attests to the strength of particularism and local patriotism in the Kingdom of Naples while at the same time it weaves and reweaves strands of the myth of a fertile Southern Italy. The power of both emotion and topos was such that the "Discourse" could easily employ glowing tones to describe even clear signs of dysfunction – the migration to the capital of people "egged on by need," and the presence in the city of Naples of an "infinite herd of servants looking for masters."[8]

Only at one point in its description did the "Discourse" sound a less than optimistic note. "All the lands in the Kingdom," the document noted,

are oppressed by very heavy debts, and they have little hope of being able to redeem themselves fully or in part. In general, too, there is very great poverty, so that there can be no hope of getting even a little more out of this Kingdom than at present is gotten, not even if war or plague came, which God forbid.[9]

Plague and war, of course, were to come to Southern Italy in the sixteenth century, and even more so in the seventeenth, and the "very great poverty," of the towns and of the people, was to become even greater as much more was "got out" of that Kingdom than had been the case even when the "Delectable and Useful Discourse. . ." was written. To a whole series of natural disasters, to the blind workings of the "invisible hand" was to be added the heavy cost of an Imperial policy run amok; and that burden was to become harshest at the worst possible moment for the Kingdom.

Obviously, neither Ambassador Tiepolo nor the author of the "Delectable and Useful Discourse. . ." could gaze into the future, at the cost of empire and the fate of Southern Italy. Nor, in all fairness, could either observer be expected to transcend the limits imposed upon him by genre or myth, time or class. Still, signs of difficulties had been noticeable in the Kingdom of Naples as early as the 1530s. By then, people living along the coasts had already been increasingly suffering from

---

[5] *Ibid.*, ff. 97v, 98r.   [6] *Ibid.*, f. 98v.   [7] *Ibid.*, f. 98v.   [8] *Ibid.*, ff. 113v, 112v.
[9] *Ibid.*, f. 101r.

raids by pirates and from the deeds of outlaws and bandits, then growing in numbers. No relief came from the troops stationed in the realm, who engaged in pillaging of their own, or from the public administration, which was riddled with disorder and corruption. And at the very same time the tax burden was rising.[10]

Conjunctural factors played an important role in the difficulties the Kingdom experienced throughout the sixteenth century, and they were to be of vital importance in Naples' seventeenth-century debacle. Beyond them, however, lay dysfunctions of a deeper, structural order, which both Tiepolo and the author of the "Delectable and Useful Discourse. . ." glossed over or obscured. Those dysfunctions had to do with the fragility and tenuousness that lay behind appearances and that, even before Tiepolo's day, were the hallmark of Southern Italian economic life.

Those provinces did not form a unified whole, an interdependent unit knit together by active economic relations. Rather, they appeared, and they were the tip of the Italian peninsula on the South, the Kingdom of Naples presented a diversified but discontinuous appearance, and it exhibited striking contrasts. Inaccessible mountains and fertile, if not numerous plains; often thriving coastal towns and a barren interior; intensively cultivated parcels of land and seemingly limitless, desolate *latifundia*; a glutted capital city and "towns" consisting of only a few hovels – such were the disparate, almost incongruous features of the twelve provinces making up the Kingdom.[11]

Those provinces did not form a unified whole, an interdependent unit knit together by active economic relations. Rather, they appeared, and they were regarded, as compartmentalized parts whose equilibrium could be easily upset.[12] Such a state of affairs reflected, as it reinforced, the great strength of localism and particularism in the Kingdom, and it was traceable to a whole constellation of factors, dictated by nature or wrought by man, which stood as obstacles to cohesiveness and coherence.

Distance and poor communications, the fruit of geography and limited technology, were no doubt the strongest of those obstacles, in the Kingdom as elsewhere in the Mediterranean.[13] From Adriatic ports such as Barletta, a galley took on average six days to reach Calabria and as many Spalato and Ragusa, in Dalmatia; it took ten days for Venice, fifteen for Naples and twenty for Genoa.[14] For transport ships, time flowed much more slowly yet: the merchantmen bringing grain to the city of Naples took as long as three to four months to make the journey from Puglia.[15]

[10] Galasso, "Momenti e problemi," p. 163.
[11] Cf. Fernand Braudel, *La Méditerranée et le monde méditerranéen à l'époque de Philippe II* (Paris, 1966) vol. I, *passim*, esp. Part I. See also Philip Jones' "Italy," Part II of "Medieval Agrarian Society in its Prime" in *The New Cambridge Economic History of Europe*, vol. I, 1966, pp. 340–431.
[12] Galasso, "Le riforme del conte di Lemos" in *Mezzogiorno medievale e moderno*, pp. 217–18, n. 19.
[13] Braudel, vol. I, Part II, pp. 326–47.   [14] ASN. *Sommaria. Consulte*, vol. 3, f. 266r.
[15] IVdDJ, envio 80/574 (4) and (3). The journey could no doubt have been made in less time: in 1597, for example, a ship loaded with grain took only six days to reach Naples from Taranto, admittedly closer to the capital than, say, Barletta or Manfredonia (ASN. *Sommaria. Consulte*, vol. 13/I, f. 396r).

To be sure, given early modern technology, sea travel was relatively fast and cheap. But it was not devoid of problems. Aside from the inevitable risks of storms and shipwrecks, it had to deal with man-made perils as well. Prominent among those, as one might expect, were the forays of pirates and corsairs, Turkish and Christian, free-lancers and organized agents of states.[16]

The Turkish danger was, of course, proverbial, and with good reason it aroused the fear of inhabitants along the coasts and the concern of many a Viceroy in Naples.[17] Turkish corsairs imperiled shipping and settlements from one end of the Kingdom to the other, on the Adriatic as on the Tyrrhenian.[18]

Almost as routinely, though not as frequently or as bloodily, Neapolitan shipping was also the easy prey of Venetian galleys. The *Serenissima*'s war ships would lie in wait for vessels which had left the grain depots of Puglia, bound for the capital or other destinations. The Neapolitan cargo ships, laden with grain, would be hijacked and diverted to Dalmatia, Venice or Corfu. There the precious cargo would be seized, and the empty boats set free. Lengthy negotiations would later attempt to resolve the important matter of "reparations."[19]

Maritime communication, as even such limited examples suggest, had its perils. Venetian terrorism on the Adriatic was one, and it occurred frequently enough to be part and parcel of life at sea.[20] Actually, though, the *Serenissima*'s seizures of

---

[16] Cf. Alberto Tenenti, *Naufrages, corsaires et assurances maritimes à Venise (1592–1609)* (Paris, 1959) and *Venezia e i corsari* (Bari, 1961); Braudel, vol. 2, pp. 190–211 and *passim*.

[17] For but one example, cf. AGS. *Estado*, leg. 1063, f. 18 (20 May 1573).

[18] For a few examples, cf. ASN. *Sommaria. Consulte*, vol. 4, ff. 101r–102r (the case of a grain ship found without crew in April, 1576, off the beach at Termoli, on the Adriatic, with its equipment destroyed "as is usually done by the Turks and other corsairs" [f. 101v]; *ibid.*, ff. 243r–v (five grain boats attacked and one seized in the waters of Porto Ercole, one of the Tuscan garrisons administered from Naples, in December 1576); *ibid.*, vol. 14, ff. 26r–v (Turkish raids on some lands in Calabria in 1594). For a later example, cf. *ibid.*, vol. 46, ff. 178r–180v (the town of Stallatti, in Calabria Ultra, sacked by 22 Turkish galleys in 1644).

[19] For some examples, cf. BPUG. Collection Favre, vol. 62, ff. 91r–108v (1570); ASN. *Sommaria. Consulte*, vol. 5, ff. 127r–136v (1575); vol. 9, ff. 169r–173r, 174r, 340r (1587); vol. 15, ff. 32r–33r (1600). For an example of negotiations, with the involvement of no less a figure than the Pope (for grain belonging to Genoese and seized by Venetians in 1570), cf. AGS. *Secretarías Provinciales*, leg. 3, f. 16 (1574).

[20] To tell the truth, Venice was not alone in its high-handed tactics: Messina too at times seized the cargo of Neapolitan grain ships bound for Naples from Puglia (cf. BPUG. Collection Favre, vol. 15, ff. 130r–v (1579), 142r–v (1580) and ASN. *Sommaria. Consulte*, vol. 13/1, ff. 40r–v, 67v–68r [1591]; vol. 47, ff. 26r–27r [1636 and 1641]. On 29 May 1580, Marc'Antonio Colonna, Viceroy of Sicily, wrote Don Juan de Zuñiga, the Viceroy of Naples: "Siempre hé ordenado al Estradico, y Jurados de Mecina, que no tomen el trigo de ninguna Nave, que de Pulla passare á essa Ciudad, y creame V. Ex.a, que las que han tomado han sido con extrema necessidad, por que como en su provision tienen tan poco cuydado, y no basta el mucho que yo les pongo, vienen à estos terminos. Pero certifico à V. Ex.a que en lo venidero havran de proceder de manera, que se escusen semejantes inconvenientes" [BPUG. Collection Favre, vol. 15, f. 215r]. On 5 July 1580, Colonna struck a more cautious, less bureaucratic note: "Quanto a la desorden que hazen los de Mecina en tomar las naves de trigo que passan por aquel estrecho, yo la tengo por tal, si bien ellos se escusan con sus privilegios y con la necessidad que les aprieta, y assi procurare que en lo venidero a lo menos en mi tiempo no se tomen mas naves" [*ibid.*, f. 247r]). But, as one might expect, those seizures continued: for some evidence from the 1670s, cf. *ibid.*, vol. 50, f. 433r.

Neapolitan grain ships seem like little more than bravado, because Venetian merchants were very deeply and profitably embroiled in a much safer venture, contraband. According to a Venetian witness, "Venetian senators and nobles" boasted that

. . .so beautiful a province as Puglia should, by right, be ours! thanks to our faithful people from Bergamo, we get so much out of it, rightly or wrongly, with and without export licenses, that we derive more profit from it than does Philip [II], especially if we consider the money he spends on the garrisons he keeps there. . .[21]

Girolamo Grimani, also "called Hunchback Grimano," had a lucrative arrangement with the monks of the monastery of Santa Maria, on the Tremiti islands.

Just as I favor the matters of their religion here [the Monastery della Carità in Venice] so must they favor my agents on the Tremiti islands, by letting them export as much grain as possible, as they have always done in the past, to their profit. This is the best way to get grain from Puglia. . .[22]

Under the leadership of their shrewd and watchful Abbot, the Tremiti monks, for their part, lived up to the arrangement.[23] The Court did suspect the monks of contraband

and sent many officials [confided one of the good brothers]. . .but we'd be so kind to them and we'd shut them in the refectory so they'd eat, and we'd serve them good omelets and the best wines we had and other good things, and we'd get them good and drunk. . .and then during the summer they'd fall asleep in the shade, because they'd arrive parched, sweaty and tired. . .

During the winter, on the other hand, the monk continued,

we'd have them dry and warm themselves by the fire, because they came running, thinking they'd catch us in the act, but we had informants, and we were warned of their coming, and while they'd eat and sleep like pigs, shut inside the refectory, we'd load carts and mules and send them off to the beach, where covered vessels would be ready and waiting, each able to take on seven *carra* of grain, and as soon as they were loaded, they'd take off. . .[24]

Not content with suborning officials sent by a worried Court, the monks kept their own troops,

all Lombards, that's who we want, so we can trust them, and we make them swear to be faithful to Our Lady of Tremiti. . .and sometimes the said soldiers, with the excuse that

[21] ASN. *Sommaria. Consulte*, vol. 2, f. 237v.

[22] *Ibid.*, ff. 237v–238r; the two monasteries belonged to the same order.

[23] One merchant alone had paid the abbot 4,000 ducats, agreeing to pay 50 ducats a *carro* for grain which the abbot had secured for 16 ducats a *carro* (*ibid.*, f. 238r). In addition, "every year the Father Abbot gives one beautiful yearling from our stable to the customs official [*mastro portolano*], which he can sell for 200 ducats, and each guard gets more than seventy ducats a year in gifts, but we ship out as much grain as we want. . ." (*ibid.*, f. 238v).

[24] If one of the boats "by misfortune" was stopped, "we'd give [the guard] as much and maybe more than the Court would. . ." (*ibid.*, f. 238v).

they're going hunting or accompanying the muleteers, go stealing, and they commit a thousand crimes, but the Father Abbot is greatly saddened by this. . .[25]

As even this limited example suggests, contraband in the Kingdom of Naples, as no doubt elsewhere, had a protean character. On the one hand, it was probably one of the Kingdom's major export networks and perhaps even, to judge by its incidence and its ubiquity, an important economic link within the Kingdom and between it and the rest of Italy.[26] On the other hand, it could also be a major obstacle – to communication as much as to civil society and to the power of the Crown. As the example of the Tremiti monks and their soldiery makes clear, it could also shade into much more serious lawlessness than "loading forty or fifty mules. . .at night, by the full light of the moon." The good brothers, after all, colluded also with "the kingdom's outlaws and bandits [who] are few, and we leave them on the island. . ."[27]

On the Kingdom's roads and highways, however, outlaws and bandits were indeed many, the dangers they posed more numerous, and the obstacles to communication much sharper, despite the Crown's great effort at road-building early in the sixteenth century.[28] Those hazards were such that grain to provision the capital had to be shipped by sea all the way from the Adriatic ports, despite Turkish corsairs, Venetian galleys and Tremiti monk contrabandists. Highwaymen and bandits, in fact, held sway in the interior, and, try as it might, the state administration was ineffective or powerless against them.[29]

In 1550, a special corps of anti-banditry police was set up with its own funding (about 15–18,000 ducats) and "with a certain number of soldiers on foot and on horse. . .to hunt down and capture the said thieves and bandits."[30] The measure had been dictated by the fact that

---

[25] *Ibid.*

[26] For some of the many examples of contraband, cf. *ibid.*, vol. 4, ff. 21v–27v (1575); vol. 9, f. 447r (1588); vol. 23, ff. 150v–151v (1611); vol. 39, ff. 290v–291r (1636).

[27] *Ibid.*, vol. 2, f. 238v.

[28] On some aspects of the road-building policy, cf. BNN. Ms. xi–B–39, ff. 27r–28r; ASN. *Sommaria. Diversi*, Prima Numerazione, F. 54, ff. 97r–98v, 100r–101v, 102r, 103r–104r, 105r–106r, 107r–108v, 109r–110r, 111r–112r, 113r–114r, 115r–116r, 117r–118r, 119r–120r, 121r–122r, 123r–124r, 125r–126r, 127r–128r, 129r–130r, 131r–v, 132r–133r, 134r, 135r–136r, 137r–138r, 139r–140r, 141r–142r, 143r–v (1563).

[29] On banditry generally, cf. Braudel, vol. 2, pp. 75–94, and Eric Hobsbawm, *Bandits* (New York, 1969). For the Kingdom, cf. Villari's analysis in *La rivolta*, ch. 2, esp. pp. 67–91. Cf. also Nunzio Federico Faraglia, *Il comune nell'Italia meridionale [1100–1806]* (Naples, 1883), p. 180; Giuseppe Pardi, *Napoli attraverso i secoli. Disegno di storia economica e demografica* (Milan, 1924), p. 74, n. 1 and pp. 78–79; Alvise Lando, "Relazione del Regno di Napoli" (1580) in Albèri, ed., *Le relazioni degli ambasciatori veneti al Senato*, ser. 2, vol. 5, p. 469 (Florence, 1858), and the despatches to the Duke of Urbino by his agents in Naples in "Documenti che riguardano in ispecie la storia economica e finanziera del regno levati dal carteggio degli agenti del Granduca di Urbino in Napoli dall'anno 1522 sino al 1622" (in the collection "Narrazioni e documenti sulla storia del Regno di Napoli dall'anno 1522 al 1667," edited by Francesco Palermo in *ASI*, 1846, pp. 201–41 [henceforth cited as "Documenti. . .Urbino"]) esp. despatches # 1, p. 203 (16 July 1522) and # 6, p. 205 (15 August 1567).

[30] BNN. Ms. xi–B–39. f. 21r. On the funding for the repression of banditry, cf. below, chapter 3, *passim*, and Appendix ii, note 23.

. . .the thieves and bandits of the Kingdom had greatly multiplied, and they continually committed very great misdeeds, with murders and robberies on the public roads, and they infested public commerce, and. . .the ordinary officials were not enough to remedy that, so excessively had the insolence, temerity and audacity [of thieves and bandits] increased in committing such public crimes. . .[31]

But the much-trumpeted "barricelli di campagna," the new anti-banditry police, left a great deal to be desired. As one proposal for improving the administration of justice in the Kingdom, the author of the "Delectable and Useful Discourse. . ." suggested that the corps be given not a regular salary,

but rather, so much per criminal, according to his quality, because that way they [the police] would try hard with informants and with their labor to catch them, because it's clear that they are good for nothing and they don't bother hunting down the bandits, thinking that in any case they receive their salary, and it's also clear that they do nothing but ruin the people with their billets, and if they are asked by someone to catch a bandit they want to be paid [extra].[32]

Such exasperation notwithstanding, and perhaps fortunately for early modern Southern Italians, the suggestion in the "Discourse" was not heeded. True, informants were employed, rewards were given for heads of bandits, and as much as 2,000 ducats were allocated for band members suborned to betray their leaders.[33] But the anti-banditry police continued its pursuits with a regularly budgeted salary.

Of course, such repressive measures were meant at best only to "treat" the symptom which banditry represented, not at all its cause, which was the economic and social crisis in the countryside.[34] In the later sixteenth century, as that crisis took on the countenance of full-fledged social warfare, the sums spent on the repression of banditry grew impressively, far above inflation, to as much as 80–85,000 ducats a year.[35]

Officials in Naples could express satisfaction, as did the Sommaria Presidents at the end of the century, at "the good success of the Count of Conversano, whom Your

---

[31] *Ibid.*   [32] AGS. *Visitas de Italia*, leg. 23/3, f. 166r.

[33] The budget for 1589–90 enters the sum of 2,000 ducats ". . .collected from the city of Campo-basso. . .for payment to that person who was to hand over to the Royal Court Ascanio De Fusco, head of the bandits, which then did not happen. . ." (ASN. *Sommaria. Dipendenze*, F. 25. f. 13v).

For some bans against bandits, detailing the names of outlaws, the misdeeds committed by them and the strategies by which bandits were induced to assassinate or capture other band members, cf. AGS. *Visitas de Italia*, leg. 20/6 (bans for the provinces of Terra di Lavoro, Principato Citra and Basilicata, 1563).

[34] For a casual contemporary analysis of the causes of banditry, cf. AGS. *Estado*, leg. 1045, f. 205 ("the outlaws grow in numbers every day. . .and though some are taken, it doesn't seem that they decrease in number. . .many are bandits because of debts, for what they owe the Court as well as private parties, and since they can't pay, they take to the hills in order to avoid going to jail. . .".

[35] ASN. *Sommaria, Dipendenze*, F. 25. The Treasury General's actual budget for 1592–93 (f. 84v) enters 63,130.46 ducats for the repression of banditry. Those expenses were met by the Treasury General itself in Naples; to them must be added the regularly budgeted amount for the payment of the anti-banditry police, whch was administered by tax officials at the local level and which, in 1600, amounted to 21,404 ducats (cf. Appendix I, Table 2). For the way expenses were met and accounted for in the various budgets, cf. Appendix II.

Excellency [the Viceroy] has lately sent to the Abruzzi."[36] But such were only the satisfactions of administrators, in Naples, which were as ephemeral and sporadic as the "successes" they celebrated. The country knew better, even if the categories used to explain banditry and lawlessness were generally stereotypical ones. The author of the "Delectable and Useful Discourse. . .," for example, could easily account for the mayhem in moralistic terms:

In general men [in the Kingdom] are sturdy and fit for labor [he wrote]; they have talent and ingenuity, and if they applied them to the good there wouldn't be as many murders on the roads, or so many false witnesses in the courts, and the jails wouldn't be as full as they are.[37]

Yet even he could not fail to grasp an essential point about the dynamics of bandit groups:

Some attribute all this to the influence of the stars. Others, to the instruction of many barons (to mention only them), who in addition to generally skinning the people make use of some of them to oppress the rest. . .[38]

Given such circumstances, it is not surprising that overland travel should have been considered safe only along certain roads and under certain circumstances. Tax monies collected in the provinces, for example, were sent to Naples only along prescribed itineraries, and then with armed escorts. To do otherwise was to court disaster and justifiably to seem disingenuous. So at least it was with Pietro Pucci, direct tax collector in the province of Capitanata, whose shipment of money to Naples was robbed of 1,200 ducats

in the forest of Sferracavallo, in the territory of Santo Martino [because the shipment] was not brought by the usual and correct route, which is through Ariano and La Tripalda. . .since the said Magnificent Pietro. . .did not order the lands to provide armed escorts as usual,. . .and he did not give the commission for it, because the said Magnificent Pietro declared the road to be safe. . .[39]

Obstacles of various sorts, then – geographical and technological, economic and social – reflected, if they did not help determine, the imbalance and precariousness of economic activities in early modern Naples. A "predominantly agricultural area," the Kingdom also had few and relatively unimportant commercial and industrial centers.[40] The coastal towns of Puglia and Tyrrhenian centers like Gaeta and Capua

---

[36] *Ibid.*, F. 25, the Treasury General's forecast budget for 1592–93, f. 33r.

[37] AGS. *Visitas de Italia*, leg. 23/3, f. 98v.   [38] *Ibid.*   [39] *Ibid.*, leg. 23/1 ("n. 4").

[40] The term is Gino Luzzatto's. See his *Breve storia economica dell'Italia medievale* (Turin, 1959). The term may seem captious or inapplicable, since Italy in the early modern period did not exhibit sharp differentiations between agricultural and "industrial" regions. The term does, however, point to a real difference between Italian regions – between those, on the one hand, that were forced to supplement their agricultural production by imports but profited from banking activities, the carrying trade and the export of local manufactures, and the "predominantly agricultural areas," those, that is, that could export agricultural products but had to rely largely on imports for their manufactures. On this point, cf. Luzzatto's *Storia economica. L'età moderna* (Padua, 1938), vol. 1, pp. 101–02.

did profit from maritime trade. In the interior, L'Aquila had long been important for the production and export of saffron, and Foggia was the principal market for the disposal of raw wool.[41] The Abruzzi, and especially Calabria, were notable silk-growing regions, and the city of Naples was the center of thriving silk manufactures into at least part of the seventeenth century.[42] But in general the industries and manufactures of the Kingdom were neither numerous nor significant. At best, they made up highly localized craft works that were gradually reduced, if not eliminated, in the course of the seventeenth century.[43]

Primarily agricultural and rural, the Kingdom showed the same traits of diversification and discontinuity in the appearance of its agrarian landscape.[44] In fertile areas, where population density was relatively high, or where the vicinity of an active urban market or of a maritime harbor favored trade, property tended to be fragmented and intensively cultivated, by landlords directly or by holders of long-term leases.[45] Such areas, however, were exceptional. For the most part, large property holdings were prevalent, either as noble and ecclesiastical *latifundia* or as private and demanial holdings.[46] Because of the landlords' absenteeism, the inalienability of the rights of usage, and the impossibility of changing the terms of tenure, those areas were generally impervious to technical innovation or to rational exploitation.

That, under the circumstances, the Kingdom should export considerable quantities of agricultural products may seem paradoxical. But that phenomenon was generally a function of low population density and especially of poor rural living standards. In 1580, for example, the Sommaria calculated the daily grain allowance of people in the grain-growing provinces of Abruzzi, Terra di Bari, Capitanata and Basilicata at 6 *tomoli* per person per year, or less than 600 grams of bread a day.[47]

---

[41] Luzzatto, *Storia economica*, vol. 1, pp. 107, 110, and Coniglio, *Il Viceregno di Napoli nel sec. XVII* (Rome, 1955), ch. 2, *passim*.

[42] ASN. *Sommaria. Arrendamenti*, Ff. 161 ff., and Coniglio, *Il Viceregno*, pp. 56, 83–84.

[43] Coniglio, *Il Viceregno*, chs. 2–3, pp. 56–93, esp. pp. 56–61, 79, and Galasso, *Economia e società*, pp. 187, 191, 194. Other products were iron, pitch, linen, cotton, hemp and paper.

[44] Cf. Galasso, *Economia e società*, pp. 138–39, 143, 185.

[45] Luzzatto, *Storia economica*, vol. 1, pp. 107–08.

[46] For useful though general information on such property holdings, cf. Coniglio, *Il Regno*, ch. 2, pp. 21–61.

[47] It did so in order to advise the Viceroy as to the amount of grain for which export licenses could be issued that year (ASN. *Sommaria. Consulte*, vol. 7, f. 204r). According to a Sommaria calculation of 1591, each *tomolo* of grain yielded on the average 33 *rotola* of bread (that is, 30 of white and 36 of ordinary ["comune"] bread [*ibid.*, vol. 11, f. 54v]). If 1 *rotolo* = 0.890997 kg., the daily allowance of ordinary bread per person would amount to about 527 grams.

A report by the Advocate of the Royal Patrimony, dated February 1594, however, argues that "the *tumolo* of grain is at least 40 *rotola*" (*ibid.*, vol. 13/1, f. 268v). That figure would bring the daily allowance per person to about 586 grams. For some perspective on such low figures, cf. Pierre Dockès, *Medieval Slavery and Liberation* (Chicago, 1982; a translation of *La Libération médiévale* [Paris, 1979]), pp. 186–88.

For metric equivalents, cf. Catello Salvati, *Misure e pesi nella documentazione storica dell'Italia del Mezzogiorno* (Naples, 1970), p. 29; Ronald E. Zupko, *Italian Weights and Measures from the Middle Ages to the Nineteenth Century* (Philadelphia, 1981), p. 291.

Still, the products of Neapolitan agriculture – grain and barley, olives and fruit, silk and wine, to mention only the major ones – made for a multiplicity of cultures in the Kingdom, and they lent the countryside its often complex appearance. They also fed an active current of trade throughout the sixteenth century and even beyond. Grain, of course, was the staple of Viceroyal production, consumption and export, reaching markets as far afield as Venice and Andalusia.[48] But, as the author of the "Delectable and Useful Discourse. . ." pointed out, the Kingdom exported a whole variety of other products, for the proverbial "million in gold."[49]

Silk from Calabria reached at least Northern Italy throughout the sixteenth century, as did wool from Puglia.[50] Neapolitan wines, true, did not travel well.[51] In the early 1560s, however, nearly 14 million liters were shipped out of the Kingdom every year and, if nothing else, they provided good cheer for many a Cardinal's table in Rome well into the seventeenth century.[52] The rich oil of the Adriatic provinces was shipped as far away as Bergamo and Milan, Venice and Dalmatia throughout the sixteenth and seventeenth centuries.[53]

Within the Kingdom, however, large markets for the free exchange of agricultural products seem to have been rare.[54] Local markets apparently fulfilled limited functions only, serving primarily those sectors of the population that were not associated with a landlord's family or clientele. In most provinces of the Kingdom, after all, the whole population was directly tied to the land, and from the land derived its livelihood, its status and quite often all its necessities. The case of landlords who moved to cities but continued to provision themselves from their estates, despite high transport costs, was hardly uncommon.[55]

Moreover, such trade as did go on within and among the provinces, and commerce between the Kingdom and other areas generally, was largely in the hands

---

[48] From 1559 to the end of August 1570, 23,791 *carra* and 28.5 *tomola* of grain were exported from the Kingdom. (AGS. *Estado*, leg. 1058, f. 126; BPUG. Collection Favre, vol. 62, f. 73. That amounted to about one-sixth the average yearly export of grain from Sicily at approximately the same time [BPUG. *ibid.*, f. 77r, for the export of nearly 1,400,000 *salme* of Sicilian grain, or about 194,000 Neapolitan *carra*, from 1557/58 to 1568/69]). According to the way it was measured, a *carro* could amount to 36 or 48 *tomola*; in this case, it equaled 36 *tomola*. (One *salma* equaled five *tomoli*; cf. *ibid.*, f. 79r).

By mid-January, 1580, export licenses for 4,500 *carra* of grain had been issued, and the Sommaria calculated that licenses for 4,000 additional *carra* could be granted (ASN. *Sommaria. Consulte*, vol. 7, ff. 204r–v).

For some examples of Neapolitan grain exports to Venice, cf. *ibid.*, vol. 5, f. 127r. For Andalusia, cf. *ibid.*, vol. 2, f. 208r (the Florentine Angelo Biffoli shipping 220 *carra* of wheat and 80 *carra* of barley in 1551). In general, cf. also Galasso, *Economia e società*, pp. 119, 125, 138–39, 143, 156; cf. also "Momenti e problemi," p. 181.   [49] AGS. *Visitas de Italia*, leg. 23/3, f. 98r.

[50] For silk, cf. the citations at notes 68–73, below; for wool, cf. Marino's *Pastoral Economics*, *passim*.

[51] Galasso, *Economia e società*, p. 152.

[52] The figure for the 1560s (about 26,000 *botti* a year) is reported in ASN. *Sommaria. Consulte*, vol. 2, f. 223r. A *botte* = 523.4 liters (Zupko, p. 35). For some examples of Cardinals seeking (and in many cases receiving) exemptions from the duty on the export of wine from the Kingdom, cf. ASN. *Sommaria. Consulte*, vol. 11, f. 53r (1591); vol. 30, ff. 22r–23v (1623); vol. 48, ff. 146v–147r (1646).

[53] ASN. *Sommaria. Arrendamenti*, Ff. 706 (September 1542–December 1545) and 745 (1651–54).

[54] Luzzatto, *Storia economica*, pp. 107–08.

[55] *Ibid.*, pp. 107–08 and Galasso, *Economia e società*, pp. 116–17.

of foreigners. Some landlords did engage in trade directly, by selling their surplus wheat, oil or wine, but it was foreign merchants who held a dominant position in Neapolitan commerce.[56] Such preeminence was not an early modern development: foreigners had in fact been masters of Southern Italian commerce since medieval times.[57] But it was, nonetheless, both an expression and a cause of the tenuousness of Neapolitan economic life.

Foreign merchants who settled in the Kingdom and engaged in trade usually returned to their homelands or withdrew from business within at most a generation.[58] New men would take their place, to be sure, but the Kingdom never developed a stable middle class of entrepreneurs who could undertake long-term operations and stimulate local initiatives.[59] Native entrepreneurs always played marginal roles, especially after Genoese merchants eroded the positions of the old Tuscan and Catalan merchants and became virtually predominant in the commercial and financial life of the Kingdom.[60] In the sixteenth century, for example, Calabrian products traveled much farther than in the past, but Calabrian producers had ever more limited contact with the extended market.[61]

The commercial mediation of foreign merchants does not reflect only the Kingdom's lack of dynamic development, a trait contemporaries noted in invidious comparisons.[62] It reflects also the dependent and tributary position of the Southern Italian economy *vis-à-vis* the Italian North. Such dependency rendered the Southern economy vulnerable, for it tied it to the vicissitudes of the Northern economy and exposed it to the fluctuations and the instability of demand.[63] That

---

[56] Merchants came from numerous Italian towns and other European centers. After 1604, English merchants gained a stable foothold in Naples, though English goods had reached the Kingdom before that date. According to Coniglio, after the 1609 truce there was an influx of Dutch merchants. On this whole question, cf. Coniglio, *Il Viceregno*, pp. 94–122, and Galasso, *Economia e società*, p. 208.

[57] For some of the literature on this problem, cf. David Abulafia, *The Two Italies* (Cambridge, 1977), *passim*. For later periods, cf. Mario Del Treppo, "Il re e il banchiere. Strumenti e processi di razionalizzazione dello stato aragonese a Napoli" in *Spazio, società, potere nell'Italia dei Comuni* (Naples, 1986); "Aspetti dell'attività bancaria a Napoli nel '400," paper presented to the Convegno di Studi nel x anniversario della morte di Federigo Melis (Florence, March 1984); "Napoli e la Corona d'Aragona: appunti per un bilancio storiografico" in *Fonti e cronache italo-iberiche del basso medioevo. Prospettive di ricerca* (Florence, 1984); Alfonso Silvestri, "Sull'attività bancaria napoletana durante il periodo aragonese," *Bollettino dell'Archivio Storico del Banco di Napoli*, 1953, pp. 80–120; Coniglio, "Annona e calmieri a Napoli durante la dominazione spagnuola. Osservazioni e rilievi," *ASPN*, 1940, pp. 105–153 (pp. 105, 109).

[58] For some examples regarding Milanese merchants, cf. Braudel, vol. 1, p. 44.

[59] Galasso, "Le riforme del conte di Lemos," pp. 226–27.

[60] Galasso, "Momenti e problemi," pp. 167–68; De Rosa, *I cambi esteri*, pp. 13, 27; Calabria, "Finanzieri genovesi." [61] Galasso, *Economia e società*, p. 207.

[62] The Calabrian economist Antonio Serra, writing at the beginning of the seventeenth century, saw in that mediation a sign of the Neapolitans' lack of industriousness and "passive" attitude to commerce. "They [Serra argued] do not traffic out of their own country (*paese*), not even in their own Italy, nor do they manage by themselves the industries of their own country. . .and despite the fact that they see the aforesaid people [non-Neapolitan merchants] managing the industries of their own country, thereby enriching themselves, they are not up to imitating them or to following their example: entirely the opposite of the Genoese. . ." Serra's diffuse indictment is quoted by Luzzatto in *Storia economica*, vol. 1, p. 103.

[63] Galasso, "Momenti e problemi," pp. 171, 183; "Le riforme del conte di Lemos," pp. 226–27.

state of affairs was to be important in the shrinking of outlets for Southern products and indeed in the regression of the Southern economy when the North, its manufactures and industries in decline, came to rely more upon its own agricultural reserves.[64]

More specifically endogenous factors, however, seem to have marked the beginnings of the secular decline of the Neapolitan economy.[65] As Silvio Zotta has dramatically shown, from the last two decades of the sixteenth century a crisis of unprecedented proportions and duration enveloped Southern Italian agriculture.[66] A good measure of that crisis is given by the trend for the free market price of grain in the city of Bari from 1550 to 1649, shown in Figure 1.1.[67]

The graph clearly shows several major phases in the trend for grain prices. After a

[64] Galasso, "Momenti e problemi," p. 180. It must be stressed, though, that such a position, important though it was, was but one of the factors at work. Sicily, for example, though a "predominantly agricultural area," subject to the tutelage of Genoese bankers and dependent upon Northern Italian commercial and industrial mediation, allegedly witnessed a "slow but steady economic expansion" in the seventeenth century. Cf. Helmut Koenigsberger, *The Government of Sicily under Philip II of Spain. A Study in the Practice of Empire* (London, 1951), p. 143.

[65] The "secular regression" of the Neapolitan economy, De Rosa reasonably argues (*I cambi esteri*, p. 63), dates from after 1630 and was contemporaneous with that of Italy as a whole. The literature on "decline" and "decadence" is extensive. For some evidence from Venice, cf. *Aspetti e cause della decadenza economica veneziana nel secolo XVII* (Venice, 1961); Domenico Sella, *Commerci e industrie a Venezia nel secolo XVII* (Venice, 1961); Brian Pullan, ed., *Crisis and Change in the Venetian Economy in the Sixteenth and Seventeenth Centuries* (London, 1968). For Lombardy, in addition to Sella's *Crisis and Continuity*, cf. Aldo de Maddalena, "I bilanci dal 1600 al 1647 di un'azienda fondiaria lombarda" in Cipolla, ed., *Storia dell'economia italiana*, vol. 1, pp. 557–604 (now also in De Maddalena's excellent collection of essays, *Dalla città al borgo. Avvio di una metamorfosi economica e sociale nella Lombardia spagnola* [Milan, 1982], pp. 137–78). Cf. also generally, especially for the urban economy, Cipolla, "Il declino economico dell'Italia" (a revised version of "The Decline of Italy: the case of a fully matured economy," *The Economic History Review*, 1952, pp. 178–87) in *Storia dell'economia italiana*, vol. 1, pp. 605–23.

[66] Zotta, "Momenti e problemi," *passim*. Cf. also Galasso, *Economia e società*, p. 353; Coniglio, *Il Viceregno*, p. 79.
     Among the worst harvests were those of 1595 and of 1597–98 (De Rosa, *I cambi esteri*, p. 58). Pardi (p. 75) reports famines for 1560, 1565, 1570, 1584, 1585, 1591. That list is incomplete, and undoubtedly it is applicable not merely to the capital but the whole realm. The famine of 1591–92 must have been particularly severe, for De Rosa calls it "the great famine" (in "Un'operazione d'alta finanza alla fine del '500," *ASPN*, 1957, pp. 267–83 [p. 268]). Pardi reports also severe epidemics for 1562, 1578, 1580 (again, that is by no means a complete list, even for the late sixteenth century).
     The change in the temper of the Neapolitan economy is reflected also in the movement of the exchange rate for Neapolitan currency, a movement which expresses the course of the balance of payments. From 1591, a normal year, to 1622, the course of exchange rates for Neapolitan currency showed quite considerable increases, and the government's attempt to curb the rises and to stimulate exports through a fourfold devaluation did not meet with success. In 1611, for example, the currency was devalued by 8.4 percent, but from February 1611 to February 1616, the exchange rate of the Neapolitan ducat *vis-à-vis* other currencies rose in greater measure than the devaluation rate. A similar pattern followed the devaluation of 1617 and that of 1621, a year when the increases in exchange rates surpassed the percentage of all devaluations undertaken. The Neapolitan balance of payments remained seriously unfavorable with respect to the rest of Italy (De Rosa, *I cambi esteri*, pp. 1, 37–39, 41, 57–58).

[67] The graph is worked out from the data in Giuseppe Mira, "Contributo per una storia dei prezzi in alcune province delle Puglie," *Società Italiana di Statistica*. Atti della IV e V Riunione Scientifica, 1942, pp. 153–73.

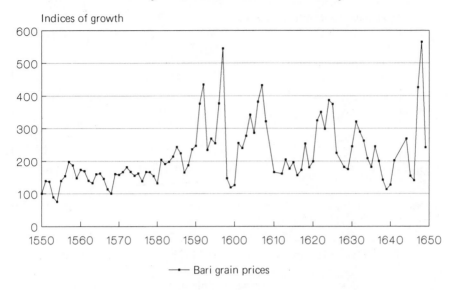

Figure 1.1 The free market price of grain. Bari, 1550–1649

relatively slow-moving rise, from the late 1540s to the late 1570s, when they doubled, prices climbed very sharply in the 1580s and 1590s, mirroring the great difficulties of Southern agriculture in those decades. The late 1590s marked both the sharpest rise and the most catastrophic fall in prices, nearly to their initial levels. After end century, grain prices rose again quite sharply, until the middle years of the new decade, only to fall precipitously after 1607 back to the levels they had reached in the early 1580s. In the last phase pictured in the graph, prices fluctuated sharply, rising almost to the peak levels of the early 1600s and sliding again, especially in the 1630s, nearly to the end-century low point.

The behavior of grain prices in the Kingdom, it is clear, provides an almost classic model of crisis in the early modern economy, from the sputterings of the late sixteenth century to the widespread difficulties of the early seventeenth. And, as one might expect, in Naples too agriculture was not the only sector of the economy to suffer dislocations in the terrible decades of the early seventeenth century. As the experience of the silk trade in the Kingdom shows, commerce and industry also witnessed sharp, even catastrophic reversals.

A case in point is that of the silk trade in Cosenza, the hub of silk traffic in Calabria, the major silk-growing region in the Kingdom. Figure 1.2 plots Cosenza's experience with the silk trade from the mid-sixteenth to the mid-seventeenth century.[68]

[68] ASN. *Sommaria. Arrendamenti*, Ff. 162 (1548), 166 (1558), 176 (1572), 178/II (1577–78), 182 (1579–80), 187 (1581–82), 209 (1597), 304 (1633–34, 1634–35), 329 (1639–40), 331 (1640–41, 1641–42), 341 (1644), 372 (1655); *Sommaria. Diversi*, Seconda Numerazione, Ff. 136 (1584–85), 141 (1586–87).

Thousands of pounds (Neapolitan)

—•— Silk shipments

Figure 1.2 The rise and fall of Cosenza's silk trade, 1548–1655

From the late 1540s to the early 1570s, between 430,000 and 560,000 pounds of silk passed every year through Cosenza's dry customs gates, much of it on behalf of the big Genoese merchant bankers, on its way to regional centers in Southern Italy, the city of Naples and the Italian North. In the 1570s and 1580s, silk exports from Cosenza fluctuated sharply, but from the mid-1580s their decline was precipitous, and by the end of the sixteenth century seems to have become permanent. Unfortunately, no figures are presently available for Cosenza silk exports for the period 1598–1633. Those for the 1630s through the 1650s, however, tell a story of very great calamity indeed. By 1639, less than 85,000 pounds of silk passed through Cosenza's customs gates, bound only for Naples and for regional centers in Southern Italy. The international entrepreneurs who had been in charge of much of that trade in the sixteenth century had been replaced by smaller local or regional merchants. Though by 1655 total exports had risen to about 116,000 pounds, Cosenza's decline as a silk-producing area proved irresistible. Even through the eighteenth-century recovery, the city's silk shipments did not regain their sixteenth-century peak: in 1737, they amounted to about 49,000 pounds; in 1759, to about 70,000 pounds.[69]

Cosenza was not alone in its experience of crisis in the silk trade. Paola always was and always remained a minor, relatively unimportant center of Calabria's silk

[69] ASN. *Sommaria. Arrendamenti*, Ff. 396 (1737–38), 397 (1759–60).

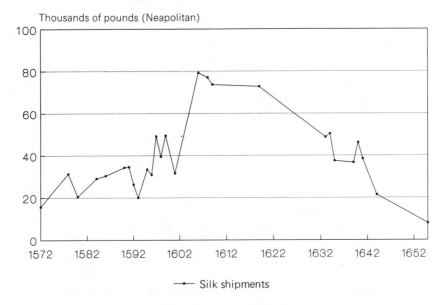

Figure 1.3 The rise and fall of Paola's silk trade, 1572–1655

production, dwarfed as it was by nearby Cosenza, but it suffered dislocations analogous to its neighbor's, even if on a different scale and perhaps also to a different rhythm. Figure 1.3 plots the vicissitudes of Paola's silk trade from 1572 to 1655.[70]

As the graph shows, in the late sixteenth century, Paola's story was one of almost unbounded success. True, its exports were only a tiny fraction of Cosenza's in that century, but they nearly doubled in the six years between 1572 and 1578, rising from about 16,000 to about 31,000 pounds. Despite some sharp fluctuations, from the late 1570s to the early 1590s, Paola's exports hovered near the 30,000 pound mark and reached nearly 50,000 pounds in the late 1590s. By 1606, nearly 80,000 pounds of silk passed through Paola's gates, or about six times the 1572 level.

Not until the 1630s did those exports begin sliding, to about 50,000 pounds in 1633, 37,000 pounds in 1639, 21,000 pounds in 1644, and only about 8,000 pounds, or roughly half the initial level, in 1655. In the Paola silk trade too, then, the seventeenth-century crisis proved to be nothing less than a catastrophe. That debacle was reversed, possibly by the eighteenth-century recovery, for 36,310 pounds of silk were declared at Paola's customs in 1737 , and 111,078 pounds in

---

[70] *Ibid.*, Ff. 176 (1572), 180 (1578–79), 184 (1580–81), 185 (1584–85), 202 (1590–91), 203 (1591–92), 204 (1592–93), 205 (1593–94), 206 (1595–96), 208 (1596–97), 209 (1597), 210 (1598–99), 212 (1599–1600), 213 (1601–02), 225 (1606–07), 227 (1608–09), 231 (1609–10), 268 (1619), 304 (1633–34, 1634–35), 329 (1639–40), 331 (1640–41, 1641–42), 341 (1644), 360 (1655); *Sommaria. Diversi*, Seconda Numerazione, F. 141 (1586–87).

Figure 1.4 The rise and fall of Monteleone's silk trade, 1572–1686

1759.[71] But for seventeenth-century Paola, all that must have seemed in the unimaginable future.

The experience of a third silk-producing center, Monteleone, in Northern Calabria, suggests the diversity of circumstances that could obtain even within the clear framework of crisis and dissolution. Like Cosenza and Paola, Monteleone's story, as Figure 1.4 shows, is one of decline, but it is also one of adaptation.[72]

Though the familiar pattern of rapid change, expansion and decline is all too present in Monteleone's case, overall that city's experience with the silk trade was not one of clear disintegration, as was the case with Cosenza or even Paola. In 1686, Monteleone's silk exports stood at their lowest level since 1584, but they amounted to about 118,000 pounds, or over five times their 1572 level of nearly 22,000 pounds. The city's shipments had risen nearly fourfold in the seven years between 1572 and 1579, and they had then tripled in the next five years, rising to about 242,000 pounds in 1584. Those exports had peaked in 1603, at nearly 330,000 pounds, and they had then fluctuated between about 225,000 and 154,000 pounds. In 1655, they amounted to over 220,000 pounds, over ten times their initial level; in 1737, they stood at about 147,000 pounds.[73]

---

[71] ASN. *Sommaria. Arrendamenti*, Ff. 396 (1737–38), 397 (1759–60).

[72] *Ibid.*, Ff. 176 (1572); 182 (1579–80), 209 (1597), 219 (1603–04), 233 and 234 (1611), 273 (1620), 276 (1621), 304 (1633–34, 1634–35), 329 (1639–40), 331 (1640–41), 338 (1641–42), 341 (1644), 345 and 346 (1646), 365 (1655), 374 (1686); *Sommaria. Diversi*, Seconda Numerazione, Ff. 136 (1584–85), 141 (1586–87).

[73] ASN. *Sommaria. Arrendamenti*, Ff. 365 (1655), 396 (1737–38).

The tale of the silk trade in the Kingdom of Naples, like the larger story of the economy of Southern Italy in early modern times, needs still to be told. The various factors behind the great changes it witnessed in the seventeenth century – from possible changes in the weather to local conditions of production to the vagaries of the international economy and the likely decline in external demand for Neapolitan silk – need to be sifted and evaluated. The evidence examined so far, however, particularly for Monteleone, shows that adaptation was perhaps as much part of the seventeenth-century crisis as dissolution.[74] But, Monteleone's case notwithstanding, it may well be that, for the silk trade as a whole, the crisis of the seventeenth century marked a clear decline, a net loss.

Unfortunately, the evidence available so far cannot give clear-cut answers to more interesting and important questions, to wit, did the crisis of the seventeenth century bring generalized decline and net loss to the entire Southern Italian economy? Was the economy of Northern Italy alone in showing signs of future growth in the midst of generalized disaster?[75] That seems highly unlikely, but, given the dearth of specialized studies, it is unclear to what extent and in what manner the various sectors of the Southern economy were affected by the difficult times of the 1620s and 1630s.[76] Some indicators, though, would seem to suggest that at least for some areas of the economy the dislocation may not have been unallayed, the dissolution not irreparable, the disaster not irreversible.[77] Of course, as subsequent chapters of this work will show, economic distress in the 1620s, 1630s and 1640s was greatly aggravated by political factors. It was Southern Italy's misfortune, in fact,

---

[74] Further study may well show, too, that geography and economic shifts traceable to geography played an important role in both adaptation and dissolution.

[75] Cf. Sella, *Crisis and Continuity*, *passim*.

[76] Aurelio Lepre stresses the crucial importance of the crisis of 1647–1656 in his suggestive article, "La crisi del XVII secolo nel Mezzogiorno d'Italia," *Studi Storici*, 1981, pp. 51–77. Cf. also the same author's *Terra di Lavoro nell'età moderna* (Naples, 1978), *Storia del Mezzogiorno d'Italia*, vol. 1: *La lunga durata e la crisi (1500–1656)* (Naples, 1986) and *Feudi e masserie. Problemi della società meridionale nel Sei e Settecento* (Naples, 1973).

[77] The indicators are the leases for the various indirect tax contracts in the Kingdom, eleven of which are graphed in Appendix 1.
   The evidence from the leases may not be unequivocal, because of the complicating factors that went into the contractors' bids (e.g. increased taxation on many consumer items, like wine sold at retail in the city of Naples). But since the leases were awarded to tax farmers through competitive bidding, they did reflect the tax farmers' expectations about the economy (cf. also below, chapter 3).
   Many of the indicators graphed in Appendix 1 follow a pattern very similar to the one brought to light by Ruggiero Romano in "Tra XVI e XVII secolo. Una crisi economica: 1618–1622," *RSI*, 1962, pp. 480–531 (available also in the author's *L'Europa tra due crisi* [Turin, 1980], pp. 76–147 and in English translation in Geoffrey Parker and Lesley M. Smith, editors, *The General Crisis of the Seventeenth Century* [London, 1978], pp. 165–225).
   Even the indicators showing catastrophic decline (i.e. in particular, those for the Naples and Puglia Customhouses) exhibited recovery in the 1630s, and they did not fall below the levels they had attained earlier in the seventeenth century. The contracts for the retail sale of wine in the city of Naples, on the other hand, showed the least dislocation and continued growth in the 1630s.
   Most of the indirect taxes in the Kingdom were given over to private parties in 1648 (cf. below, chapter 3); it is therefore impossible to follow the vicissitudes of the indirect tax contracts much beyond the admittedly abrupt end of the series graphed in Appendix 1, the late 1630s.

that some of the most trying years for its economy should also have been the ones to see the cost of Empire become harshest and most burdensome.

The difficulties experienced by Neapolitan agriculture starting late in the sixteenth century, and the fall in production and demand for Neapolitan products, which accompanied those difficulties, coincided with and contributed to the transfer of thousands of hectares of land to stock farming.[78] The breeding and pasturing of livestock, particularly of sheep, did not, of course, date from the sixteenth or seventeenth centuries. That important sector of the Southern economy had been developed in the fourteenth century, and it had been given a strong stimulus by Alfonso of Aragon in the fifteenth century.[79]

The introduction of *merino* sheep had improved the quality of Neapolitan wool, while the institution of a Sheep Customs based on the Spanish model and the ordering of transhumance had stimulated the production and commerce of raw wool.[80] The pasturing of livestock, in fact, became increasingly widespread in the later sixteenth century. Lucrative though it also was for some, that increase may well serve as an indicator of the shift and regression in the Neapolitan economy, and it may point as well to its essentially "depressed" nature.[81]

That shift did not escape the attention of contemporaries. Addressing the Venetian Senate in 1580, Ambassador Alvise Lando struck a different note from Paolo Tiepolo seventeen years earlier. The Kingdom, Lando argued, was "an unwieldy body," afflicted not only by the "evil disposition" of its subjects but also by the "pestilential humors" that had been daily accumulating in it: "The infirmity [Lando continued] has become so contagious that its cure has always been judged, if not indeed desperate, at least dangerous."[82]

While economic regression by itself made for the "infirmity" that Lando diagnosed, population movements no doubt contributed to the doubtful prognosis. Although precise demographic data is not available, the trend in Neapolitan population is nonetheless clear.[83] After the strong oscillations of the second half of

---

[78] Galasso, *Economia e società*, pp. 137–38; Coniglio, *Il Regno*, pp. 169–70; *Il Viceregno*, p. 79. Cf. also Massimo Petrocchi's note, "Il feudo chiuso della città di Gallipoli," in his *Lo stato di Milano al novembre 1535 ed altre ricerche sulla storia dell'economia e degli ordinamenti degli Stati italiani* (Naples, 1957), pp. 61–63.

[79] Galasso, *Economia e società*, p. 163; Braudel, vol. 1, pp. 79–82.

[80] Luzzatto, *Storia economica*, p. 110; Lodovico Bianchini, *Storia delle finanze del Regno di Napoli* (Naples, 1859), pp. 196–98. Now, cf. Marino, *Pastoral Economics*.

[81] For Luzzatto, stock farming is a characteristic feature of underdeveloped areas. Cf. his *Breve storia economica*, ch. 8, part 4. Whatever its merits for other areas, this term does not seem inappropriate for the Neapolitan economic system.

[82] Alvise Lando, "Relazione del Regno di Napoli" (1580) in Albèri, ed., *Le relazioni degli ambasciatori veneti al Senato*, ser. 2, vol. 5, p. 449 (Florence, 1858).

[83] Aside from contemporary descriptive accounts, the sources available for the Kingdom as a whole in the sixteenth and seventeenth centuries are censuses drawn up for the allocation of the hearth tax. Such censuses are not numerous, though, because while in theory they were to be undertaken every fifteen years, in practice they were not. Allegedly to avoid the expense of a new census, in fact, the Estates of the Kingdom would grant extraordinary parliamentary aids to postpone a new count. (Cf. Faraglia, *Il Comune*, p. 183). In the second half of the sixteenth century, censuses were drawn up only

the fifteenth century, the population of the Kingdom underwent a strong upsurge, nearly doubling from the beginning of the sixteenth century to the middle of the seventeenth.[84] The rate of increase was greatest through the middle of the sixteenth century.[85] Subsequently, the population leveled off and, because of epidemics and plague, it declined. The phenomenon of population growth and of coinciding economic contraction nonetheless obtained in the Kingdom, as in other parts of Europe at the same time.

The city of Naples paralleled the demographic trend of the Kingdom at large, as it did many of its other economic, social and financial rhythms. Through the fifteenth century, its rulers had encouraged its growth, and its population had risen to about 115,000–120,000 in 1505.[86] The sixteenth century marked a great increase in the city's population, which amounted to about 225,000 people in 1596. Despite the heavy losses endured because of the plagues of the seventeenth century, particularly the one of 1656, Naples in 1671 had 300,000 souls; it was the largest city in Italy and one of the most populous in Europe.[87]

Early on in the sixteenth century, that growth had no doubt been abetted by the end of warfare following the Spanish conquest. Afterwards, the policy of public works undertaken by Viceroy Don Pedro de Toledo and the development of the capital generally helped promote the city's growth.[88] No doubt the centralizing

in 1561 and 1596. Though obviously censuses do not register exemptions and evasions, they do give a valid picture of demographic trends.

The following fiscal documents containing census data are used in this work (cf. chapters 3 and 4): AGS. *Estado.*, leg. 1030, f. 180 (1532: 335,395 hearths); *Visitas de Italia*, leg. 348/18 (1549–50: 426,162 hearths); *Estado*, leg. 1103, f. 214 (1595: 526,946 hearths); BNN. Ms. Branc., VI–B–8, ff. IV–2r (1561: 479,760 hearths); Ms. XI–B–39, f. 5v (1595: 499,449 hearths [*sic*]); IVdDJ, envio 80/579 (1545: 425,959 hearths). By 1722, the Kingdom numbered 362,122⅓ hearths (HHStA, *It.-Sp. Rat, Neapel, Collectanea*, vol. 50, "Stato generale...del Real Patrimonio...dell'anno 1722," 18 March 1722 [the same figure is in the "Stato generale...formato nell'anno 1717," 30 March 1717, *ibid.*; it is 369,223 in the early eighteenth-century, undated "Bilancio del numero effettivo de Fuochi," *ibid.*]).

84 Karl Julius Beloch, *Bevölkerungsgeschichte Italiens*, vol. I (Berlin, 1937), pp. 169–277, esp. p. 215 for the censuses from 1505 to 1669; cf. also his "La popolazione d'Italia nei secoli sedicesimo, diciassettesimo e diciottesimo" in Cipolla, ed., *Storia dell'economia italiana*, vol. I, pp. 449–500.

85 Beloch, *Bevölkerungsgeschichte Italiens*, vol. I, p. 215. Cf. also the fiscal documents cited at note 83 above.

86 AGS. *Secretarías Provinciales*, leg. I, f. 115, which states that Naples had about 10,000 people ("2,000 hearths") in the late thirteenth century and about 100,000 ("20,000 hearths") in about the 1560s. For the 1505 estimate, cf. Pardi, p. 66. In assessing the city's population, Pardi reports data derived from censuses drawn up for the allocation of the salt tax, and (for 1505) for the distribution of bread, generally during famines (cf. also p. 71 for 1547 and p. 76 for 1591, 1593, 1595). Like all such documents, those censuses without doubt do not include the entire population.

87 For the 1596 figure, cf. BNM. Ms. 2659, f. 96r (reported also in Francesco Caracciolo, *Sud, debiti e gabelle.Gravami, potere e società nel Mezzogiorno in età moderna* [Naples, 1983], pp. 226–27). For the others, cf. Coniglio, *Il Viceregno*, pp. 23–24. Cf. also Beloch, *Bevölkerungsgeschichte Italiens*, pp. 169–90; Cesare De Seta, *Storia della città di Napoli dalle origini al Settecento* (Bari, 1973); Claudia Petraccone, *Napoli dal Cinquecento all'Ottocento. Problemi di storia demografica e sociale* (Naples, 1974) and *Napoli moderna e contemporanea* (Naples, 1981).

88 Luzzatto, *Storia economica*, p. 111. Note also the report on the Kingdom of Naples to the Grand-Duke of Tuscany by Francesco Marcaldo, in "Documenti sulla storia economica e civile del Regno cavati dal carteggio degli agenti del Granduca di Toscana in Napoli dall'anno 1582 sino al 1648" (in the

tendency of government did too, bringing to Naples, for administrative and social reasons, a growing portion of the nobility and such provincial middle class as there existed.[89]

Like capitals and administrative centers generally, then, Naples attracted a vast array of people. From outside the Kingdom, a late sixteenth-century document notes, came "an infinite number of foreigners[,] vassals of other lords of Italy and of areas outside Italy, who come to enjoy the peace and tranquility of the Catholic Majesty's most happy rule in the best climate of Italy."[90] The well-to-do, wrote the author of the "Delectable and Useful Discourse. . .," could live in the capital, "in quiet, without paying protection money to the Barons and the. . .officials of the Kingdom."[91] There, too, they could easily "engage in business. . .and buy from one day to the next estates, territories, revenues and houses worth hundreds of thousands of ducats. . ."[92] For their part, artisans and merchants, a document tells us, no doubt with exaggeration, also "flock[ed] to Naples. . .and most of them are very poor when they come, but they return to their lands rich and well-off."[93]

A more important reason for the growth of the city of Naples, however, was the migration there of poor people, of "the infinite herd of servants looking for masters," as the author of the "Delectable and Useful Discourse. . ." put it.[94] From the beginning, in fact, extensive pauperism and parasitism characterized the city's demographic expansion.[95]

The gates [of the city] should be kept closed [argued a member of the Collateral Council in the 1560s], so that useless persons are not allowed in, and the vagabonds should be kicked out, as is provided for by Your Excellency's [the Viceroy's] ban. . .[96]

Like the imposing presence of "useless persons" and "vagabonds," the wide incidence of prostitution was a clear sign of Naples' problematical and chaotic growth. By the early 1580s, the number of prostitutes in the capital had allegedly risen so much that

---

collection entitled "Narrazioni e documenti sulla storia del Regno di Napoli dall'anno 1522 al 1667," edited by Francesco Palermo in *ASI*, 1846, pp. 243–353 [henceforth cited as "Documenti. .Toscana"] pp. 247–49. Writing in 1594, Marcaldo noted that in the preceding thirty years Naples had grown greatly in dwellings and people, and that it had expanded by more than two *miglia* in circumference ("essendovi state aggiunte due gran miglia di circuito," p. 247).

[89] Luzzatto, *Storia economica*, p. 105.

[90] AGS. *Visitas de Italia*, leg. 24/3 ("Ragioni che si adducono per ottener la revocatione ò almeno la reformatione del bando delle fabriche in Napoli dal Rè nostro signor."), f. 168r.

[91] *Ibid.*, leg. 23/3, f. 112v.   [92] *Ibid.*   [93] *Ibid.*, leg. 24/3, "Ragioni che si adducono," f. 169v.

[94] *Ibid.*, leg. 23/3, f. 112v. For the importance of internal migration generally, cf. Galasso, *Economia e società*, pp. 101, 103–05, 107, 114.

[95] Pardi, p. 66; Galasso, "*Momenti e problemi*," p. 172. Cf. also BNN. Ms. Brancacciano II–E–5, ff. 112r–123r. Marcaldo clearly showed little perception and much exaggeration when he wrote of the "ease with which the poor can earn a living [in Naples], since at any time there is always an enormous amount of work to be found there" (". . .la comodità che hanno i poveri di guadagnarsi il vivere: essendovi da lavorare in qualsivoglia tempo abbondatissimamente" ["Documenti. . .Toscana," p. 247]).   [96] AGS. *Secretarías Provinciales*, leg. 1, f. 115.

all the streets are full of them...and they have grown in infinite numbers. In fact, over the last few years they have come to this city from all the places in the world, because of the freedom they have to live here. They pick the best streets and the best squares, as was seen last year, when the Lord Duke of Osuna [the Viceroy] kicked them out of Toledo street, which was full of them from one end to the other...[97]

The women's trafficking was regulated by an appropriate gabelle,

...which is necessary and useful to the city of Naples...to curb and punish the women who live dishonestly, to hold in check the iniquity and licentiousness of the prostitutes and pimps, who, being evil-doers, continuously commit enormous crimes and excesses, because...the nesting places of thieves, blasphemers, gamblers, pimps and other criminals are almost always the houses of prostitutes.[98]

Actually, though, prostitution's milieu was not merely one of "thieves, blasphemers, gamblers, pimps and other criminals." It was also one in which even middling officials of the capital's own government circles were actively involved. The line between those circles and the "low life" seems to have been a thin one indeed:

...the secretaries and the civil and criminal officials of the High Court of Justice protect some of the whores, who are their friends and concubines, and they frustrate the work of said gabelle with the writs they issue...which the judges sign simply on the secretaries' report... and because of the connections they have with the police and the ministers of justice, it is commonplace during the holidays to see some of the secretaries going around in coaches, accompanying the whores, and so also at night, and they make them wrongly dress up [*stravestire*] as men...[99]

In the 1570s, the Church of the Holy Ghost alone in the capital served as a hospice to 300 girls,

daughters of prostitutes, whose mothers, it is suspected, would impose on them the same [type of life], and they stay in said house until they are of age to get married, and then the

---

[97] AGS. *Visitas de Italia*, leg. 24/2 ("Gabella de las Meretrices"), f. 491r. The Duke of Osuna was Viceroy of Naples from 1582 to 1586. On prostitution in Naples generally, cf. Salvatore Di Giacomo, *La prostituzione a Napoli nei secoli XV, XVI e XVII* (Naples, 1899; reprinted, 1968).

[98] AGS. *Visitas de Italia*, leg. 24/2, f. 488v. The gabelle, the document continues, "is also very useful in curbing the other women who have not yet given themselves over to an evil life, and in making them live in fear and chastity." For some very sensitive pages on the plight of the unfortunate women in this occupation, particularly those who were entrapped into prostitution by none other than the gabelle officials, cf. Mantelli, *Burocrazia e finanze pubbliche*, pp. 208–11.

[99] AGS. *Visitas de Italia*, leg. 24/2, ff. 489r–v, 490r–v ("...perche secondo s'intende [salvando sempre la verità] li scrivani, mastrodatti civili, è criminali, e gli subattuarij dela gran corte della Vicaria, tengano protettione de alcune puttane e loro amiche e concubbine, et inhibiscono la detta gabella, spedendo provisioni contra la forma della regia pragmatica...Li signori Giudici della Vicaria...fermano le provisioni a semplice relatione de li scrivani di Vicaria...gia per l'ordinario alcuni scrivani criminali le feste si mettano in cocchio con le putane e le acompagnano, e cosi ancora la notte con farle stravestire da homo, per la confidenza che hanno con gli capitani, e ministri de giustitia," f. 489v).

house gives them something for their dowry, and if they don't want to get married, they become nuns. . .[100]

Four hundred girls, on the other hand, "orphans, daughters of honorable people [who are] natives of the city of Naples," were housed in the Church of St. Lewis, "and they stay there until they are of age, and if they want to get married, they are given sixty ducats in dowry. . ."[101] The Hospital of Our Lady of the Annunciation, for its part,

ordinarily employs 7,000 [*sic*] wet-nurses to bring up the babies who are left at the door of the church [of the Annunciation], and they look after them up the age of seven and after that the boys are put to work, and the girls are placed in the convent. . .where there are usually 1,200 of them, and each year about 200 of them get married, and they are given 90 ducats each in dowry. . .[102]

The wide presence in Naples of so many marginal people – the orphans and the abandoned, the prostitutes and the slaves, the "useless persons" and the "vagabonds" – was a telling sign of conditions in the Kingdom, one that was not entirely lost on Court circles.[103] In 1560, in fact, a royal despatch to the Viceroy argued that if "the poor and others" were prohibited from going to Naples, "since in other places there aren't as many opportunities to live, work and earn a living, it's clear that they would have to take to the hills and become outlaws. . ."[104]

---

[100] AGS. *Visitas de Italia*, leg. 24/2 ("Relacion de algunas cosas de la ciudad y reyno de Napoles"), ff. 495r–502r [f. 498r], a very free Spanish version of the "Delectable and Useful Discourse."

[101] *Ibid.*, f. 498r (St. Eligio).

[102] *Ibid.*, f. 497v. This is by no means an exclusive list; a very large number of hospices, monastic institutions and hospitals were to be found in the capital. According to a document from 1583, "the monasteries, convents and churches inside the city have increased to the point that they take up almost a third of it" (AGS. *Visitas de Italia*, leg. 24/3, f. 170r).

[103] AGS. *Secretarías Provinciales*, leg. 1, f. 117 (29 July 1562; in answer to the royal letter of 13 October 1560, cited below). On slaves, cf. AGS. *Visitas de Italia*, leg. 24/2, f. 4v: the case of one Antonio Contichio, who would bring Greeks, Turks and Slavs to Naples, asserting they were Muslims, so that he could sell them as slaves (Christians could not be enslaved). On 11 August 1579 seven women brought to Naples by Contichio "by decree of the Collateral Council. . .were declared free, and Christians;" two of them had apparently been "in the household of Jo:Vicencio de Julijs," no doubt as domestic servants. A year and a month later, on 16 September 1580, slave driver Contichio ran into some difficulties again. Of the five men he had brought to Naples to sell as slaves, two, "Memet and Jacoda were declared free"; the remaining three, "Memia, Boliza and Pervan [,] were declared slaves."

A seventeenth-century manuscript on fiscality discusses the customs duties to which slaves were subject: "Infidel [i.e. Islamic] slaves who are redeemed in Naples to go back to their homelands are to be considered as live animals and pay the *jus gabelle* and *buondinaro* duties in the [Naples] Customhouse. They do not pay the *jus fundaci* because they are live animals, but since they go off by sea, they pay the new gabelle of six *grana* per *onza*. And the Chamber [i.e. the Sommaria] decreed on 8 July 1580 that black slaves cannot be taken out of the Kingdom without pledge that they will be returned" (BNN. Ms. XI–B–39, f. 60r).

[104] AGS. *Secretarías Provinciales*, leg. 1, f. 113 (13 October 1560; in answer to the Viceroy's letter of 21 March 1560, which contained a dire assessment of the problems brought on by the growth of the city of Naples and which suggested some extreme remedies to stop that growth [*ibid.*, leg. 1, f. 116; AGS. *Estado*, leg. 1050, f. 23]: ". . .de mas del que seria en quitar que los pobres y otros no puedan venir a

Still, and increasingly over time, the growth of the city of Naples was a cause of great concern to the Spanish authorities, for the problems it created and the specters it evoked. "What must kept clearly in mind and what most matters," the Duke of Alcalá wrote the Court in 1560, "is that ordinarily the new arrivals are poor, and they are people of such caliber that, at any time of unrest, they would have to be considered as familial enemies. . ."[105] To hear the Viceroy, "they would have to be feared more than avowed [enemies] because, being poor, they are wont to look with favor on changes in the state, thinking that they have something to gain and nothing to lose."[106]

As one might expect, the author of the "Delectable and Useful Discourse. . ." found himself in some measure of agreement with the Duke of Alcalá. Since the people of the city of Naples are "numerous, agile and quick-witted," that writer noted, it would be very difficult for the King to secure the countryside in time of war if he did not already have mastery of it and if the inhabitants "did not resolve on their own to stay devoted to him."

And this is why [he went on]. . .a few years ago there was a great deal of talk, and many reports were drawn up and models built to plan a fortress that would have in its sights most of the new dwellings towards the Mountain of San Martino and Pizzofalcone, and in which an army could easily stay without having to guard itself from the inhabitants of the city and from the enemy outside it. And such a fortress could have heavily damaged the city, and thus prevented any change of allegiance [*opinione*] in time of war. . .[107]

Not surprisingly, Spanish and Italian administrators devoted much attention and debate to what was an important problem of state, Naples' peculiar type of growth. Time and again they discussed measures to forbid it; periodically (and vainly) they issued orders to stop it.[108] Despite bans and coercive measures, it was "almost impossible," as the Duke of Alcalá wrote the King in 1562, to prevent "so many vagabonds and lazy people" from remaining in the city.[109] The building of houses, shops, walls, and the occupation of empty structures and lots also went on despite the orders forbidding them. According to a document urging the revocation of a ban forbidding building within the city, by the 1580s the face of Naples had been

Napoles, pues sta cierto que no haviendo en otra parte tanto aparejo de vivir, travajar, y ganar la vida, se havrian de salir a la campaña y hazerse foragidos").

The Viceroy was not convinced by that argument. "In any part of the Kingdom," he answered the King in 1562, "anybody who wants to work and not live in idleness can do so; indeed, if those who come here stayed in their homes. . .more land would be tilled than is the case now, and the Kingdom would have more abundance, and they could keep themselves busy in the mechanical arts, that is, in working cloth, linen and other things" (AGS. *Secretarías Provinciales*, leg. 1, f. 117).

[105] *Ibid.*, leg. 1, f. 116 (21 March 1560; cf. also AGS. *Estado*, leg. 1050, f. 23).   [106] *Ibid.*

[107] AGS. *Visitas de Italia*, leg. 23/3, f. 113r. Cf. also leg. 24/2, the "Relacion de algunas cosas de la ciudad y reyno de Napoles" [f. 497r].

[108] Bans attempting to stop the growth of the city of Naples were issued at least in 1552, 1554, 1560 (three bans), 1566 (two bans), 1569, 1582, 1583. Cf. AGS. *Visitas de Italia*, leg. 24/1, ff. 89r–102v.

[109] Cf. AGS. *Secretarías Provinciales*, leg. 1, f. 117 (29 July 1562): "y por bandos que se echen y provisiones que se hagan es quasi impossible prohibirles la estancia en ella."

changed, and speculation in real estate and rental properties had received a strong stimulus:

since construction is forbidden outside [the city walls], the houses within [the city limits] rise up to the stars, and palaces get gutted at ground level to make dwellings for the baseborn, while monasteries and palaces tear down their delightful gardens to make room for those who want to build. . .[110]

Forbidding construction would have deleterious effects, the document argued, both on the "many thousands of artisans who have earned their living with said construction and who today are starving to death, possibly endangering, or even losing their honor,"[111] and on the

many gentlemen and other citizens who got rid of their orchards and mortgaged their farms for building [in Naples], and today are stuck with buildings which are unfinished or were never even started, gaining no pleasure or profit from their orchards and with no other investment income. . .and they can't get over being ruined. . .[112]

As was no doubt the case with the "many thousands of artisans" allegedly employed in the construction industry, the prospect, or the mirage, of work in the city served as a powerful lure attracting poor people to Naples. Equally persuasive were the capital's unique exemption from direct taxes and its provisioning policy. The former derived from Naples' ancient privileges; it had been granted by the Aragonese rulers, no doubt to encourage the city's economic and demographic expansion.[113] The latter had been forced on the authorities by reason of state. In order to maintain order and avoid riots in an increasingly populous, congested and volatile city, in fact, bread had to be made available through the bakeries at fixed, political prices, often below cost.[114]

Naples' provisioning policy and its citizens' exemption from direct taxes may have been strong inducements for impoverished provincials to take up residence in the capital. For the rulers, however, they were problems, even if, in a letter to the

---

[110] AGS. *Visitas de Italia*, leg. 24/3 ("Ragioni che si adducono"), f. 170r. [111] *Ibid.*, f. 170r.

[112] *Ibid.*, ff. 170r–v, 171r.

[113] BNN. Ms. xi–b–39, ff. 1r–3r; AGS. *Secretarías Provinciales*, leg. 1, f. 115.

[114] For an example of such transactions, cf. "Documenti. . .Toscana," pp. 264–65 (27 July 1606). The Tuscan agent noted that the government had contracted for the purchase of grain at 26 *carlini* per *tomolo*, whereas "in the past months" the contracting price had been 18 *carlini* per *tomolo*; he also noted that the retail sale price to citizens was 17 *carlini* per *tomolo*. That policy did not always suffice to prevent scarcities: cf. "Documenti. . .Toscana," p. 251 (30 December 1597); p. 266 (23 April 1607); p. 288 (26 July 1621); pp. 290–93 (January–March 1622). For the revolt of 1585, whose immediate cause was the city administration's decision to raise the price of bread, cf. Villari, *La rivolta*, pp. 33–58, and Michelangelo Mendella, *Il moto napoletano del 1585 e il delitto Storace* (Naples, 1967). On the question generally, cf. Braudel, vol. 1, p. 317.

For the Neapolitans' alleged volatility, cf. the "Delectable and Useful Discourse" (AGS. *Visitas de Italia*, leg. 23/3, f. 112v): "It is believed that the people of this city would be as quick to take up arms and cause turmoil, especially if it were a matter of the Inquisition, as it is to throw itself, to the beat of drums and with flags unfurled, to devotions and almsgiving."

Viceroy Duke of Alcalá in 1560, Philip II had minimized them both.[115] The loss of revenue suffered by the exchequer because of the tax exemption, the King had written, would probably be made up by the increased yield from taxes on the consumption of necessity items like wine and meat and on the higher volume of business conducted in a populous city. As for provisioning the city, the King suggested "an opportune and easy remedy" to avoid scarcities of grain, that is, securing stockpiles of it in time, so that the city could be well provided during the summer, "when one must fear the Turkish fleet." During the winter, of course, ships had "every opportunity" to bring grain from Puglia to Naples, but, in addition,

in order to avoid the dangers of the sea and to be sure of having the grain transported overland, it would be a good idea to repair the roads from Puglia, near Ascoli. . .so that the grain can be taken to Naples overland, as is done in Germany and other countries, with the certainty of having plenty of it, without having to fear riots for lack of grain. . .[116]

Such "remedies" found little sympathy with the Viceroy Duke of Alcalá, whose day-to-day tasks in Naples impressed him with the threat posed by a city overpopulated with the poor. As for the matter of the direct tax exemptions, he answered the King in 1562,

the kind of people who are swelling the city are not of such quality as to bring any profit to business, and while they do buy wine and food, that amounts to so little that it ought not even be taken into account, considering the damage done to direct tax receipts.[117]

With regard to the royal suggestions about provisioning the city, the Viceroy was even more blunt:

I don't want to talk about opening up the roads in order to cart victuals over them to this city (though road repairs are being attended to with all possible diligence) [the Viceroy went on], but I will say that if one works out the cost of bringing what grain can be brought here from Puglia, it would be so expensive that few people would want to undertake such a task.[118]

Supplying the capital with grain, for which the royal letter blithely found "opportune and easy" solutions, was instead "the most substantial" of all problems,

without doubt the biggest job. . .I have in running the whole Kingdom, because it's easy to say that supplies should be obtained in time and grain brought during the winter from Puglia. . . but this can only be done by dint of money. . .[119]

Those funds, furthermore, had to come from the city's own treasury, at a time when the capital was indebted to the tune of more than 600,000 ducats, "and I must

[115] AGS. *Secretarías Provinciales*, leg. 1, f. 113 (12 October 1560).
[116] *Ibid*. Of course, winter shipping could still become prey to Turkish privateers. For an example, cf. above, note 18, the second citation.
[117] AGS. *Secretarías Provinciales*, leg. 1, f. 117 (29 July 1562).
[118] *Ibid*. According to Coniglio ("Annona e calmieri"), grain shipped by sea cost two *carlini* less per *tomolo* than that shipped overland.   [119] AGS. *Secretarías Provinciales*, leg. 1, f. 117.

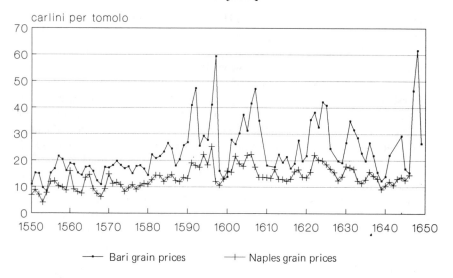

carlini per tomolo

—•— Bari grain prices   —+— Naples grain prices

1 carlino = 0.1 ducat

Figure 1.5 The price of grain on the free market and in the city of Naples

go begging that money from the merchants, and I have to put more effort into this alone than into all the other matters of governing the Kingdom. . ."[120]

Still, the Spanish authorities had no choice but to make grain available in Naples at cheaper than market prices, and, as Figure 1.5 suggests, they did.[121]

As the graph shows, the difference between the price for grain on the free market at Bari and in the regulated environment of the capital could be substantial. Not surprisingly, then, supplying the city of Naples with bread at political prices became an expensive affair. What made it more burdensome, indeed almost prohibitive, was the bewildering amount of mismanagement and of outright fraud committed by those involved in grain supply. Provisioning the city, in fact, became a very lucrative business, both for the merchant bankers supplying the grain and for the city and state officials awarding the contracts and profiteering from the ventures.

The Treasurer General, for example, was to bargain with the merchants, but instead he colluded with them, to his profit. "A few years ago," a source argues, "he

---

[120] *Ibid.*

[121] The graph is worked out from the data in Giuseppe Coniglio, "La rivoluzione dei prezzi nella città di Napoli nei secoli XVI e XVII," *Società Italiana di Statistica*. Atti della VIII Riunione Scientifica, 1949, pp. 205–40. Since the data is compiled from the records of retail grain purchases by monastic houses, it may not be an accurate reflection of the price of grain paid by commoners in Naples. It is an important indicator nonetheless, if nothing else because of the destruction of pertinent archival sources. As Coniglio himself points out, other data for grain contracts is not readily usable (cf. "Annona e calmieri").

had a lot of debts, but from what one can figure, he has spent more than 80,000 ducats, which is an incredible sum to put together in twenty years with savings from his own money and his salary [alone]. . ."[122] The Duke of Alcalá's own staff, for their part,

enjoyed their share of very great profits, because in those thirteen years that he [the Viceroy] ruled this Kingdom contracts for something like 4 million *tomola* of grain were made, whence, reckoning profit at one or two *carlini* per *tomolo*, one can image the huge sums to be made.[123]

As one might expect, the merchants worked to drive up prices, and they managed to "buy the worst possible grain they can find in Puglia, in order to buy cheap and sell at an even higher profit. . ."[124]

After three or four months at sea, the grain would arrive in Naples "very poorly conditioned" and "always about the time of the new harvest." It would be stored for the future, and since it did not improve with time, it would spoil, or not sell for three or four years, or sell only at a loss.[125] To "good" grain, to be delivered to the bakeries for the city's bread, the merchants would then add "spoiled and old" grain; the bakers, for their part, "with the excuse that they are forced to take bad grain, at times add earth, but more commonly they mix in peeled barley, rotten broken tack and other mixtures. . ."[126]

Despite the city's provisioning policy, then, Neapolitan citizens, especially the less fortunate among them, seem to have paid dearly enough for their bread – with money to the bakers, the merchant bankers and the officials, and with the pain brought on by the not infrequent scarcity of grain, which, to believe a remark (or a slip) by the Duke of Alcalá himself, ". . .isn't due to chance."[127]

But supplying Naples with enough grain, and doing so at reasonable prices, might not have been so problematical a matter. The question was periodically debated by the top administrators in the Kingdom. Time and again, the suggestion would be made that Sicilian grain be imported to feed Naples, as had been done in the past.[128] Time and again, too, the clear advantages of such a move would be restated. Grain from Sicily was of better quality than its counterpart from Puglia; it could reach Naples in much less time, and it would cost less. Pugliese grain could then be sold to the Venetians, who had to procure it on the high seas and to buy it as far away as Turkey, and His Majesty's exchequer would gain in both Sicily and Naples.[129] But

---

[122] IVdDJ, envio 80/574 (4), "Relacion de Angelo costanzo que trata de la desorden que ay de proveer a la ciudad de Napoles de trigo," n.d., but from the early 1570s (AGS. *Visitas de Italia*, leg. 337/6). Cf. also a free Spanish version of the above, envio 80/574 (3).

[123] *Ibid.*; the Duke of Alcala was Viceroy of Naples from 1558 to 1571.   [124] *Ibid.*   [125] *Ibid.*

[126] IVdDJ, envio 80/247; 1 December 1579.

[127] AGS. *Secretarías Provinciales*, leg. 1, f. 117. Cf. also AGS. *Visitas de Italia*, leg. 24/2, ff. 583r–591v for additional material on frauds by officials involved in the administration of the capital (for provisioning, ff. 585v–586v).

[128] IVdDJ, envio 80/574 (4). For some figures on Sicilian grain exports, cf. note 48.

[129] ASN. *Sommaria. Consulte*, vol. 2, ff. 67r–68r; vol. 5, ff. 145r–150r; cf. also Galasso, "Momenti e problemi," pp. 180–81 and IVdDJ, envio 80/572 (1), "Relacion en que se muestra el beneficio que puede dar el proveerse la ciudad de Napoles de trigo en el Reyno de Sicilia" (1570); envio 80/573 (2).

inevitably the discussions would be tabled, and the suggestions would remain moot, most probably because the lobby importing grain from Puglia was too strong to defeat. The city of Naples, and its citizens, paid the price: in the late sixteenth and seventeenth centuries the city was to see its tax burden multiply, its expenses rise well above its income, its debts skyrocket.[130]

In that unhappy process, the cost of supplying the poor and the disinherited in the capital with bread, though heavy enough, probably did not play the starring role attributed to it by some historians. In that facet of its experience, as in so many others, Naples reflected the wider rhythms and the wider fortunes, or misfortunes, of the Kingdom at large. Like the Kingdom, it came to bear the spiraling fiscal pressure and the economic contraction that were the hallmarks of Southern Italian life in the late sixteenth and seventeenth centuries and that impelled people to leave the provinces, indeed to abandon entire towns and flee – to the capital and even beyond the capital, to Sicily, or even to North Africa and Turkey – or to become beggars and bandits.[131]

[130] There is no doubt that the inflated cost of provisioning Naples had a negative effect on the city's finances, but it was not the only reason for the capital's financial straits. An account of the city's finances for 1583, which reports the city's debt as 1,606,423.50 ducats, states that from 1547 to 1579 630,000 ducats had been granted as aids to the Monarchy. In addition, in 1574, at the suggestion of Viceroy Cardinal Granvelle, the city had mortgaged revenues for 200,000 ducats for other aids; in 1583, it was receiving 8 percent on those mortgages. Between 1575 and 1582, the document goes on, the city had lost about 200,000 ducats on grain contracts that had been underwritten in its name (AGS. *Visitas de Italia*, leg. 25/2, ff. 178r–179v).

The city's debt had stood at "more than 600,000 ducats" in 1562 and at 963,000 ducats in the early 1570s. It rose to 1,627,223.22 ducats in 1584, 3,250,000 ducats in 1596 and 10,143,601.29 ducats in 1616. By 1584, it already took up nearly four-fifths of the capital's expense budget, which stood at little over 150,000 ducats. By 1616, it made up nearly 90 percent of expenditures, which had risen more than fourfold, to about 635,000 ducats a year. In 1584, on the other hand, the city's income had amounted to little over 160,000 ducats, nearly 90 percent of it from taxes on foodstuff. In 1616, it had risen to about 635,000 ducats, or about 50,000 ducats less than expenses; 97 percent of it came from taxes on foodstuff, new and old.

For 1562, cf. AGS. *Secretarías Provinciales*, leg. 1, f. 117; for the early 1570s, cf. IVdDJ, envio 80/574 (4); for 1584, cf. AGS. *Visitas de Italia*, leg. 24/2, ff. 347v–353r and Mantelli, who discovered and first analyzed this document, *Burocrazia e finanze pubbliche*, pp. 254–57; for 1596, AGS. *Secretarías Provinciales*, leg. 7, unfol., 4 May 1596, letter by Ascanio Muxettula (Muscettola) to the King; for 1616, Bartolommeo Capasso, *Catalogo ragionato dei libri registri e scritture esistenti nella sezione antica o prima serie dell' Archivio Municipale di Napoli* (Naples, 1876), p. 53. The data for the city's finances reported in Caracciolo's *Sud, debiti e gabelle*, pp. 231–41, are unreliable because of some serious errors. On this question, cf. chapter 2, note 7, and Appendix 1, below.

[131] For but a few of the many examples of towns abandoned by their inhabitants, cf. Faraglia, *Il Comune*, pp. 179–80. Galasso, (*Economia e società*, pp. 107–08) stresses the precarious nature of many Calabrian settlements and the relative ease with which new centers were alternately populated and abandoned. He writes, indeed, of a complex process of "redistribution of the population" in the region throughout the sixteenth century (p. 114). For the reference to migration to Turkey and North Africa, cf. Pontieri, "Il volto storico della Calabria nel Viceregno spagnolo di Napoli" in *Nei tempi grigi*, p. 372.

2

The fiscal system in early modern Naples

The passage of Naples from Aragonese to direct Spanish rule in 1504 brought no more immediate changes in the structure of the fiscal system or in the intensity of fiscal pressure than it did alterations in the political or representative system of the Kingdom.[1] Even the early years of Emperor Charles V's reign were marked by no substantial innovations. The weight of taxation remained as it had been, more or less constant, since the reforms started by Alfonso the Great, in 1444, and the retention of Don Ramón de Cardona as Viceroy until his death in 1522 attested to the sovereign's respect for the privileges and traditions of his newly-acquired realm.[2]

Yet the period bounded by the consolidation of Spanish power in Italy and the great anti-Spanish revolts of Sicily and Naples in the 1640s did see profound changes in fiscal life in the Kingdom. Those changes were most clearly felt in a significant and sustained growth of fiscal pressure which came to ignore the economic capacities of the Kingdom as it reflected the growing needs of Imperial policy.

Until the devolution of Milan to the Spanish Crown in 1535, the Kingdom was the beachhead of Spanish action in Italy, and the relatively light fiscal pressure it bore reflected its status as a newly-acquired strategic outpost. The decade following Cardona's death was an interlude, in both political and fiscal terms. Significant change in the function of Naples and in the fiscal pressure it bore, in fact, did not take place until the exceptionally long tenure of Don Pedro de Toledo, Viceroy from 1532 to 1553. Toledo's tenure reflected the new unitarian, Castilian imprint of the Spanish monarchy, and it made the Kingdom an integral part of the Imperial military and political system.[3]

That new role meant that for much of the sixteenth century Naples was part of a new strategic system that sought to contain or to roll back the tide of Islam, that was deeply involved in the wars in the Italian peninsula and that was enmeshed as well in ambitious and costly operations in Central Europe. With that, of course, went the costs of Empire, which laid heavy burdens on the Kingdom in the course of the sixteenth and, even more, the seventeenth century.

The growing population, the wealth and the "Indian summer" buoyancy of the

---

[1] Villari, *La rivolta*, p. 13. For an excellent example of the continuity in fiscal administration, cf. ASN. *Sommaria. Consulte*, vol. 2, ff. 102r–103r (on managing the gabelle for *Censali*).
[2] Galasso, "Momenti e problemi," p. 164.   [3] *Ibid.*, pp. 155–57, 164–65; Villari, *La rivolta*, pp. 98, 123.

economy enabled the Kingdom for a good part of the sixteenth century to raise taxes without unduly compromising economic activities. But inflation ate up much of the proceeds from tax increases, and it also raised expenses, forcing fiscal pressure to spiral upwards merely to keep pace with rising costs.[4]

Pressure on the Kingdom decreased somewhat in the 1580s, after the truce with Turkish power and the shift in the focus of Spanish activity from the Mediterranean northwards.[5] That change, however, proved to be only an interlude. Soon Naples was drawn once again into the thick of things. True, it was no longer a frontline for warfare in the Mediterranean. But Madrid's strategy demanded that it provide important sums of money, as well as men and arms, in support of Spanish goals and Spanish war efforts in the North.

Unfortunately for the Kingdom, the new demands it had to meet coincided with the economic reverses that began in its agriculture and its economy generally in the late 1500s. Early in the next century, Spanish demands grew increasingly urgent and burdensome, with a brief respite only during the Twelve Years' Truce (1609–21). They reached their peak in the later stages of the Thirty Years' War (1618–48) – precisely at the time, that is, when the economy in the Kingdom was showing unmistakable signs of dislocation and dysfunction. Naples thus became an ever more strained supply base for the defense of Lombardy and the support of Spanish activity in Central Europe. That trend found its climax in the great anti-fiscal revolts of the mid-seventeenth century.[6]

These generalizations are, of course, rather schematic, but they can serve to sketch out in broad detail the phases of fiscal pressure which the Kingdom of Naples sustained in the sixteenth and seventeenth centuries. They can also help as background to the detailed examination of the fiscal system, of the means and expedients used in the Kingdom to meet the demands of a new age.

Naples' tale in the sixteenth and seventeenth centuries naturally reflects historical circumstances and traditions that were specific to the Kingdom, rooted in its medieval past. The intriguing aspect of that tale, however, is that in many ways Naples' experience in the sixteenth and seventeenth centuries was far from unique. Indeed, it was a common one for kingdoms and states in Europe in that age. French cardinals and Dutch patricians, like Viceroys in Naples and Count-Dukes in Spain, all had to face the difficult problems presented by rising prices, mounting expenses and generalized warfare. Though local circumstances obviously made for variety in the responses to those problems, and in the success or failure of those responses,

---

[4] See chapters 3 and 4, which peg government income and expense in the Kingdom to the price movement.

[5] On the events in those years, see the gripping pages by Braudel, esp. Part III.

[6] On this important topic, cf. John Elliott, *The Revolt of the Catalans* (Cambridge, 1963); Boris Porchnev, *Les soulèvements populaires en France de 1623 à 1648* (Paris, 1963; a translation of *Narodnie vosstaniya vo Frantsii pered Frondoi, 1623–1648* [Moscow, 1948]); J.H.M. Salmon, "Venality of Office and Popular Sedition in Seventeenth-Century France," *Past and Present*, 1967, pp. 21–43; Robert Forster and Jack P. Greene, *Preconditions of Revolution in Early Modern Europe* (Baltimore, 1970).

Naples' experience can serve as a commentary on a pattern that transcended the borders of Southern Italy.

Like other European states in the early modern period, the Kingdom drew its revenues from taxation as well as from measures such as the sale of offices, the alienation of towns in the royal domain and various types of loans and financial expedients. Both taxation and the other revenue-generating measures showed appreciable increases in the sixteenth and seventeenth centuries, and they worked together throughout that time. For the sake of clarity, though, it is best to consider those two sources of income separately.

The core of the fiscal system in the Spanish period, as in the Aragonese, was a direct ordinary impost, the base hearth tax (*focatico* or *fiscali*). The amount of this levy was assessed by the Sommaria for each of the twelve provinces in the Kingdom on the basis of the number of hearths in each province. Within the provinces, communal administrations (*università*) then allocated the tax among the households. They did so not in direct relation to the number of hearths, but to the property, movable and not, owned by members of each household.[7] The size of the group living under one roof, furthermore, affected the amount levied upon each hearth, since a certain amount of property for each member of a family unit was exempt from the tax.[8]

The base hearth tax was not levied on the clergy, the inhabitants of the city of Naples, and the allodial holdings of the capital. It was not levied either on the old or the "poor," that is those who lived from the earnings of their labor but owned no immovable property.[9] These last exemptions perhaps attested to the Spanish government's desire to avoid fiscal inequities and to refrain from measures prejudicial to the lower classes.[10] As often happens in such cases, however, a gap existed

---

[7] Toward the end of the sixteenth century, however, there seems to have been a trend in the municipalities for the substitution of the hearth base tax with indirect taxes. The old system of tax allocation was reportedly discarded in order to raise more revenue and to meet rising fiscal demands. This trend is documented by Galasso (*Economia e società*, pp. 354–58). Caracciolo has suggested that such a trend was an expression of class interests by those in control of communal administrations (cf. "Fisco e contribuenti in Calabria," *NRS*, 1963, pp. 504–38; *Sud, debiti e gabelle* [Naples, 1983]).

Caracciolo's argument, however, has drawn very heavy criticism. Cf. in particular, Galasso, *Economia e società*, pp. 325–406, esp. pp. 354–58. *Sud, debiti e gabelle* has likewise been very damagingly criticized in an important review by Alessandra Bulgarelli-Lukacs (in *NRS*, 1985, pp. 170–7; reprinted in the same journal in 1986 [pp. 646–52], with Caracciolo's response [pp. 653–58] and with another very critical review by Mantelli [pp. 659–70; for Caracciolo's reply, cf. *Clio*, 1988, pp. 283–306]).

As both Bulgarelli-Lukacs and Mantelli point out, a basic problem lies in Caracciolo's use of data (on this question, cf. also this work, chapter 1, note 130, and Appendix 1). The problem of local finance in the Kingdom is an important one, but it will probably remain unclear until the publication of Bulgarelli-Lukacs' research.

[8] According to Coniglio, *Il Regno*, p. 76, which, however, does not specify the amount of property.

[9] *Ibid.*, p. 77.

[10] Antonio Domínguez Ortiz, *Política y Hacienda de Felipe IV* (Madrid, 1960), p. 163.

between theory and practice. Towns, for example, were often ascribed more hearths than they had, and exemptions were not always respected.[11]

From the fifteenth until at least the seventeenth century, the base hearth tax was assessed at 1.51 ducats per hearth. Naturally, though, given the pressure of rising prices and mounting expenses, the government added other direct "extraordinary" taxes to it over the course of time. The nineteenth-century Liberal writer Lodovico Bianchini, whose history of taxation in the Kingdom still holds historians' interest, noted with disapproval and dismay that, because of such extraordinary levies, the hearth tax allegedly rose from 1.51 ducats under Ferdinand the Catholic to 4.87 ducats in 1643.[12] Bianchini counted six tax increases between 1542 and 1566, five between 1605 and 1611 and three between 1617 and 1640.[13]

Actually, though, the increases in direct taxes were probably even more numerous than that. New taxes would be introduced on a contingency basis for "extraordinary" needs, such as defense, internal police, road-building, land reclamation and so forth. As is often the case in such matters, "temporary" levies tended to became permanent, despite the fact that the alleged need for them had abated, passed or been forgotten. At times, too, the reasons mustered to promote new taxes would be disingenuous or flimsy. In 1544, for example, Viceroy Toledo instituted a tax, which he later had to rescind, "for the salt and vinegar to be used in the soldiers' salads."[14] In 1608, Viceroy Count of Benavente, a source informs us,

having received many complaints and lamentations by the people and communities of the Kingdom about the oppression they suffered from soldiers, both Spanish and Italian...set up certain places called fixed garrisons in which said soldiers were to stay, and for the maintenance of all utensils, such as beds and every other thing necessary for said garrisons and soldiers, it was ordered that all the towns of the Kingdom should contribute to said impost of fixed garrisons at the rate of 30 *grana* per hearth per year...[15]

All that despite the fact that a billeting tax had been collected ever since Aragonese times and that it had been refurbished and increased on more than one occasion since the mid-sixteenth century![16]

Probably the most important of "extraordinary" direct taxes were parliamentary aids, subsidies dating back to Aragonese times.[17] Between 1504 and 1642, the dates marking the first and last meeting of the Neapolitan Estates in the Spanish period,

---

[11] Faraglia, *Il comune*, pp. 134, 184, 187. See also the "Corrispondenza tra il Nunzio di Napoli e la Corte di Roma intorno a cose di giurisdizione e di amministrazione economica e civile dall'anno 1592 sino al 1605," *ASI*, 1846, pp. 433–69 (despatch of 13 June 1599; p. 466).

[12] Bianchini, p. 206.

[13] *Ibid.*, pp. 206–07. The following chapter discusses some of the tax increases in their historical context. [14] Mantelli, *Burocrazia e finanze pubbliche*, p. 225, n. 28.

[15] BNN. Ms. XI–B–39, f. 31r. [16] Cf. chapter 3, note 19 and the references there cited.

[17] Elena Croce, "I parlamenti napoletani sotto la dominazione spagnuola," *ASPN*, 1936, pp. 341–79 (p. 347).

those subsidies were voted by the Parliament of the Kingdom.[18] After 1642, they were granted instead by a committee made up of nobles from the communal administration of the city of Naples.[19]

Representatives of the nobility, the clergy and the towns in the royal domain attended the Estates of 1504 and voted aids for 300,000 ducats.[20] After 1504, though, only the nobility and the towns contributed to aids, because the clergy had been exempted from direct taxes.[21] The burden was not divided equally between the two groups, as it was in Sicily: the towns, in fact, usually paid three-quarters the sum voted.[22]

[18] The Neapolitan Estates have not been the subject of intensive or substantive investigation (cf. A. Marongiu, "Pagine dimenticate di storia parlamentare napoletana del Cinquecento," *Studi in onore di R. Filangieri* [Naples, 1959], vol. 2, pp. 317–27). Symptomatic of that neglect is the fact that until 1957 scholars assumed that the first assembly of Parliament after the Spanish conquest had taken place in 1507 (cf. P. Gasparrini, "Un ignorato parlamento generale napoletano del 1504 e un altro poco noto del 1507," *ASPN*, 1957, pp. 203–10).

This state of affairs is in part due to the fact that the Estates, like the Viceroyal period generally, have long been viewed with a jaundiced eye. The Estates have in fact been considered mere rubber stamp assemblies, convened for the approval of decisions already taken. The image of Parliament in Naples as a purely formal institution, devoid of any substance, has continued into this century thanks in part to Benedetto Croce, who wrote in his history of the Kingdom that the Estates' positive aspects amounted to "useless litigations," and their negative ones to complicity to imposition of heavy fiscal pressure.

Essentially similar, though somewhat less harsh, was the position of Croce's daughter, Elena, who argued in the article cited above that the Estates had never been a "lively force" in Neapolitan political life, that they had sprung not from the Kingdom's needs but from a mechanical adoption of foreign institutions, and that after the Spanish conquest they had become even more formal institutions. Parliament, Croce argued, was usually submissive in voting the subsidies demanded, and its infrequent protests were superficial. Still, she concluded, they had been of some importance, because at least they had regulated extraordinary imposts, which would have been heavier without them. (For a similar argument, and on the role of the Sicilian Estates in regulating imposts, cf. Koenigsberger, pp. 160, 196.)

The need for study of the Estates remains, despite a step in the right direction taken with Guido D'Agostino's *Parlamento e società nel Regno di Napoli* (Naples, 1979).

[19] B. Croce, *Storia del Regno di Napoli*, p. 116; E. Croce, p. 358.

[20] Gasparrini, p. 206.

[21] Carignani, "Le rappresentanze e i dritti (*sic*) dei Parlamenti napoletani. Notizie tratte dai libri detti Praecedentiarum," *ASPN*, 1883, pp. 659–60; E. Croce, p. 352; Gasparrini, p. 207. The clergy as a body attended none of the Estates after 1504. Individual clergymen did, but in their capacity as barons, not clerics. In the Estates, the nobility was divided into titled and non-titled orders. By 1642, the towns had stopped sending representatives to Parliament, probably because they had lost importance with their numerical decline and their alienation from the royal domain (cf. Carignani, "L'ultimo Parlamento generale del regno di Napoli nel 1642," *ASPN*, 1883, pp. 34–57 and "Le rappresentanze," pp. 655, 659). The mayor and the representatives of the city of Naples played some role in the proceedings of the Estates. The former presided over the assembly after the opening session, which, like the last one, was led by the Viceroy; the latter, twelve strong, joined twelve representatives of the baronage in a committee that drew up the lists of privileges requested (E. Croce, pp. 349–50). The role of those officials attests to the capital's influence, especially since the city of Naples was exempt from direct taxes and thus was not usually affected directly by the Estates' decisions.

[22] In Sicily, the clergy paid $\frac{1}{6}$ the amount of parliamentary aids granted; the barons and the towns, $\frac{5}{12}$ each (Koenigsberger, p. 125). For the apportionment in Naples, cf. Galasso, "Momenti e problemi,"

Aids were paid only periodically from 1504 to 1534, when they began to be voted generally every two years.[23] The sums they provided varied a good deal until 1566, when they were set at 1,200,000 ducats, payable over two years, or 600,000 ducats a year.[24] Between 1534 and 1546, they provided 3,585,000 ducats, or about 276,000 ducats a year; but they ranged from 75,000 to 500,000 ducats a year.[25] From 1549 to 1552, they amounted to 600,000 ducats, to be collected in eight instalments, that is 225,000 ducats a year.[26] In 1552, they supplied 800,000 ducats over two years.[27] Ten years later, in 1562, they provided 1,000,000 ducats over two years.[28]

The sum stipulated in 1566, moreover, did not reflect the entire amount of subsidies generally paid after that year. From time to time, in fact, the government would request additional "extraordinary" aids for varying amounts.[29] Occasionally, the Estates themselves would vote supplementary monies, as they had done before 1566, in exchange for the suspension of new hearth censuses.[30] Oftentimes also, the Estates or the barons alone would grant relatively small sums to the Viceroy or other officials, even though in 1564 Parliament had been expressly ordered to refrain from such practices.[31]

Year	Amount
1534	150,000
1536	1,000,000
1538	360,000
1539	285,000
1541	800,000
1543	150,000
1544	600,000
1546	240,000
Total	3,585,000

p. 175; Coniglio, "Note sulla società napoletana ai tempi di Don Pietro di Toledo," *Studi in onore di R. Filangieri*, vol. 2, p. 359, note 34.

In the Kingdom, the nobility's contribution included a monetary grant that had replaced the older, feudal military obligation due the King (*adoa*); the towns' share was apportioned among the hearths in the same manner as the hearth base tax. (Until 1504, the *adoa* had amounted to 52.5 percent of noble revenues; that year, the barons were allowed to pass half of it on to their subjects [Faraglia, *Il comune*, p. 119, n. 1]. For the apportionment of aids on the towns, cf. Caracciolo, "Fisco e contribuenti," p. 505. A Tuscan agent, however, informed the Grand-Duke in 1612 that since there was no ready cash with which to meet that year's aids payment, gabelles had been imposed on silk, shoes, wine, sugar and meat [cf. "Documenti...Toscana," p. 274; despatch for 29 June 1612]). [23] Bianchini, p. 204.

[24] Galasso, "Momenti e problemi," p. 175.

[25] AGS. *Guerra Antigua*, leg. 29, f. 10. That sum was broken down as shown in Table 2.1.

[26] AGS. *Estado*. leg. 1042, f. 120 (until December 1552).   [27] *Ibid.*, leg. 1042, f. 135.

[28] *Ibid.*, leg. 1053, f. 126.

[29] Those were not always granted. For an example, cf. "Documenti...Urbino," pp. 215–16, despatches for 30 December 1582, and 3 January 1583: a request for an extraordinary grant of 200,000 ducats met with "stalwart opposition" and was rejected.

[30] For some examples of this common phenomenon, cf. Carignani, "Le rappresentanze," p. 667.

[31] E. Croce, p. 355. For examples of grants by the barons alone, cf. *ibid.*, p. 379; Carignani, "Le rappresentanze," p. 667. As was the case in Sicily, such grants may have been inspired only by the

While hearth taxes and parliamentary aids were increased in the course of the sixteenth and seventeenth centuries, their levy did not represent a substantial structural innovation in the fiscal system refurbished by the Aragonese dynasty. Nor, as the next chapter will show in some detail, did government receipts from direct taxes manage to keep abreast of inflation at any time from the mid-sixteenth century to the 1630s.[32]

The same is not true for indirect taxes. Although those imposts were by no means unknown before the passage of Naples to direct Spanish rule, their extension and multiplication after 1504 amounted to a true fiscal novelty.[33] Not only that, but from the 1550s to the 1630s they made up an increasingly larger share of government receipts, and they more than made up for the sluggishness of direct taxes by far outpacing the price movement.[34]

Primarily responsible for this trend were gabelles on consumption and on economic activities, which began proliferating in the last years Emperor Charles V's rule.[35] Wine, oil, silk, soap – nearly every commodity for export or use within the Kingdom was the target of new levies, which were added to whatever "ordinary duties" existed. In 1558, for example, the excise on the export of cereals and leguminous products was increased from 2 to 10 and, after a few years, to 30 ducats per *carro*.[36] In 1556, the tolls on the pasture of sheep in the reserves of Puglia and Abruzzi were increased by 50 percent.[37] In 1557, a similar increase affected the tax on the retail sale of wine in the capital and its environs.[38]

As might be expected, indirect taxes were generally decreed for a limited number of years, but they usually wound up becoming permanent. A duty on the export of saffron, levied soon after the French invasion of the Kingdom in 1528 and subsequently abolished, was imposed again in 1554 for two years; in 1556, it was indefinitely extended. Similarly, after the 1528 invasion a duty on the export of oil was levied on the two provinces of Terra di Bari and Terra d'Otranto; it too was first abolished and, in 1554, reimposed throughout the Kingdom.[39]

Pervasive and lasting as they were, such imposts were naturally also subject to increases over time. The tax on silk in Calabria, for example, rose from 5 *carlini* (0.5 ducat) per pound in 1540 to 22 *carlini* (2.2 ducats) in 1590.[40] The duty on the export

---

desire to make a good impression, and they may have been accompanied by the tacit understanding that they should not be accepted (cf. the case of Viceroy Villena, who in 1609 took seriously the offer of 60,000 *scudi* made to him by the Sicilian Estates [Koenigsberger, p. 97]. Cf. also "Documenti. . . Urbino," p. 216, despatch for 7 January 1583, which reports the opinion, apparently current in Naples at the time, that the aids of 25,000 ducats voted to the Viceroy would not be accepted, and which cites the cases of the Marquis of Mondéjar and of the Cardinal of Granvelle, who, on the King's orders, had refrained from accepting grants, and that of the Duke of Alcalá, who had accepted, but subsequently returned a grant made to him).   [32] See chapter 3, below.

[33] Most of the contracts for the administration of indirect taxes, in fact, sprang up in the Viceroy period. Cf. De Rosa, *Studi sugli arrendamenti*, p. 8.   [34] See chapter 3, below.

[35] Galasso, "Momenti e problemi," pp. 176–78.   [36] *Ibid.*, p. 179.

[37] *Ibid.*, p. 177; Bianchini, p. 197.   [38] Galasso, "Momenti e problemi," p. 178.

[39] *Ibid.*, p. 177.   [40] Galasso, *Economia e società*, p. 146.

of oil, which had amounted to one *tarì* (0.2 ducats) per *salma* in the early 1540s had increased over sixteenfold, to 3.3 ducats per *salma*, by 1654.[41]

In addition to such taxes on consumption and export, the government levied also a whole plethora of other duties – on business transacted and commodities imported; on scarce items, like iron and pitch, and on new products, like tobacco.[42] It exacted anchorage taxes on ships in the harbors, and it assessed excises on the retail sale of goods, the slaughter of animals, the introduction of produce in the towns. At times, it resorted to bizarre, if ingenious, measures: in 1605, it proposed (but soon had to abandon) a duty of one ducat per window, applicable to the capital and payable by landlords.[43]

The administration and collection of taxes was marked by a strong disparity between theory and practice. On paper, the system was clear and centralized. In fact, it was chaotic, marred by overlapping and often competing jurisdictions, and plagued by a bewildering variety of exemptions and loopholes.[44] Though it had elements of centralization, in actual practice, more often than not, these were negated by even stronger elements of particularism.

Thus theoretically the allocation and administration of the tax burden was a relatively simple and streamlined affair. The Sommaria set the yearly quota of direct taxes; communal administrations allocated them by household, and officials responsible to provincial treasurers collected them. Analogously, the Sommaria held bids for indirect tax contracts, the tax farmers who won the bids administered them, and a spate of officials dependent on the tax farmers collected them. The Sommaria oversaw the administration of all taxes, direct or indirect, and it exercised a similar control over the Foggia Sheep Customs, the lucrative pastoral organization in the Kingdom.[45]

In practice, though, the feedback mechanism between the center and the periphery was slow, often unresponsive and easily blocked. Officials did present their books to the Sommaria, who did audit the accounts. As in other parts of the Empire, however, the process was proverbially slow and cumbersome. Repeated attempts at rationalizing procedure and speeding up audits in the course of the sixteenth century did not improve matters, despite unquestionable good faith and even better intentions.[46] Jurisdictional trivia could tie up matters for years on end,

[41] ASN. *Sommaria. Arrendamenti*, Ff. 706 (September 1542–December 1545) and 745 (1651–54).

[42] Bianchini, pp. 210–21; Coniglio, *Il Regno*, pp. 192–203. For the gabelle on tobacco, which was introduced in 1637, cf. the informative article by Renato Urga, "La privativa del tabacco nel Napoletano durante il Viceregno," *Studi in onore di R. Filangieri* (Naples, 1959), vol. 2, pp. 551–72.

[43] No doubt this could be described as a type of luxury tax. "Documenti. . .Toscana," pp. 259–60, despatches for 5 July and 16 August 1605. For additional examples, cf. p. 261 (16 June 1606: a gabelle on paper); p. 278 (22 March 1619: a gabelle on foodstuffs).

[44] For some examples, cf. the exemptions from duties in the Naples Customhouse, in BNN. Ms. XI–B–39, ff. 58r–60r, 63r–65v.

[45] On the Foggia Sheep Customs, cf. the works cited in chapter 3, note 42.

[46] For some examples, cf. ASN. *Sommaria. Consulte*, vol. 5, ff. 104r–106r, 212r–214r; vol. 7, f. 192v; vol. 11, ff. 67r–v, 76r–78r; vol. 13/1, ff. 5v–8v, 333r–336v, 370r–373r, 421r–424v, 454r; vol. 15, ff. 235r–v;

and burning issues could become moot with the passage of time.[47] The Sommaria accountants were clearly overworked, and their salaries, like those of officials generally, did not keep up with inflation.[48] The pressures of clienteles and interest groups, furthermore, must have been immense, and temptations were rife. Like their counterparts in other states, and not just in early modern times, Sommaria personnel, from the Lieutenant to the accountants on down, could be, and often were, suborned.[49]

From a modern perspective, probably the most damning aspect of fiscal administration is the fact that only part of it was centralized. For much of the sixteenth century, in fact, only about two-fifths of expenses were handled by the Treasury General, in Naples. The other expenses were met directly at the local level, by the same tax farmers who leased the gabelles and by the same fiscal officials who collected direct taxes.[50] Furthermore, those men's profits, and for some of them even their salaries, depended on the "success" of their tenures. Direct tax collection, in particular, often took the form of armed incursions and raids.[51] This state of affairs, of course, encouraged rapacity and profiteering, at the tax payers' expense. But it, too, was not peculiar to Naples; it was the norm rather than the exception in early modern Europe.

Actually, it is doubtful that even a more directly centralized system could have been more efficient and honest. The Sommaria, at least, does not seem to have thought so. In 1564, it was asked to consider whether the Court should repurchase an important policiary/judicial office involved in provisioning the city of Naples.[52] That office had been "sold" to one Jacobo Terracina for the hefty sum of 32,000 ducats.[53]

In considering its recommendation, the Sommaria discussed

whether the office should be run by a royal official. . .for good government and the public good, so that keeping it and administering it in the royal name [the office] would be run more honestly and with greater authority and respect, without the frauds committed by the people involved in said office, especially in the matter of selling foodstuffs at higher prices than those set for provisioning this city.[54]

Sommaria. *Carte Reali*, vol. 1, ff. 35r–36r, 69r–v, 179r–v, 236v–237v; *Sommaria. Diversi*, Prima Numerazione, F. 51, ff. 59r–63r, 69r–70r, 71r–72r, 176r–177r, 177v–178r, 178v–179v, 180r–v, 181r–184r, 188r–189r, 197r–v, 201r–v, 203r–204r; BSNSP. Ms. xxvii–c–3, ff. 65r–v, 278r–279r.

47 An excellent example of jurisdictional squabbles used to thwart a thorough audit of accounts is given in the petition by Joan Antonio and Joan Francesco Grimaldi, sons of Cristoforo Grimaldi and heirs to their father's office of direct tax collector in the province of Terra di Lavoro, in AGS. *Secretarías Provinciales*, libro 516, ff. 150r–151v (19 May 1593).

48 For some of the descriptions of the accountants' work, their duties and their workload, cf. ASN. *Sommaria. Consulte*, vol. 2, f. 2r, ff. 185v–186r and vol. 13/1, f. 358r. For the question of salaries and inflation, cf. the section on civil expenditures in chapter 4.

49 For but some examples, cf. AGS. *Secretarías Provinciales*, leg. 235, *passim*; *Visitas de Italia*, leg. 345/5 ("#142"). 50 Cf. Calabria, *State Finance*, p. 185.

51 Cf. Coniglio, *Il Regno*, pp. 63–74. 52 The office of *Justitiero de la grassa* in the city of Naples.

53 ASN. *Sommaria. Consulte*, vol. 2, ff. 56v–58v. Note, for comparative purposes, that a Viceroy's annual salary at that time was 10,000 ducats. 54 *Ibid.*, f. 56v.

Its decision was emphatically negative. Even if the Court were to regain control of the office, it argued, "the frauds and excesses that are committed in [its] jurisdiction" would not stop.

Rather [it went on], it seems they would increase, because. . .the Court. . .would have to put in charge of it an administrator with an assistant, and even if they were trustworthy and respectable, it does not seem the Royal Court could be as confident of good and honest administration as with the said Magnificent Jacobo. . .[55]

Part of the reason was "the quality of [Jacobo's] person"; but there was also the fact that, with "poor administration," Jacobo risked having his office confiscated, thus losing his investment, "which penalty would not apply to a royal administrator." Proper administration in that office, the Sommaria went on, "is due to fear," and involves collecting fines. A royal official need not be afraid, "and in the matter of fines, it is doubtful that [he] would use as much diligence in investigating and levying them on the Royal Court's behalf as does the said Jacobo for his own utility and profit."[56]

Finally, the Sommaria concluded, with a royal official

it would be necessary that said administrator and his assistant employ several people, who are needed in such an administration, but who would pose the danger, as usually happens, of secret understandings with butchers and shopkeepers, which redound more to their private gain than to the royal service or the common good. . .[57]

The case of Jacobo Terracina and his office speaks eloquently of the limits of royal authority in an age of allegedly growing "absolutism." Unfortunately for the cause of centralization in early modern Europe, it is also not simply an isolated, random incident, or one peculiar to the Kingdom of Naples.[58] It is, rather, an emblematic

---

[55] *Ibid.*, f. 57r.

[56] *Ibid.*, f. 57r ("In le quale pene è da dubitar si lo administratore Regio usasse tanta Diligentia ad Investigarle et exigerle per la regia Corte quanta usa Il detto Jacobo per l'utile et benefitio suo proprio").

[57] *Ibid.*, ff. 57r–v. There would also be, the Sommaria argued, the matters of determining how much the office yielded, of paying appropriate salaries to the royal officials, and of coming up with the 32,000 ducats to repay Terracina.

The latter, for his part, felt aggrieved "because of new bans [to the effect] that lawbreakers can be punished with a monetary fine only once. . .saying expressly that he would not have bought [the office] at such a price of 32,000 ducats if he had considered running it any other way than used to be done before said new bans" (ff. 57v–58r).

Terracina sued for redress but lost, even though the Sommaria believed his claim that his income from the office had decreased. His legal undoing had been twofold. First, the fact that "said new bans depend on the [royal] guidelines for good living [i.e. the rules for provisioning the capital], under which guidelines he purchased said office." Second (and this is a statement that seems to define the sphere of royal authority) "because the nature of said office entails varying the penalties according to the quality of the times and the public good, which is understood to be reserved for His Majesty and Your Excellency [the Viceroy] in His name" (f. 58r).

[58] To give but one of many possible examples, in 1626, sixty-six years after the Sommaria had made its recommendation on the Terracina case, the Collateral Council, Naples' top political magistracy, most strongly urged that the salt tax contract in the provinces and of Terra d'Otranto and Basilicata be leased to a tax farmer because, one speaker argued, "keeping the contracts in the Royal domain is like

case: like a microcosm, it reveals assumptions and attitudes that helped shape and delimit realities in early modern times – realities that were at once fiscal and cultural, public and private, social and political.[59]

Taxation was the primary source of government income, but it was complemented by expedients that were commonplace in early modern fiscal systems and that often provided important sums for administrations beleaguered by rising prices and mounting expenses.

The proceeds from the sale or "ampliation" of offices in the Kingdom increased in the course of the sixteenth and seventeenth centuries, but they were not a large source of government income. Between 1564 and 1574, such revenue amounted to 93,605 ducats, or less than 10,000 ducats a year – a paltry sum indeed if one considers that from 1551 to 1554 alone the Kingdom provided Milan with 369,000 ducats.[60] By the end of the century, the price of offices had increased, and some offices, formerly not sold, had become venal, so that the proceeds from this source, a document from the 1590s states, could be estimated at 20,000 ducats a year, "and perhaps more."[61] In 1600, they amounted to about 18,000 ducats; in 1621, to about 29,000; in 1626, they were estimated at about 40,000 ducats. Though with some variation, they seem to have stayed at about that level into the late 1630s.[62]

Clerical contributions, like the proceeds from the sale of offices, were also unimpressive. While the latter source of revenue was objectively limited, the former was largely untapped and potentially vast. The clergy of the Kingdom was exempt from direct and indirect taxes alike; it enjoyed the privilege of immunity, and it owned considerable amounts of property.[63] Its members must have been numerous

putting them in the hands of the devil" (quoted in Galasso, "Le riforme del conte di Lemos," p. 208. The original has a pun: "lo stare l'Arrendamenti [indirect tax contracts] in demanio, è come stessero in mano del demonio"). For another example, from 1637, cf. below, p. 103.

59 Cf. the important paper by Federico Chabod, "Y a-t-il un état de la Renaissance?" (English translation: "Was there a Renaissance State?" in Heinz Lubasz, ed. *The Development of the Modern State*, [New York, 1964], pp. 26–42).

60 Federico Chabod, *Lo stato di Milano nella prima metà del secolo XVI* (Rome, 1955), p. 119. The figure for offices is from a document from 1591–92 (ASN. *Archivi Privati. Giudice-Caracciolo*, F. 33), cited in Galasso, "Momenti e problemi," p. 174.

61 Galasso, "Momenti e problemi," p. 174.

62 For 1600, cf. ASN. *Sommaria. Dipendenze*, F. 25, f, 225r (17,675 ducats); for 1621, AGS. *Estado*, leg. 1884, f. 105, c. 18r (28,976 ducats); for 1626, Galasso, "Contributo alla storia delle finanze del Regno di Napoli nella prima metà del Seicento," *Annuario dell'Istituto Storico Italiano per l'età moderna e contemporanea*, 1959, pp. 5–106 (the budget, "Bilancio del anno 1626 del stato del real patrimonio per l'intrate et pesi tiene per anno in questo Regno di Napoli," is in ASN. *Archivio Farnesiano*, busta 1338, 1 [40,107 ducats; pp. 78–79]); for 1638, ASN. *Sommaria. Consulte*, vol. 41, f. 189r (43,001 ducats; estimate); for 1639, BNN. Ms XII–B–46, p. 924 (65,129.50 ducats, estimate based on alleged income of 87,324 ducats for 1637 and 42,935 ducats for 1638).

63 On occasion, the clergy took advantage of the privilege of immunity by engaging in contraband. Cf. Coniglio. "Annona e calmieri," pp. 108–09, and chapter 1 of this work (for the case of the Tremiti islands monks).

Bianchini (p. 192) writes that the clergy owned two-thirds of all Neapolitan properties, but Coniglio (*Il Viceregno*, pp. 73–75) is justifiably skeptical; still, he argues, that figure points generally to the greater extent of ecclesiastical property *vis-à-vis* both baronial and demanial holdings.

indeed. In 1580, the Venetian Ambassador Alvise Lando wrote that the Kingdom had twenty archbishoprics and one hundred bishoprics, and in 1621 in the province of Calabria Ultra alone there were 7,319 priests and minor clerics.[64] In the capital, as in the Kingdom at large, furthermore, there were innumerable convents and monasteries. With its wealth, its privileges and its numbers, the clergy was a force to be reckoned with. Indeed, according to one writer, its strength imposed a serious limit on the civil and political power of the Monarchy.[65] Clerical presumptions were by no means uncontested by the state, but they were strengthened by the clergy's aggressiveness and by the theoretical subjection of the Kingdom to Rome as a Papal fief.[66]

As one might expect, the clergy's financial contributions to the state were hardly commensurate with its wealth and position. Apparently, half the proceeds from the ecclesiastical tithes levied in the Kingdom went to civil authorities, but aside from occasional aids dispensed through Papal authority in times of emergency, no other revenue from ecclesiastical sources seems to have been available to the state.[67]

Much more lucrative than either the sale of offices or clerical contributions was the sale of lands. This expedient had been used at least since Aragonese times, and it imported the outright alienation of towns and properties in the royal domain.[68] It had figured prominently as a source of revenue in the first quarter century of Spanish rule, when a limit to the number of alienable properties seemed to have been reached. But it continued throughout the sixteenth and seventeenth centuries, even though other expedients came to dominate the fiscal scene from the 1540s on.[69] It returned in full force in the 1630s and 1640s, when the strains of the Thirty Years' War led to the wholesale alienation of towns and lands formerly left untouched.

---

[64] For Lando's report, cf. Albèri, ser. 2, vol. 5, 1858, p. 449. The 1621 figure is in Galasso, *Economia e società*, p. 325. The presence of a minor cleric in a household reportedly exempted the entire family from taxes (Coniglio, "Annona e calmieri," p. 463).

[65] V. Castaldo, "I vescovi e il vicerè Cardinal di Granvela (Dalle lettere esortatorie)," *Studi di storia napoletana in onore di Michelangelo Schipa* (Naples, 1926), p. 443.

[66] Galasso, *Economia e società*, pp. 325, 335; Castaldo, p. 443. The other side of the coin is demonstrated by the Venetian Ambassador Girolamo Soranzo, who in 1602 reported that the King greatly esteemed "this Kingdom. . .having always been the true instrument for keeping in check those pontiffs that might have aspired to stir movements in this province" (Niccolò Barozzi and Guglielmo Berchet, eds., *Le relazioni degli stati europei lette al Senato dagli ambasciatori veneziani nel secolo decimosettimo* [Venice, 1868], vol. 1: *Spagna*, p. 332).

[67] AGS. *Estado*, leg. 1882, folio missing, 6 February 1619: the Council of State to the King, which summarizes the letters of the Viceroys Duke of Osuna and Cardinal Borja y Velasco. The latter had written of his futile efforts to get the Pope to increase the aid for the effort in Bohemia.

[68] For some examples of the towns' reactions to this measure, cf. Faraglia, *Il comune*, pp. 120–121.

[69] Note the periodization in Galasso's important "Momenti e problemi," pp. 174, 178. From the fifteenth to the end of the sixteenth century, the number of lands in the royal domain declined, from about 7 to about 4 percent of the total. They had been 102 in the times of Alfonso I, out of 1,550 properties, and they fell to 53 out of 1,619 properties in 1579. In 1586, they had increased to 69 out of 1,973 properties; at the end of the century, they numbered 76 out of 1,974 properties (the source for the figures up to, and including, 1586 is Bianchini, p. 186; those figures, and the ones for the end of the century, are reported in Galasso, "Momenti e problemi," pp. 173–74 and note 29).

Properties, of course, varied greatly in value, and thus in both price and their utility to the fisc, but two examples, from different points in time, can give a sense of the amount of revenue they could muster. At the meeting of the 1536 Estates, Emperor Charles V requested 3,000,000 ducats, allegedly so as to redeem all lands and properties which had been alienated.[70] In 1619, on the other hand, the Council of Italy informed the King that he could obtain five or six million ducats from the sale of demanial lands.[71] Although the Council subsequently reversed its opinion, the figure it had cited suggests the magnitude of sums that could be involved in the sale of royal properties. That figure is no doubt also a reflection of a changing policy toward demanial lands. Ordinarily, in fact, towns of strategic importance or lands whose alienation might have compromised state security had not been sold. Even in 1619, some such precautions were still being taken. In the following years, though, as financial needs became more pressing, all caution was thrown to the winds.[72]

The "sale of revenues" and a complex system of loans were much more important than any of the expedients discussed so far in providing money for the exchequer. Those financial expedients were the effective underpinnings of the Imperial fiscal machinery.[73] In Naples as in other parts of the Empire, they were used to meet urgent needs, to make up chronic deficits and to bridge the gap between tax levies. A wide variety of short-term loans made up the floating public debt, while the proceeds from the "sale of revenues" made up the consolidated, long-term public debt.

Among the more important types of short-term loans were exchange transactions (*cambi*) and contracted loans (*partiti*). Exchange transactions made up the core of the credit system in the Spanish Empire and tied its different areas into the major

---

[70] Coniglio, "Note sulla società," p. 354.

[71] Pidal and Miraflores, Marquises of, and Don Miguel Salva, eds., *Colección de documentos inéditos para la historia de España*, vol. 47 (Madrid, 1865), pp. 306–07. Cf. corroborating evidence in "Narrazioni tratte dai giornali di Don Pietro Girone duca d'Osuna Viceré di Napoli scritti da Francesco Zazzera" in Francesco Palermo, ed., "Narrazioni e documenti sulla storia del Regno di Napoli dall'anno 1522 al 1667" in *ASI*, 1846, pp. 471–617 [p.564]. For additional examples from the sixteenth century, cf. Calabria, "Finanzieri genovesi."   [72] For some examples, cf. Villari, *La rivolta*, p. 124.

[73] The literature on the system of loans in the Spanish Monarchy is immense. Some of the more important works discussing it are: H. Lonchay, "Etude sur les emprunts des souverains belges au XVIe et au XVIIe siècle," *Académie Royale de Belgique. Bulletin de la Classe des Lettres et des Sciences Morales et Politiques et de la Classe des Beaux Arts*, 1907, pp. 921–1013, *passim*; Ramón Carande, *Carlos V y sus Banqueros*, (Madrid, 1945–67); *Otros siete estudios de historia de España* (Barcelona, 1978); Modesto Ulloa, *La hacienda real de Castilla en el reinado de Felipe II*, (Madrid, 1977); Henri Lapeyre, *Simon Ruiz et les "Asientos" de Philippe II* (Paris, 1953); Felipe Ruiz Martín, *Lettres marchandes échangées entre Florence et Medina del Campo* (Paris, 1965); "Un expediente financiero entre 1560 y 1575. La hacienda de Felipe II y la Casa de la Contratación de Sevilla," *Moneda y Crédito*, 1965, pp. 3–58; "Las finanzas españolas durante el reinado de Felipe II," *Hispania. Cuadernos de Historia*, 1968, pp. 109–73; and the important articles by Alvaro Castillo Pintado, "Dette flottante et dette consolidée en Espagne de 1557 à 1600," *Annales. Economies, Sociétes, Civilizations*, 1963, pp. 745–59; "Los juros de Castilla. Apogeo y fin de un instrumento de crédito," *Hispania*, 1963, pp. 43–70; "'Decretos' et 'medios generales' dans le système financier de la Castille. La crise de 1596," *Mélanges en l'Honneur de Fernand Braudel* (Toulouse, 1973), vol. 1, pp. 137–44. A model of clarity is A.W. Lovett, "The Castilian Bankruptcy of 1575," *The Historical Journal*, 1980, pp. 899–911.

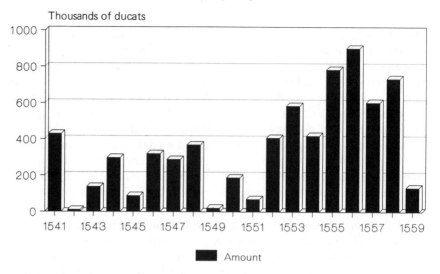

Figure 2.1 Exchange transactions: sums drawn on Naples, 1541–1559

circuits of international finance. Contracted loans served identical goals, but they worked well also with local needs and local emergencies, like budget deficits or defense costs in the Kingdom itself. Both types of loans represented Naples' share of the cost of Empire. Exchange transactions, though, might be underwritten either in Naples or abroad; contracted loans were stipulated by the Viceroy in Naples. The one and the other involved very large amounts of money throughout the sixteenth and seventeenth centuries.

From 1541 to 1559, loans for nearly 7,000,000 ducats were assigned for payment on Naples or sent from the Kingdom to support Imperial efforts in Italy, North Africa and Northern Europe.[74] As Figure 2.1 makes clear, the time of most intense borrowing through these financial expedients was the 1550s, in particular the years 1555–1558.

From the 1540s to the early 1580s, on the other hand, over 8,000,000 ducats in contracted loans were underwritten in the Kingdom.[75] High points in that series

[74] Roberto Mantelli first brought those loans to the attention of scholars. Cf. his *Burocrazia e finanze pubbliche*, pp. 333–52, also for a discussion of the "events' those loans helped finance. Figure 2.1 is derived from the original document, AGS. *Visitas de Italia*, leg. 346, "Sumario de los dineros ["Notamento delli dinari che sono stati tratti a pagare"].

[75] Available figures cover the years 1541, 1548–62, 1564–66, 1568, 1571–80, 1582–84. The data on loans for 1541–59 is in AGS. *Visitas de Italia*, leg. 20/8, ff. 79r, 92r–94r, 137r–v; for 1560–76, in AGS. *Estado*, leg. 1070, f. 6, and for 1563–84 in AGS. *Vititas de Italia*, leg. 25/1, ff. 595r–602r.

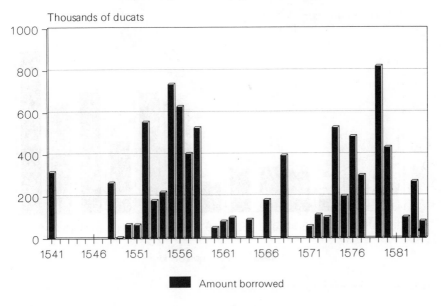

Thousands of ducats

Figure 2.2 Contracted loans, 1541–1584

occurred in the 1550s, especially the years 1552 and 1555–58, then again in the mid-
and late 1570s and the early 1580s. Figure 2.2 plots these data.

As both Figures 2.1 and 2.2 clearly show, sizable sums of money were involved in
both exchange transactions and contracted loans. Providing those sums became very
big business indeed in the Kingdom, as in Castile itself, and gave merchant bankers,
particularly the Genoese, unique opportunities for profit.[76] Thanks to such loans,
Imperial administration was able to secure advances on future revenues, and to meet
pressing military obligations from one corner of Europe to the other. But those very
same measures made also for a vicious cycle of indebtedness that frustrated attempts
at increasing revenue and that helped place much of the economy and the finances of
the Kingdom, as of Castile, in the hands of foreign entrepreneurs.

The root cause of such a state of affairs, of course, lay in the demands imposed by
Imperial policy on the resources of the Kingdom, as of Castile. But the royal
officials' attitude towards the Crown's resources did not help matters. As A.W.
Lovett has aptly pointed out, those officials were "credit raisers and debt managers
[who] saw Crown resources and tax grants not as items of recurrent revenue to be
husbanded carefully but as capital assets to be pawned hurriedly."[77]

This was particularly true of the "sale of revenues," the other financial expedient

---

[76] Cf. Calabria, "Finanzieri genovesi," *passim*.   [77] Lovett, p. 910.

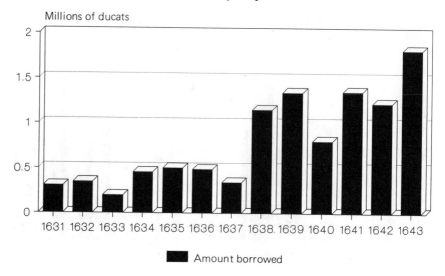

Millions of ducats

Amount borrowed

1643: Actual and Projected; other years, actual

Figure 2.3 Loans for the defense of Milan, 1631–1643

that provided Imperial administration with huge sums of ready cash. As the term suggests, the "sale of revenues" involved mortgaging at interest future revenue from a source of income, such as a gabelle or a direct tax, in return for a lump sum of money. A gabelle yielding, say, 50,000 ducats after the usual operating expenses could provide (at least theoretically) a lump sum of 500,000 ducats if securities guaranteed by its income were "sold" (or mortgaged) at 10 percent interest, or 625,000 ducats if the interest were 8 percent, and so forth.

Floating securities in such a fashion could prove a boon to a financially hard-pressed administration, though, of course, only in the short run. Once the government had obtained its lump payment, in fact, it had also "alienated," or mortgaged, future revenues from the specific tax source guaranteeing the securities sold. Those monies would provide the yearly interest payable to the investors in the usual three yearly instalments.

The last chapter of this work will discuss in some detail the creation of market in government securities in the 1540s and 1550s, the "financial revolution," as that venture has been called, and it will explore the social dimension of the funded debt in the Kingdom through a computer study of nearly 4,500 investors in the later sixteenth century. Here perhaps it suffices to state that thanks to such ingenious measures as the creation of a government bond market, the Crown was able greatly to expand its indebtedness in the course of the sixteenth and seventeenth centuries. As chapter 4 will show in detail, the public debt in the Kingdom in fact nearly quadrupled in the last forty-odd years of the sixteenth century and then nearly tripled in the first forty or so of the seventeenth.

That indebtedness, as subsequent chapters will suggest, was out of proportion to the economic capacities of the Kingdom in the late sixteenth and seventeenth centuries. It was a clear reflection, though, of the increasing cost of the policy of war and grandeur in which the Spanish Empire, and all Europe, came to be embroiled. A clear measure of that change will emerge from the next two chapters, which will analyze in detail government income and expense from the mid-sixteenth century to the times of the Thirty Years' War. Yet it can be anticipated even now by a last figure, for loans underwritten in the Kingdom between 1631 and 1643.[78] Those loans amounted to about 11,000,000 ducats, or about 840,000 ducats a year – about one and a half times the average yearly amount of indebtedness incurred through exchange transactions and contracted loans together in the sixteenth century.[79] They represented Naples' burden for the defense of Milan and Lombardy in those years, its share of the cost of Empire, and a mortgage that was to haunt the future of the Kingdom for years to come.

[78] The data used in Figure 2.3 are derived from ASN. *Sommaria. Consulte*, vol. 47, ff. 107r–126r. They differ slightly from those published in Coniglio, *Il Viceregno*, pp. 268–72, which are based on a Spanish translation of the Sommaria's *consulta* (AGS. *Estado*, leg. 3267, f. 255). The difference is due to the fact that in rendering the document into Spanish, the translator entered the entry for 1636 as "100,000 ducats" in the written text and as "10,000 ducats" in the addition column. Coniglio used the first amount, but, as the Italian original makes clear (f. 115r; fourth entry on the folio), the second is correct.

[79] That, of course, is a rough and ready measure for indebtedness for the years represented in Figures 2.1 and 2.2 above.

3

Government income, 1550–1638

The preceding chapter focused on elements of continuity and change in the fiscal administration of the Kingdom of Naples in the early modern era and showed that both tradition and innovation were the hallmarks of the Spanish presence in Southern Italy. The Neapolitan fiscal system underwent little structural innovation in the two centuries of direct Spanish rule. Significant change did come to the Kingdom during that time, however, and it concerned the intensity and rhythms of fiscal pressure as well as the introduction of certain expedients, such as the creation of a market in government securities, which greatly expanded the state's return from the yield of taxation.

Though from a different perspective, this chapter too will be concerned with both continuity and change. Its aim is to trace the history of government income in Naples from the 1550s to the 1630s, and to do so in quantitative terms. It will therefore concentrate on innovation, on the results of fiscal policies which sought to increase state revenue in the face of mounting commitments in several theaters.

The story this chapter will tell is, of course, grounded in the specific historical context of the Kingdom of Naples in the sixteenth and seventeenth centuries. But in its general outline at least, it is a story of much wider resonance than that, because the fiscal and financial problems of the Kingdom of Naples were also those of Spain and of many other states in Europe in an age of rising prices and of increasingly expensive warfare. The solutions to those problems, and their consequences, differed in the several states of Europe, but on this score too Naples' experience illustrates a larger pattern, one which the Kingdom shared with Spain and at least partly with France as well.[1]

---

[1] For Spain, see the works cited in chapter 2, note 73. For France, cf. the recent essay by Alain Guéry, "Les finances de la monarchie française sous l'Ancien Régime," *Annales: Economies, Sociétés, Civilizations*, 1978, pp. 216–39 (but cf. also David J. Buisseret, "Les budgets de Henri IV," *Annales: Economies, Sociétés, Civilizations*, 1984, pp. 30–34; Julian Dent, *Crisis in Finance: Crown Financiers and Society in Seventeenth-Century France* (New York, 1973); Martin Wolfe, *The Fiscal System of Renaissance France* (New Haven, 1972). For England, cf. the classic works by Frederick C. Dietz, *English Government Finance 1485–1558* (London, 1964 [Urbana, 1921], *English Public Finance 1558–1641* (London, 1964 [New York, 1932], *Finances of Edward VI and Mary* (Northampton, Mass., 1918), *The Exchequer in Elizabeth's Reign* (Northampton, Mass., 1923), *The Receipts and Issues of the Exchequer during the Reigns of James I and Charles I* (Northampton, Mass., 1928). For a slightly later period, cf. also *La fiscalité et ses implications sociales en Italie et en France aux XVIIe et XVIIIe siècles* (Rome, 1980).

Vast and dramatic fiscal changes came upon the Kingdom in the eighty-odd years from the middle of the sixteenth century to the end of the 1630s, and they affected the fortunes of the state and the lives of its citizens in deep and lasting ways. It is no secret that the most critical factor making for those changes was the heavy warfare dictated by Spanish Imperial policy. War ran almost uninterruptedly through those years, because of Emperor Charles V's attempt to enforce religious uniformity and political control in Germany, or because of Imperial efforts against the Turks, or, finally, because of the Habsburgs' renewed efforts at hegemony in Central Europe.

As an integral part of the Spanish system, Naples was intimately involved in all that warfare. The Kingdom shared its burden and its cost, serving as a financial and military base for the war effort in Germany, as a strategic outpost for Imperial efforts on the Mediterranean and in North Africa, and again as a reservoir of men, money and supplies for the defense of Milan and the pursuit of Habsburg goals in the Netherlands and Central Europe.[2]

A series of financial records enables us to plot the growth in government income in Naples from 1550 to 1638.[3] As the Figure 3.1 shows, in 1550 the revenues of the Kingdom amounted to about 1,330,000 ducats. By 1638, they had more than quadrupled, rising to about 5,800,000 ducats. That change is all the more remarkable because it fell upon a population base whose dramatic sixteenth century growth had peaked in 1595, to be replaced by contraction and decline.[4] Under such circumstances, the tax burden rose from about three ducats per hearth in 1550 to about eleven ducats per hearth in 1638.[5]

These, of course, are only rough and ready measures, which acquire true meaning only if they are related to the movement of prices in the same period. In the case of essentially agricultural economies like those of early modern Europe, the price of grain can serve as a good indicator of price fluctuations.[6] Though a reliable price history for the Kingdom is still to be written, commodity price series, including some for grain, are available for the capital city of Naples and for the city of Bari, a chief center in the grain-growing Adriatic province of Terra di Bari.[7] Though the price of grain in both Naples and Bari followed a similar pattern of change, it is best to peg the growth in government income to the figures for grain in Bari, which were closer to market quotations than those for Naples. In the capital, as we have seen, the

---

[2] Villari, *La rivolta*, p. 123.
[3] For the citations and a discussion of the sources, cf. Appendix II at the end of this volume.
[4] See the archival census data discussed in chapter 1, note 83.
[5] Cf. also Bianchini, p. 207; Mantelli, *Burocrazia e finanze pubbliche*, p. 265.
[6] For an introduction to these problems, cf. the essays and the editor's introduction in Ruggiero Romano, ed., *I prezzi in Europa dal XIII secolo a oggi* (Turin, 1967). Cf. also Romano's "Tra XVI e XVII secolo," and "La storia economica" in *Storia d'Italia* (Ruggiero Romano and Corrado Vivanti, editors, [Turin, 1974]), vol. 2: 2, pp. 1813–1931.
[7] Coniglio, "La rivoluzione dei prezzi nella città di Napoli," and Mira, "Contributo per una storia dei prezzi". Cf. also Coniglio's "Annona e calmieri," and Lorenzo Palumbo's *Prezzi e salari in Terra di Bari (1530–1860)* (Bari, 1979).

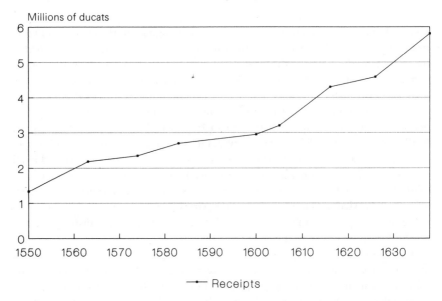

Millions of ducats

Figure 3.1 State revenues, 1550–1638

task of assuring public order and of feeding a swelling populace dictated a provisioning policy with political prices for grain and other foodstuffs.

Figure 3.2 presents the data for income and for Bari grain prices. It plots the growth of government revenues in its various phases, and it relates revenues and prices to demographic movements from the mid-sixteenth to the seventeenth century.[8]

The graph points clearly to four distinct stages in the growth of government revenues from 1550 to 1638. The first, from 1550 to the early 1560s, coincided with the wave of "new imposts" levied in the Kingdom in the 1550s and with the regularization of parliamentary aids in 1566.[9] Onerous as those tax increases were, at best they did no more than keep state revenues abreast of price levels. The second stage, from the early 1560s to the early 1580s, in fact, saw government revenues and prices move closely together. The third stage, from the early 1580s to the 1610s coincided with the economic difficulties of the late sixteenth century in the Kingdom and with the expansive phase of the seventeenth-century crisis, and saw prices definitely outdistance government income.[10] By contrast, the last phase, from the 1610s to the end of the series in 1638, saw government revenues rise markedly faster than price levels, most clearly after 1608. Starting in 1618, prices recovered,

---

[8] Unless otherwise noted, the figures for prices here and in all figures are expressed as ten-year rolling averages, by midyear.   [9] See chapter 2, above, and Galasso, "Momenti e problemi," pp. 173–79.
[10] Cf. Romano, "Tra XVI e XVII secolo," *passim.*

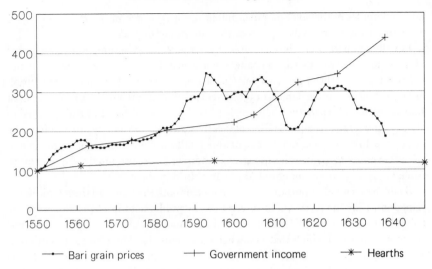

Indices of growth

Figure 3.2 Prices, government income and hearths, 1550–1638

but they did not catch up with revenue, and they fell again, well below the level of income, in the late 1620s and in the 1630s.

For most of the later sixteenth century, then, state revenues generally failed to keep up with inflation. They started to do so, and actually began outdistancing prices, at the worst possible time for the Kingdom's economy and society, that is, only in the 1610s, after the end of the sixteenth-century boom cycles and just as economic activities in the Kingdom embarked on a period of secular decline.[11]

Interestingly enough, the beginnings of this last phase coincided not with renewed warfare but actually with a period of respite from it (1609–21, the Twelve Years' Truce in the revolt of the Netherlands) and with the tenure in Naples of a reforming Viceroy, the second Count of Lemos.[12] Then, as the Thirty Years' War heated up, prices and government income diverged more and more, until their maximum point in 1638, five years before the Spanish defeat at Rocroi and ten before the peace of Westphalia.

Profound changes, then, marked the fiscal history of the Kingdom of Naples from the last years of Charles V's activities in Germany through the climactic period of Habsburg involvement in the Thirty Years' War. Those changes were marked by

---

[11] Cf. De Rosa, *I cambi esteri, passim.*
[12] On Lemos' reforms, cf. Galasso, "Le riforme del conte di Lemos." Cf. also Muto, *Le finanze pubbliche, passim.*

heavy increases in the levels of government receipts, which in the 1620s and 1630s came more and more to diverge from the movement of prices.

Equally dramatic were the changes in the structure of government income in that same period. The most striking changes concerned the relative weight of direct and indirect taxes and the appearance in 1638 of a new category of income, the retention of interest on the public debt. In 1550, direct taxes made up more than 80 percent of state revenues. By 1638, they had nearly tripled in amount, but they had declined to about 55 percent of receipts. Indirect taxes, by contrast, rose nearly fifteenfold in the same time, to over 1,800,000 ducats, or about half a million ducats above the total of all tax revenues in 1550. Whereas in 1550 indirect taxes accounted for 9 percent of receipts, by 1638 they amounted to nearly a third of them.

Such changes had important consequences for both the state and the people in the Kingdom. Like the retention of interest on the public debt in 1638, they were the tangible manifestation of fiscal crisis and an important element in the social and economic upheaval which that crisis helped accentuate. The interest retention of 1638 is a good case in point. It signaled the abandonment of a policy which in the sixteenth century had built up investor confidence in the government and thus helped lure massive amounts of capital into the state securities market.[13] It heralded in place of that policy a new course of thinly veiled confiscation which ruined large numbers of state creditors.[14]

In order to see how Naples traveled that road, how the elements of fiscal, economic and social crisis came to be entwined and to work together in the Kingdom, it is necessary to examine more closely the growth of government income and the changes in its composition in the sixteenth and seventeenth centuries. Fig. 3.3 presents these data. It groups the figures for income into five major categories – direct and indirect taxes, the revenues from the Foggia Sheep Customhouse, "various proceeds" and, for 1638, "other" income, or the retention of interest on the public debt.[15]

The first category of income to examine is direct taxation. As we saw in the preceding chapter, it was at the core of the fiscal system in the Kingdom in the sixteenth and seventeenth centuries, as it had been since the Aragonese reforms in the 1450s.[16] It included a whole gamut of taxes, ranging from the hearth levy and parliamentary aids to imposts for the billeting of soldiers, the repression of banditry and the building and repair of roads and fortresses.

In nominal terms, direct taxation nearly tripled between 1550 and 1638. In real terms, however, as the graph in Figure 3.4 shows, it stayed well below the price

[13] See chapters 2, 4 and 5.
[14] Cf. chapter 4 and Villari, *La rivolta*, pp. 121–57.
[15] The categories are similar to those used by Galasso in his analysis of the 1626 budget. Cf. his "Contributo" and "Le riforme del Conte di Lemos." They are also comparable to those used in one of the budgets, Visitor General Guzmán's report on Neapolitan finances for 1583–84 (AGS. *Visitas de Italia*, leg, 25/1).
[16] Cf. chapter 2.

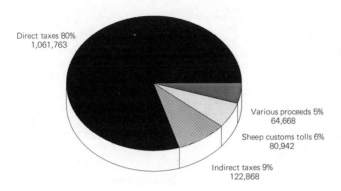

1550

Direct taxes 80%
1,061,763

Various proceeds 5%
64,668

Sheep customs tolls 6%
80,942

Indirect taxes 9%
122,868

Total revenue: 1,330,241 ducats

1563

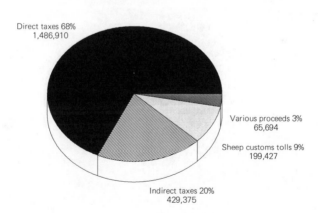

Direct taxes 68%
1,486,910

Various proceeds 3%
65,694

Sheep customs tolls 9%
199,427

Indirect taxes 20%
429,375

Total revenue: 2,181,406 ducats

Figure 3.3 Government income, 1550–1638

59

The Cost of Empire
1574

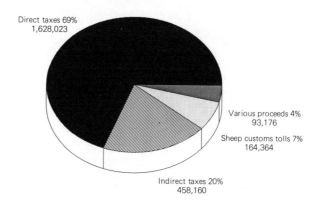

Direct taxes 69%
1,628,023

Various proceeds 4%
93,176

Sheep customs tolls 7%
164,364

Indirect taxes 20%
458,160

Total revenue: 2,343,723 ducats

1583

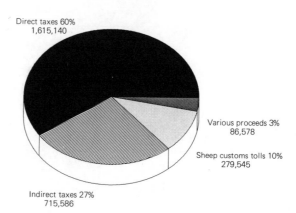

Direct taxes 60%
1,615,140

Various proceeds 3%
86,578

Sheep customs tolls 10%
279,545

Indirect taxes 27%
715,586

Total revenue: 2,696,849 ducats

1600

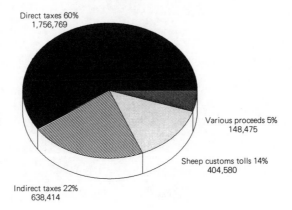

Direct taxes 60%
1,756,769

Various proceeds 5%
148,475

Sheep customs tolls 14%
404,580

Indirect taxes 22%
638,414

Total revenue: 2,948,238 ducats

1605

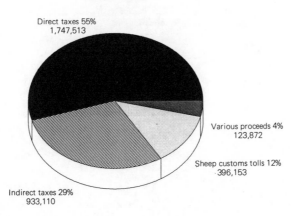

Direct taxes 55%
1,747,513

Various proceeds 4%
123,872

Sheep customs tolls 12%
396,153

Indirect taxes 29%
933,110

Total revenue: 3,200,648 ducats

The Cost of Empire
1616

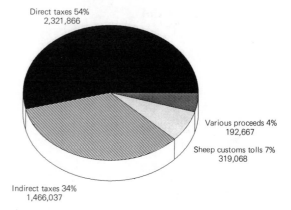

Direct taxes 54%
2,321,866

Various proceeds 4%
192,667

Sheep customs tolls 7%
319,068

Indirect taxes 34%
1,466,037

Total revenue: 4,299,638 ducats

1626

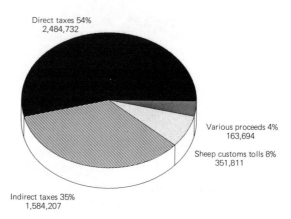

Direct taxes 54%
2,484,732

Various proceeds 4%
163,694

Sheep customs tolls 8%
351,811

Indirect taxes 35%
1,584,207

Total revenue: 4,584,444 ducats

1638

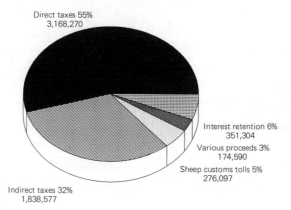

Direct taxes 55%
3,168,270

Interest retention 6%
351,304

Various proceeds 3%
174,590

Sheep customs tolls 5%
276,097

Indirect taxes 32%
1,838,577

Total revenue: 5,808,838 ducats

curve for most of that period, especially from the 1580s to about 1605, and in the 1620s.

Such a lag behind the price movement was largely a function of the fact that direct taxation was geared to the hearth base, which grew only modestly from the census of 1545 to those of 1561 and 1595.[17] Those relatively small increases set limits on the "natural" growth of direct taxation, and the way those taxes were collected, through a plethora of officials in the twelve provinces and at various intervals, must have reinforced those limits.

Still, through the 1590s, increasing population allowed for the introduction of new imposts or the intensification of old ones. From the 1540s to the 1560s, for example, taxes for the building and maintenance of roads and fortresses, for the repression of banditry and "for the pay of the Spanish infantry" (the 48 *grana* per hearth tax) were introduced or regularized.[18] At the same time, the cost of billeting

---

[17] See the census data for those years in chapter 1, note 83.

[18] The tax for the pay of the Spanish infantry was introduced on 1 May 1542, and until August 1544, it was assessed at 3 *grana* per hearth per month, or 36 *grana* per hearth per year. In that period, it yielded 255,689.79½ ducats (so it must have been levied on 293,896 hearths). From August, 1544 on, it was levied at the rate of 4 *grana* per hearth per month, or 48 *grana* per hearth per year. Through 22 August 1546, it yielded 276,845.35⅝ ducats (AGS. *Guerra Antigua*, leg. 29, f. 8). On the tax generally, cf. BNN. Ms XI–B–39, ff. 9r–v; on the others mentioned in the text, *ibid.*, ff. 10r–28v.

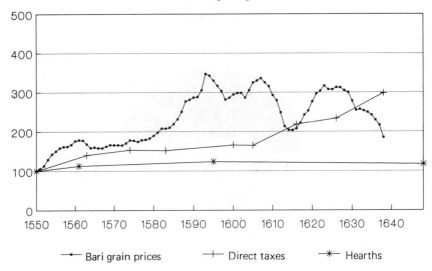

Indices of growth

Figure 3.4 Direct taxes, prices, and hearths, 1550–1638

soldiers was apportioned among a number of the hearths, and parliamentary aids were set at 600,000 ducats a year.[19]

˙Other increases came even when the population had begun declining, between the census of 1595 and the one of 1648, and they added considerably to the direct tax burden, even if they did not bring it on a par with prices. Between 1600 and 1605, they amounted to about 21 percent; between 1626 and 1638, to more than 34 percent.[20] Some of those increases represented the formalization of *de facto* situations, as was the case with the Reclamation tax, which had been collected from at least the 1560s but which became ordinary only in 1612.[21] Others were new taxes dictated (or rationalized) by the necessity for public order, as with the imposts for "fixed garrisons" and for mint and weights and measures, introduced between 1608 and 1610.[22] Others yet were quasi-hidden taxes, like those imposed on salt in 1606. That year, in fact, the government stopped providing the *tomolo* of salt which it had traditionally distributed to each hearth, though it continued levying the 52 *grana* from the base hearth tax which had been allocated to cover the costs of that

---

[19] For the billeting tax, cf. BNN. Ms. xi–b–39, ff. 10r–20v; ASN. *Sommaria. Consulte*, vol. 5, ff. 71v–76v.

[20] Cf. Figure 3.4, above.

[21] Even then, the Reclamation tax was applicable only to the four provinces mentioned in the 1560 budget (Terra di Lavoro, Contado di Molise, Principato Citra and Principato Ultra): BNN. Ms xi–b–39, ff. 29r–30v.   [22] *Ibid.* ff. 31r–36v.

distribution.[23] From then on, the sale and distribution of salt were given over to tax farmers, as with any other gabelle. Such a maneuver, of course, amounted simply to an additional tax, which yielded about 300–360,000 ducats a year.

Often, as had been the case with the "tax for the pay of the Spanish infantry" in the 1540s and 1550s, new levies might be decreed for limited times or as "extraordinary" measures, only to be extended, increased, or made permanent. This classic strategy proved especially useful in the seventeenth century. Special aids amounting to 300,000 ducats a year were granted in 1611, in exchange for the suspension of the hearth census.[24] They were still being collected in 1626, and they were extended until 1642.[25] An "extraordinary" levy of 16 *grana* per hearth per month (or 1.92 ducats per hearth per year, more than the entire hearth tax base of 1.51 ducats per year) was introduced in 1636.[26] Though it was to be rescinded in 1637, it was still being collected in 1638, when it was scheduled to yield over 850,000 ducats, and in 1642, when it was to bring in more than three-quarters of a million ducats.[27]

Between the 1620s and the 1640s, as these examples suggest, "extraordinary" direct taxes became increasingly frequent and burdensome. They averaged 159,935 ducats a year between 1622–29; 777,434 ducats a year between 1630–39, and 614,098 ducats a year between 1640–44.[28] Those sums, of course, were to be collected *in addition* to the "ordinary" direct taxes, and along with other "extra-ordinary" levies on goods and services, so that the annual yield from all such special, extraordinary taxation alone between 1640–44 was only about 80,000 ducats less than the total tax burden in 1550![29]

All this was made much worse by the privatization of direct tax collection, which was first suggested in 1609 and which was to become a reality by the 1620s and 1630s. In 1609, Philip III had wanted to accede to what should have been a startling proposal. Battista Serra, a Genoese financier, had requested the authority to use his own private officials in collecting payment for a loan of 390,000 ducats which he had made to the Crown and which had been assigned for payment on parliamentary aids in Naples. The Council of Italy had strenuously objected, arguing that such innovation would hurt the venal tax collectors financially and might lead to "many problems...very prejudicial to Your Majesty's service." For the people, the Council had argued, the measure would be "a much more hateful and vexing burden than the payment of the money itself." The King had complied with the Council's recommendation, and Serra's request had been denied, but he had added "if those officials [the state tax collectors in the Kingdom] do not pay punctually, do what

[23] Bianchini, pp. 215–16.   [24] *Ibid.*, p. 203.

[25] At least according to Bianchini, p. 203, and Davide Winspeare, *Storia degli abusi feudali* (Naples, 1883; reprinted, Bologna, 1967), p. 190.

[26] BNN. Ms. XI–B–39, f. 197v; Coniglio, *Il Viceregno*, pp. 256, 262, 266.

[27] BNN. Ms. XI–B–39, f. 213r (769,221.35 ducats).   [28] Calculations based on *ibid.*, ff. 187r–214v.

[29] That yield averaged 409,834 ducats a year between 1622 and 1629; 1,076,144 ducats a year between 1630 and 1639, and 1,334,311 ducats a year between 1640 and 1644.

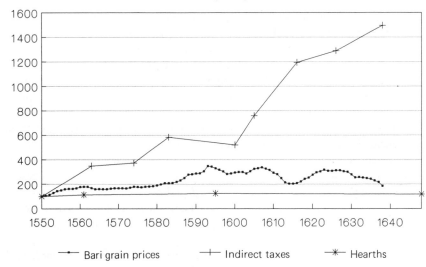

Indices of growth

Figure 3.5 Indirect taxes, prices, and hearths, 1550–1638

Serra asks without delay."[30] In the 1620s and 1630s, substantial portions of direct
tax monies were routinely collected by the state creditors' own fiscal delegates. As
the Council of Italy had foreseen, their privateering worked to the venal officials'
"disadvantage" and the people's added "burden."[31]

This last element, the "burden" represented by taxation, however, is revealed
even more starkly by indirect taxes, a quintessential component of Old Regime fiscal
systems and an increasingly prominent one in the Kingdom. The history of those
revenues in Naples in the sixteenth and seventeenth centuries was in some ways very
different from that of direct taxation. Indirect taxes in the Kingdom rose from about
120,000 to about 1,800,000 ducats a year between 1550 and 1638. As the graph in
Figure 3.5 shows, those increases were drastic not merely in nominal but in real
terms as well. Indirect tax receipts, in fact, soared above prices, far outpacing them
at all points in the series between 1563 and 1638.

Figure 3.5 points clearly to two major phases in the growth of indirect taxation,
with receipts for 1600 as the break between them. Between 1550 and 1600, indirect
taxes more than quintupled; between 1600 and 1638, they more than tripled. The
most notable increases in the first phase took place between 1550 and 1563, and they
are traceable to the "new imposts," duties which were either introduced or raised in
the mid-1550s and which brought an increase of over 238 percent in the level of

---

[30] AGS. *Secretarías Provinciales*, libro 634, ff. 197v–198v.
[31] ASN. *Sommaria. Dipendenze*, F. 25, 28: budgets for 1627, 1630, 1636; Villari, pp. 121–57.

Table 3.1

Time	Movement of indirect taxes (% increase or decrease)	Movement of prices (% increase or decrease)
1550–1563	+238.13	+68.11
1563–1574	+10.25	+9.59
1574–1583	+56.22	+29.87
1583–1600	−10.78	+87.18
1600–1605	+46.16	+30.17
1605–1616	+57.11	−117.35
1616–1626	+8.06	+105.25
1626–1638	+16.06	−127.96

indirect taxation. Between 1563, 1574 and 1583, the percentage increases were smaller, but they still outpaced the rise in prices. Only between 1583 and 1600, no doubt because of the economic problems becoming apparent in the Kingdom from the 1580s, did the level of indirect taxation register a downturn, while prices continued their ascent.[32] The second phase, from 1600 to 1638, saw other steep, continued increases in the level of indirect taxes. They came at the worst possible time for the economy and society of the Kingdom, when commercial and industrial crisis joined agricultural slumps and led prices to swing markedly, crashing between 1605–16, recovering over the next decade and crashing again between 1626 and 1638.[33]

Administrators and politicians in Naples, of course, could not view matters from such perspective. Theirs were different, more short-term concerns. Chief among them, for most of the sixteenth century, were the troublesome ones of coping with inflation and of making the exchequer's ends meet on a year-to-year or even day-to-day basis. From that point of view, and under circumstances as trying as the ones they had to deal with, targeting indirect taxation for substantial increases made good sense, at least for part of the period under consideration.

For one thing, indirect taxes were farmed out to private contractors, who were held to pay their leases in a convenient yearly lump sum.[34] The fact that some of the most remunerative gabelles were administered on the spot, in Naples, no doubt proved more convenient yet for the exchequer. Gabelles like the one for the Naples Customhouse, for the retail sale of wine or other consumer goods in the capital, for

---

[32] Zotta, *passim*.

[33] The years cited in this paragraph are, of course, the years of the fiscal records. They are not meant to be strict indicators of the onset or end of "crisis" or of price reversals. Using those same indicators, we can plot the movement of indirect tax receipts and of prices (see Table 3.1).

[34] For an example, see the contract between the Court and the Genoese merchant banker Antonio Fornari Casella for the lease of the Oil and Soap gabelle from 1559 to 1563 (AGS. *Visitas de Italia*, leg. 345/5, "Antonio Casella servitor").

example, yielded anywhere from 26 to 40 percent of total levies from indirect taxation.[35] On appearance, very little of those monies wound up in Treasury General coffers, because of the expenses assigned on them and met by the contractors directly. In reality, though, available revenue from increases in those sources could be very large. The sale of securities guaranteed by the yield of tax revenues, in fact, generated sums of ready cash worth several times any increase in a given source of revenue.[36] And in all that there was no doubt a further element of expediency, because the share of Naples-based investments in state securities was large, perhaps even massive. Financially hard-pressed administrators, then, would almost naturally look to increases in those gabelles and duties, as in all indirect taxes generally, to resolve their difficulties.

In their attempts at securing the highest possible leases, furthermore, administrators were aided by the system of tax farming itself. With its appeal to the contractors' profit motive, in fact, the system encouraged contractors to make the highest possible bids. If a given contractor was successful in his bid, he could try to recoup his investment by passing his risks and his costs on to consumers in a whole variety of legal and extra-legal ways. But to be viable, bids had also to be realistic, that is, they had at least partly to be in tune with such economic factors as expected product supply and demand, consumer liquidity and purchasing patterns, volume of turnover and so forth. The contractors' profit and the government's interest in securing tax revenues thus went hand in hand. Unrealistic bidding, after all, could mean the government's loss of revenue as well as the contractors' bankruptcy and ruin.[37]

---

[35] The gabelles of Naples Customs, Retail Sales of Wine, Eggs and Goats, *Censali, Manna Forzata* and Playing Cards yielded the following share of direct taxes:

36.20% (1550)
25.71% (1563)
32.07% (1574)
35.76% (1583)
39.50% (1600)
34.01% (1605)
29.76% (1616)
38.49% (1626)
30.77% (1638)

[36] Cf. chapters 2 and 5.

[37] For some examples of this phenomenon, cf. Mantelli, *Burocrazia e finanze pubbliche*, pp. 250–54, and the archival sources there cited. Between 1561 and 1585, twenty-one tax farmers went bankrupt and one was on the verge of doing so. Of those, eight fled, eight died (four of them in jail) and one became a cleric. About three we know only that they went bankrupt; one was in jail. Of those bankruptcies, one affected a lease contracted in the 1560s; six, leases spanning the 1560s and early 1570s; two, the 1570s; four, the late 1570s and early 1580s; six the 1580s. The leases involved major gabelles (like those for Naples Customs, Silk and Saffron, Puglia Customs and others) and minor ones alike (like those for Eggs and Goats and the disastrous one for Playing Cards).

Insolvency and bankruptcy were common risks for tax farmers, and they meant loss of revenue for the exchequer; they continued in the seventeenth century. For but one example, cf. AGS. *Estado*, leg. 1884, f. 105 (the budget for 1621): the salt contractor for the provinces of Terra d'Otranto and Basilicata, Domitro Capuzmadi, was dismissed, stripped of his goods and jailed. He left his contract owing the Court "many thousands of ducats" (c. 71r).

Economic calculations such as these, and not just the government's demands for higher revenue must be held to account for the spectacular increases of indirect taxation through the 1610s or, at the outside, the 1620s. By the 1630s, however, Spain's mounting demands for aid in the Thirty Years' War had forced the administration in Naples to abandon whatever semblance of rationality its quest for higher tax revenues might have had.

The case of a gabelle on flour introduced in 1638 is emblematic of that change. The gabelle added ten *grana* on each *tomolo* of flour consumed in the city of Naples.[38] It was valued at 2,000,000 ducats, capitalized at 4 percent interest, or 80,000 ducats a year. It was ceded to tax farmers for a lump payment of 800,000 ducats, that is, at 40 percent its alleged value.[39]

Similar operations took place in the following years, with tax revenues passing into contractors' hands at 30 and even 20 percent of alleged value.[40] This process culminated in 1648, when all the gabelles in the Kingdom, except for a few minor ones, were ceded to private parties in return for the relatively paltry sum of 300,000 ducats a year, or less than a third what indirect tax receipts had been forty-three years earlier, in 1605![41]

This course of action amounted to nothing less than the wholesale privatization of state resources, the abrogation of the authority of the state, and the rejection of that policy of state-building which fifteenth-century kings had so laboriously crafted. The new course was set by Habsburg ambitions in Central Europe; it sealed the fate of Southern Italy for centuries to come.

A major category of fiscal income in the Kingdom, after direct and indirect taxation, consisted of the revenues from the Foggia Sheep Customhouse (*Dogana della mena delle pecore di Foggia*), the pastoral organization which paralleled the Castilian Mesta.[42] In addition to the income from the Foggia Customhouse proper, that is, the tolls on transhumance from the Abruzzi to Puglia, those revenues included the proceeds from a smaller, Abruzzi-based customhouse (the *Doganella*),

---

[38] That was a substantial sum, especially because it hit the poor hardest and because it fell on a high necessity item in their diets. It might have added, by very rough measure, an average of as much as three-fifths of a ducat a year on the tax burden of each inhabitant in the capital. (The figure is only approximate, because it uses the 1580 Sommaria calculation for the yearly allowance of wheat [not flour] per person in grain-producing provinces [6 *tomoli*, hence a tax of 60 *grana* a year]; cf. the citation at chapter 1, note 47).　　[39] BNN. Ms. XI–B–39, f. 202r.

[40] As was the case, for example, with the extraordinary duties on the export of oil in 1643 and 1644 (BNN. Ms. XI–B–39, ff. 214r–v).

[41] On that operation, see De Rosa's informative *Studi sugli arrendamenti*.

[42] The definitive work on the Foggia Sheep Customhouse is Marino's *Pastoral Economics*. Also useful are the following older treatments: Giuseppe Maria Galanti, *Della descrizione geografica e politica delle Sicilie* (F. Assante and D. De Marco, eds. [Naples, 1969]), vol. 1, ch. 4, pp. 151–57 and ch. 23, pp. 516–31; Bianchini, pp. 195–98; Raffaele Colapietra, "Vicende storiche ed ordinamento della Dogana di Foggia fino a Carlo di Borbone," *Rassegna di Politica e di Storia*, 1959, pp. 13–29; Dora Musto, *La regia dogana della mena delle pecore di Puglia* (Rome, 1964). For archival works, cf. the excellent discussion in BNN. Ms. XI–B–39, ff. 101r–128r. Cf. also ASN. *Archivi Privati. Giudice–Caracciolo*, F. 33, ff. 273r–276v.

Indices of growth

Figure 3.6 Sheep tolls, prices, and hearths, 1550–1638

and the rental fees for pasture lands given over to farming (*terre salde*) and for the fief of Monteserico, the Customhouse's mutton-raising preserve.[43]

As Fig. 3.6 shows, net revenues from the Foggia Customhouse rose fivefold from 1550 to 1600 (from 80,942 ducats to a high of 404,580 ducats). After that, they declined, so that in 1638 they stood at about three and a half times their 1550 level (or about 276,000 ducats). At all times in that period, however, they outdistanced prices, and they made up anywhere from 5 to 13 percent of total yearly state revenue. With good reason, then, administrators and kings held the Customhouse in high regard, and they followed its fortunes with care.[44]

The rise in Customhouse revenues took place in two distinct phases, from 1550 to 1563 and from 1574 to 1583 and 1600. The increase in the first of those periods coincided with the "new imposts" levied in the Kingdom: in 1556, in fact, the tolls on transhumance to Puglia were raised by 50 percent, from 88 to 132 ducats per thousand sheep.[45] The increase in the second period, from 1574 to 1583 and 1600, on the other hand, was due not to higher rates but rather to the reorganization of the Customhouse and of its revenues, which began in 1574.[46]

That reorganization was motivated by the steep fall in income which had affected

[43] For the fief of Monteserico, cf. BNN. Ms. XI–B–39, ff. 121r–124r and ASN. *Archivi Privati. Giudice–Caracciolo*, F. 33, f. 275v. [44] Cf. the quotations in Marino, p. 154.
[45] Galasso, "Momenti e problemi," pp. 177–78; Bianchini, p. 197; BNN. Ms XI–B–39, f. 102v; ASN. *Archivi Privati. Giudice–Caracciolo*, F. 33, f. 275v. [46] Colapietra, p. 19; Musto, p. 39.

the Customhouse over the preceding five years, despite the rise in the toll rate. It was the work of a committee made up of Fabrizio Di Sangro, scion of a family long involved in the Foggia Customhouse, and of Sommaria experts Francesco Reverter and Annibale Moles.[47] It culminated in Viceroy Cardinal Granvelle's Pragmatic order of 30 July 1574 and in Fabrizio Di Sangro's ascension to the Customhouse's top administrative office (*Doganiere*).

An important part of the 1574 Foggia reforms concerned the system by which those registering with the Customhouse (*locati*) declared their sheep. That system, *professazione*, had been introduced in 1553 to replace the actual counting of sheep by royal officials. After 1574, it became the hub of a complex network that sought to provide the state with an assured source of income as it abetted large-scale private speculation in pasture lands and extended the Customhouse's own jurisdiction to those involved in the pastoral organization.[48]

This last aspect of the *professazione* system was remarkable, for it provided many with a welcome avenue of escape from baronial lawcourts. Customhouse justice extended to all sheep declarers, to their families (except for married daughters), their servants and *their* families. It included merchants, indeed all who were in any way connected with any Customhouse activity, from the bakers of the declarers' bread to the basket weavers of Customhouse cheeses. Customhouse justice was personal, not territorial or chronological. It could thus be enforced in the summer, in the declarers' mountain homes, and it could apply retroactively to litigations begun in baronial or even ordinary tribunals before the declarer's enrollment in Customhouse rolls.

This extraordinary avenue of escape from feudal jurisdiction is alleged to have spurred the registration of sheep declarers with the Foggia Customs and, consequently, to have made for increases in royal revenue. The celebrated eighteenth-century reformer Giuseppe Maria Galanti, for example, made a direct, causal link between the Sheep Customs' judicial system and the rise in Customhouse revenue from 157,000 ducats in 1573 to 396,000 ducats in 1577 and 450,000 ducats in 1578.[49]

There is little doubt that special jurisdiction was a contributing factor in the rise of Sheep Customs revenue. A more important reason for that rise, however, is to be found in the workings of *professazione* itself. The system hinged upon the declaration, and not necessarily or even primarily the ownership, of sheep. In effect, it encouraged the declaration of sheep which existed only "in the air," that is, which were fictitious, but which still were assessed a toll, albeit a lower one than for real sheep.

The *professazione* system might seem bizarre by modern standards, but it had a logic and an economic rationality of its own.[50] It assured the state a toll on real sheep and, in effect, a tax on speculation in pasture land as well. In other words, it produced a profit for the state from the conflict which pitted agriculturalists against

[47] Colapietra, p. 19; Musto, p. 39.   [48] Colapietra, pp. 23–25; Galanti, pp. 523–24.
[49] These are Galanti's figures (p. 152).   [50] Marino, *passim*.

pastoralists in the sixteenth and seventeenth centuries, as it had from time immemorial.

Thanks to such practices, Customhouse revenues soon began rising, reaching 225,775 ducats in 1575 and 325,117 ducats in 1576.[51] Further increases came after 1584, when the declaration of sheep began to be made in secret between each declarer and the *Doganiere*. The new twist in the system, in fact, encouraged competition and helped inflate the number of sheep declared, thus assuring the exchequer sizable amounts of revenue, as reflected in the financial records for 1583–1605.[52]

The *professazione* system continued in existence until 1615, when its very reason for being, like the Customhouse's own viability, was undermined by natural disasters. Starting in 1611, in fact, unseasonably cold weather and ovine epidemics worked together to kill nearly 70 percent of the sheep.[53] Such sharp reduction in flocks was reflected in the decline of Customhouse revenues, from the 1610s well beyond the 1620s and the 1630s.

Despite such circumstances, though, the state's fiscal interest still had to be met, and a new system, *transazione*, was devised for that purpose. Like *professazione*, which it replaced in 1615, *transazione* was designed to guarantee the exchequer a regular income from the Foggia Customs. By the new convention, sheep declarers were to pay the fisc a regular yearly sum, which was set at 192,000 ducats and which was raised to 220,000 ducats in 1620.[54] Naturally enough, though, the speculation on pasture lands continued after the end of *professazione*, and financial records from the 1620s through the 1640s continued reporting staggering expenses for "unusual extraordinary," that is, fictitious, fodder.[55]

---

[51] Colapietra, p. 19.

[52] According to Galanti (p. 523) the number of sheep declared rose from 2,000,000 in 1577 to more than 3,700,000 in 1592. (A tally from 1591–92 [ASN. *Sommaria. Dipendenze*, F. 25, ff. 37r–38v; "Introyto della Regia Dohana delle Pecore di Puglia del anno Ve Ind.s 1591 et 1592"] enters 3,057,430 sheep). Colapietra (p. 25) reports 5,500,000 declared in 1604. Simple arithmetic, however, suggests that even this last hyperbolic figure cannot account for the inflated gross totals for revenues that appear in some of the financial reports (like those for 1583, 1600, 1605 and 1638, which report gross revenues ranging from about 500,000 to about 690,000 ducats). Granting even capacity herds at pasture in Puglia, or about 1,500,000 sheep, the income from them, at 132 ducats per thousand, would be 198,000 ducats. The tolls on the remaining 4,000,000 fictitious sheep, at the lower rate of 32 ducats per thousand, would amount to 128,000 ducats, so that the highest possible gross income from sheep would be 326,000, not 500,000 or 690,000 ducats.

   The solution to this puzzle lies in a last quirk in the Customhouse accounting system, which made gross income and expenses also appear as inflated as the sheep which were declared "in the air". In November, when sheep were declared, in fact, participants in the Customhouse economy would be listed as owing 132 ducats per thousand sheep on all their sheep, real and fictitious. In May, when the toll fees were due, they would receive a rebate, on paper only, of 100 ducats per thousand (fictitious) sheep. Hence the swollen figures for "extraordinary unusual fodder" in some of the financial records. Cf. Calabria, *State Finance*, pp. 131–35, and the sources there cited, esp. BNN. Ms. xi–b–39, f. 106v.

[53] Musto, p. 42.   [54] Colapietra, pp. 20–21; Galanti, p. 523; Musto, p. 43.

[55] This is the most logical explanation for the continued usage of terms dating from the *professazione* period. There is no mention of "erbaggi insoliti" in the 1616 budget (ff. 4v–5v); expenses for ordinary and extraordinary fodder are reported as 23,000 ducats (f. 10r). The 1621 budget, on the other hand

The Foggia Sheep Customhouse was most profitable for the state in the course of the generation ending with the great mortality of 1611. Its revenues during that period had ranged between 10 and 13 percent of government income – an amount that was considerable in itself and that, better yet, was conveniently made available to the state in a lump sum, in May, when the toll fees were paid. In the 1610s, Customhouse revenues embarked on a decline from which they were not to emerge until the eighteenth century. The beginning of that secular process coincided almost perfectly with the full swing of the seventeenth-century crisis. It coincided also with the phase of heaviest fiscal burdens the Kingdom had to bear in the sixteenth and seventeenth centuries. By 1638, Customhouse revenues had fallen to about 5 percent of state income, or about 75,000 ducats less than one of the "extraordinary" measures enacted that year, the retention of interest on public debt payments, and only about 3,000 ducats more than what they had yielded back in 1583.

Two categories of state income remain to be considered in this analysis: the retention of interest on the public debt in 1638 and the entries in the rubric labeled "Various Proceeds." The first of these items is best discussed in the wider context of the problem of the public debt in the Kingdom. Accordingly, it will be considered in chapter 5, which analyzes the public debt in the Kingdom in the sixteenth and seventeenth centuries.

The second category, or "Various Proceeds," consists of monies from a wide variety of sources, ranging from taxes on feudal succession and the administration of

---

(AGS. *Estado*, leg. 1884, f. 105, c. 79r), enters 11,353.41⅝ ducats for "Herbaggi ordinarij," 10,087.38 ducats for "Herbaggi ordinarij soliti," and 31,048.93 ducats for "Herbaggi ordinarij insoliti." It then lists 287,066.69 ducats for "herbaggi impossedibili delle locationi ordinarie," 13,545 ducats for "herbaggi impossedibili della locatione di Terra d'Otranto," and 14,684.50 ducats for "herbaggi extraordinarij insoliti dispensati, et non posseduti." For 1625–26, fodder expenses appear as 24,739.32½ for "erbagi ordinarii et extr'ordinarii soliti et insoliti posseduti," and as 291,289.69 ducats for "erbagi extr'ordinarii insoliti non posseduti" (Galasso, "Contributo," p. 76, note h [1]).

The phrase "erbaggi aerei" occurs in the budgets for 1627, 1630, 1633, 1636 and 1648. The 1627 reports 176,522.88 ducats "che Importarono li erbaggi Aerei non posseduti et ordinato farsi buoni," that is, rebated, as had been accounting practice during *professazione* (ASN. *Sommaria. Dipendenze*, F. 25, f. 9v, n.d.), whereas that for 1630 lists 188,952.71 ducats "Per tanto Importano li herbagi aerei ordinari per il presente anno 1630 fatti buoni alli locati à Ciascuno la Rata Giusta il repartimento de magnifici Credenzieri" (*ibid.*, f. 149v., November 1633). For 1633, the "herbaggi aerei delle locationi ordinarie" are entered as 188,273.09 ducats (*ibid.*, ff. 4v, 14v, n.d.). For 1636, 192,025.21 ducats are listed "Per tanti fatti boni a locati per erbaggi aerei et caccito" (*ibid.*, F. 28, f. 12r; 6 September 1638). For 1648, 196,328.56 ducats are listed as expenses for "herbaggi aerei delle locationi ordinarie fatti buoni alli locati" (*ibid.*, F. 25, f. 3r; 17 December 1655; cf. also f. 46r). No such expenses appear in the 1673 budget (*ibid.*, F. 25, 23 December 1673). The 1638 financial report lists 204,510.19 ducats "fatti buoni a locati di detta dohana per herbagi et altre cause" (ASN. *Sommaria. Consulte*, vol. 41, f. 185r).

Clearly, in order to have a realistic view of the trend in Customhouse revenues, expenses for fictitious fodder must be subtracted from the totals for all years. For some years, however, the texts do not distinguish between ordinary and fictitious fodder but lump instead all fodder expenses into one sum (as in 1600: 364,947.23 ducats). To counteract possible distortions due to that fact, the tables reporting Customhouse revenues in this work subtract all fodder expenses for all years; they list, in other words, *net* Customhouse income.

73

justice to the proceeds from fines on contraband, the rental of fiefs and mills in the Crown's domain, the sale of animals from the royal stables of Puglia and Calabria or of those unfortunates held to be little better than that, the "old and useless slaves."

The sums involved in this last category of income, though not negligible, were relatively unimportant. Only in two of the financial reports here analyzed, those for 1550 and 1600, in fact, do those sums amount to 5 percent of yearly income. The entries making up those proceeds, furthermore, tend to vary greatly with each report, and they are not always strictly comparable.[56] Variation and discontinuity at times obtains because of the summary or inconsistent ways in which the reports treat those entries,[57] or because of the fiscal vicissitudes which brought about changes in the make-up of a given entry.[58] Often they can be traced to mere contingency, as, for example, with the yield from taxes on feudal succession, which depended on the deaths of feudal landowners, or with the payments of debts and of arrears or overdue accounts. Little can be gleaned about income or about fiscal policy from this last category of revenue, and it seems best to dispense with direct analysis of it, leaving to the notes the explanations that might be of interest to specialists.[59]

In the course of the sixteenth century, Spanish politicians and diplomats from one end of Europe to another complained about the shortfalls in the revenues they administered. In almost monotonous tones, the despatches of all the Viceroys in Naples, from the Cardinal de Jaén to the Marquis of Mondéjar to the Duke of Olivares, lamented the "exhaustion" of the Kingdom, its mounting deficit, the abysmal plight of its exchequer. On the whole, as this chapter has shown, those were not just the self-serving conceits of career-minded administrators. Each Viceroy, to be sure, was interested in showing how revenues had grown and expenses fallen during his tenure.[60] But it became more and more difficult to do that while presiding over what Braudel has aptly called "the growing defenselessness of states before the

---

[56] The 1600 financial report, for example, enters a lump sum of 50,000 ducats with the generic explanation "per tanti che possano Importare l'exattione di diversi altri debitori vendita de beni, et Intrate che se devolveno a la regia Corte et altre cause per detto anno" (ASN. *Sommaria. Dipendenze*, F. 25, f. 225r). The budget for 1574, on the other hand, takes up about four folios and thirty-eight items to account for approximately 5,600 ducats (AGS. *Estado*, leg. 1064, f. 146, cc. 21r–25r and the first entry on c. 25v).

[57] For most items, the financial reports here analyzed generally list the previous year's yield, or a three-year average, but the entries are not always strictly consistent. The yield from taxes on feudal succession, for example, is a twenty-year average in 1563, a three-year average in 1574, a "customary" yield in 1583 and one year's receipt (1599–1600) in 1600.

[58] In 1574, to cite one example, the income from the rental of the fief of Salpi, in Terra di Bari, was listed a 1,400 ducats, and that of the fief of Presentino, in Capitanata, as the likely 269.66 ducats that a rental would yield (AGS. *Estado*, leg. 1064, f. 146, cc. 21r–v). By 1584, both fiefs had been subsumed in the income of the Foggia Sheep Customhouse, since no renter could be found for either of them (AGS. *Visitas de Italia*, leg. 25/1, f. 17v).

[59] Cf. Appendix I, Table 5. Only two items might relate to larger issues of fiscal policy, the proceeds from the sale of offices in 1626 and 1638 and from fines on intercepts and contraband in 1638.

[60] Cf. ASN. *Sommaria. Consulte*, vol. 2, ff. 78r–83r, for an example of that practice.

rising cost of living."[61] With the economic crisis of the seventeenth century and the coming of the Thirty Years' War, as this chapter has suggested and as the next one, on government expense in the sixteenth and seventeenth centuries will show in detail, it became impossible. In the Kingdom, as across Europe, politicians – Viceroys, Count-Dukes and Cardinals all – came to preside over "the ruin of the States they served."[62]

[61] Braudel, vol. 1, p. 484.   [62] Guéry, p. 224.

4

Government expense, 1550–1638

On 8 November 1595, Ferrante Fornaro signed a "Brief Budget of Income and Expense and of what is due to Merchants and the Militia."[1] The budget was sent to Spain, where no doubt it was carefully studied. Fornaro, after all, enjoyed a good reputation as fiscal expert at Court, and he was not new to the task of reporting on the condition of the exchequer.[2] In 1592–93, furthermore, he had served as regent and fiscal advisor at the Spanish Court, and he had been entrusted with the sensitive task of reforming finances in the Kingdom.[3] Immediately afterwards he had been sent to Naples as Sommaria Lieutenant, a prized and responsible position at the center of fiscal administration in the Kingdom.

Fornaro's budget is instructive, for it brings to light the difficult straits of the Neapolitan exchequer at the end of the sixteenth century. It projected income at about 2,500,000 ducats and expense at nearly 2,930,000 ducats. But even the sizable deficit, nearly 430,000 ducats, paled in comparison to debts due, which the Lieutenant assessed at about 1,950,000 ducats, or more than three-quarters of a full year's revenue. About a fifth of that sum, almost 340,000 ducats, consisted of arrears due the cavalry, infantry and galleys as of the end of October, the week before the budget was signed. The rest, over 1,600,000 ducats, was due to merchant bankers and had been assigned to them for payment on the next six years' proceeds from the Foggia Sheep Customhouse and from parliamentary aids.

As Figure 4.1 shows, the income side of the Lieutenant's ledger, structurally at least, presents few surprises. More than half the revenue came from direct taxation; nearly a quarter from gabelles and other indirect taxes. The tolls from the Sheep Customhouse amounted to about 15 percent of total receipts, and a variety of duties and proceeds made up the rest.

The expense side of the ledger, on the other hand, as Figure 4.2 shows, is striking indeed. The most sizable expenditure in the Lieutenant's budget was for the interest due every year on the public debt, more than 1,150,000 ducats, or about two-fifths total outlay. Very high also was the sum for military expenses, over 800,000 ducats,

---

[1] AGS. *Estado*, leg. 1094, f. 124.
[2] For but one example, cf. the financial report for 1585–86, which Fornaro had drawn up (BNM. Ms. 2659, ff. 128r–144v).
[3] AGS. *Secretarías Provinciales*, leg. 6, unfoliated, 29 January 1593 ("Los meses passados") and *ibid.*, n. d. ("A la consulta que se hizo"). Cf. also *ibid.*, libro 479, ff. 75v–80v; libro 478, ff. 146r–v; libro 429, f. 526r; libro 428, f. 278r.

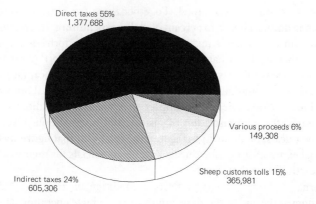

Government expense, 1550–1638

Direct taxes 55%
1,377,688

Various proceeds 6%
149,308

Sheep customs tolls 15%
365,981

Indirect taxes 24%
605,306

Total revenue: 2,498,283 ducats

Figure 4.1 Ferrante Fornaro's 1595 budget: the structure of income

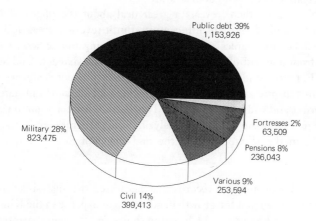

Public debt 39%
1,153,926

Fortresses 2%
63,509

Pensions 8%
236,043

Various 9%
253,594

Civil 14%
399,413

Military 28%
823,475

Total expenditures: 2,929,960 ducats

Figure 4.2 Ferrante Fornaro's 1595 budget: the structure of expense

nearly one-third the year's total. Together those two entries accounted for nearly 2,000,000 ducats, almost 70 percent of global expenditure. Interestingly enough, the lowest sum in Fornaro's text was that budgeted for fortresses, roads and watch-towers, that is, for what touched the Kingdom's most immediate and direct defensive needs. That sum was dwarfed even by the allocation for pensions and stipends, which amounted to only about 8 percent of the total but which was almost four times as large. The amount apportioned for civil expenditures – for the salaries of officials, the administration of justice, and internal police work – was nearly 400,000 ducats, or about 14 percent of the total. But that figure was swollen by the unusual expense of 120,000 ducats payable to officials for their work in conducting the hearth census that year.[4]

Fornaro's budget clearly reflects a condition of great fiscal difficulty in the Kingdom at the end of the sixteenth century – a huge operating deficit, vast unpaid arrears due the armed forces and even vaster obligations to merchant bankers, all of which required the mortgaging of revenue far into the future. Beyond that, the Lieutenant's budget reflects the fiscal priorities operative in Neapolitan finances and thus the political, economic and social choices made about the Kingdom in both Madrid and Naples. And to a large degree, those priorities and choices revolved around military expenditures and the funding of a huge public debt, by themselves heavy mortgages on the Kingdom's future.

Fornaro's budget, then, reveals a great deal about the plight of Neapolitan finances at the end of the sixteenth century. But it reveals a great deal in a larger sense as well, because Naples' experience, far from being unique, was a common one for states from one end of Europe to the other in the sixteenth and seventeenth centuries. Fornaro's budget is thus emblematic of early modern fiscal systems, of the strategies that inspired them and of the difficulties of kingdoms and states in an age of rising prices and widespread warfare. This chapter will focus on those problems and seek to illuminate them by analyzing the structure and trend in state expenditure in the Kingdom from the mid-sixteenth to the early seventeenth century.

The same series of financial records that permitted the analysis of government income enables us to plot the growth in government expense in the Kingdom from 1550 to 1638, as in Figure 4.3. As the graph shows, in 1550 state expenses in Naples amounted to about 1,350,000 ducats. By 1638, they had risen nearly sixfold, to about 7,800,000 ducats. As we saw in chapter 3, receipts in the same period rose less

---

[4] The entry labeled "Various" in Figure 4.2, for 253,593.89 ducats, lumps together disparate items which State of the Patrimony budgets generally kept distinct. Fornaro's notation, in fact, was for "several ordinary expenses for the feudal homage presented to His Holiness, construction, supplies, mail, secret expenses, interest paid to merchant bankers, and other things." This composite entry, which included payments on the floating public debt, civil expenses and outlays for fortresses, no doubt appeared in the Lieutenant's budget for the sake of expediency and conciseness.

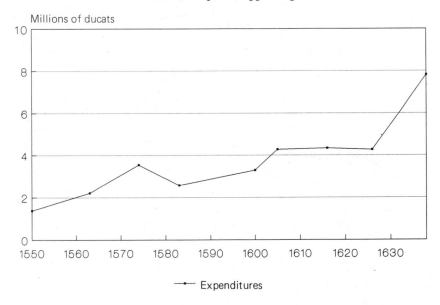

Millions of ducats

— Expenditures

Figure 4.3 Government expenses, 1550–1638

markedly, from about 1,330,000 to about 5,800,000 ducats.[5] The result was that the exchequer in Naples, as in so many other states across Europe at that same time, was in a condition of permanent insolvency: it operated at a deficit every year from 1550 to 1638, with the exception of 1583.

By itself, such a state of affairs was difficult enough. What gave it special poignancy was the fact that at critical junctures, the level of expenditures was higher yet than that of prices. Figure 4.4 illustrates this situation by relating the growth of expenses in the Kingdom to the price movement from 1550 to 1638. As with the income data analyzed in chapter 3, it pegs expenses to the price of grain in Bari.[6] As the graph clearly shows, expenses stayed below the price level only in 1563, 1583, 1600 and 1605. They rose markedly above it in 1574 and 1616, and somewhat less so in 1626, as prices temporarily recovered from their early-seventeenth-century slump. But in 1638, the last year in the series, expenses skyrocketed, soaring far above prices. No wonder that, in their despatches and financial reports to Madrid in the sixteenth and early seventeenth centuries, Viceroys and administrators in Naples lamented the "exhaustion" of the Kingdom, its mounting deficit, and the abysmal plight of its exchequer!

Those conditions, and the fact that expenses outstripped prices (and income) in

---

[5] Or 6,500,000 ducats if we consider the entire proceeds from the flour gabelle sold that year (cf. chapter 3 and Appendix II, note 30).   [6] See above, chapter 3.

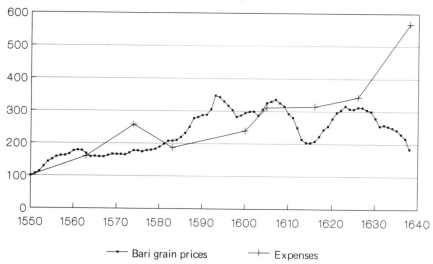

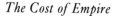

Indices of growth

Figure 4.4 Prices and expenditures, 1550–1638

many of the years under consideration, can be easily related to the high cost of financing warfare, either directly, in the Mediterranean, or indirectly, in Central Europe. This is especially clear for 1574, before the post-Lepanto demobilization and the shift in the grand strategy of Spain from the Mediterranean to the North. It is equally clear during and just before the Thirty Years' War, when Spanish policy imposed its heaviest burdens on the Kingdom, as on Castile, in the pursuit of its goals from the Netherlands to Germany.

For most of the late sixteenth and early seventeenth centuries, then, state expenses in Naples outstripped both income and prices. They did so markedly enough to offset even the considerable increases in taxation which fell upon the Kingdom in the course of those decades. The relationship (and the gap) between receipts, expenditures and prices, as Figure 4.5 shows, can best be discussed in six distinct stages.

The first stage in the relationship between prices, income and expenses went from 1550 to the early 1560s, and it corresponded to the introduction or intensification of "new imposts" and parliamentary aids in the Kingdom. Those increases in taxation did not succeed in bringing revenue levels on a par with expenses, and inflation in those years outdistanced both receipts and outlays. The second stage, in the 1570s, was dominated by the great expenditures for war in the Mediterranean, and it saw expenses rise markedly above both income and price levels, which tracked closely together at that time. The third stage, corresponding to the early 1580s, provided an

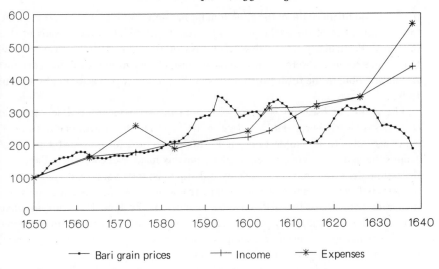

Government expense, 1550–1638

—•— Bari grain prices   —+— Income   —*— Expenses

Figure 4.5 Prices, government income, and expenses, 1550–1638

interlude of relative calm in the fiscal history of the Kingdom. Income was higher than outlay, while expenses, which had shrunk considerably from 1574, were below the price level. Such a situation seems to have lasted only through the mid-1580s: it was soon vitiated by the sharp increases in prices, themselves an expression of the dysfunctions in the Southern Italian economy in those decades.[7] The gap between expenditures and income widened in the fourth phase, from about the mid- or late 1580s to 1616, despite the heavy increases in taxation which started early in the seventeenth century. In that same period, as we have seen, prices initially continued their ascent and then, starting in 1608, plunged below both income and expense levels. In the last two phases, from 1616 to 1626 and from 1626 to 1638, both income and expense levels outdistanced inflation, despite the recovery of prices between 1618 and 1628. Income stayed near, even if below, expense levels through 1626, but it was definitely and markedly outdistanced by them as the Thirty Years' War heated up.

Under such circumstances, it hardly seems an exaggeration to view the period from the mid-sixteenth to the early seventeenth century as one of almost permanent, structural fiscal crisis. More often than not, expenses in the Kingdom rose higher than prices, and revenues regularly failed to keep pace with expenditures. Deficits became not the exception, but the rule of fiscal administration. Change did come to

[7] Cf. Zotta, *passim*, and chapter 1, above.

the fiscal and financial life of the Kingdom in that time, but it brought no resolution to the difficulties of the exchequer, as it brought no relief to the travails of the economy. Particularly in the desperate days of the Thirty Years' War, as the Kingdom's resources were strained to the utmost, change meant involution, decline and dissolution, in the royal patrimony as in the productive capacities of Southern Italy.

The reality of fiscal crisis in the Kingdom in the sixteenth and seventeenth centuries is clearly borne out by a closer examination of the growth in government expenses and of their composition. Figure 4.6, which presents the data for analysis, groups the figures for government expense into six major categories of outlay – for the public debt; the military; pensions and stipends; fortresses, roads and watch-towers; civil expenses and "various" items. Ironically, though, it can do so only for the years 1550–1626. By 1638, in fact, finances in the Kingdom were in such shambles that the budgetary process had become moot. Expenses for the government's normal operations, in fact, simply could not be met, and the old categories of fiscal administration gave way before the most pressing concern, that of raising the money which the Kingdom was to supply in support of Spanish policy.[8]

The most striking aspect of the data in figure 4.6, and the one that had a prominent role in making crisis a permanent feature of financial life in the Kingdom, is the enormous share of outlay taken up by the public debt and by military expenditures in every year of the series. At no time between 1550 and 1626 did expenses for the public debt and for the military together amount to less than 71 percent of yearly expenditure. The share of military expenses did shrink over time, going from 45 percent of outlay in 1550 to about half that percentage in 1626. But that decline was more than made up by the awesome growth in the public debt, which climbed from nearly a third (31 percent) of payments in 1550 to nearly three fifths (56 percent) in 1626. In 1638, remittances to Milan alone amounted to 1,148,000 ducats, more than military expenses and outlays for fortresses and other internal defense in the Kingdom in 1626, and expenses for the public debt may have come to about 4,000,000 ducats.[9]

The consequences of such a state of affairs are not hard to disentangle. Heavy military expenditures no doubt served to stimulate certain sectors of the economy, such as those associated with troop provisioning, galley construction and the like, but they were of no benefit to long-term, structural economic development. Even more, the awesome growth of the public debt dictated by the military needs of Spanish policy encouraged, if it did not engender, a certain type of parasitical development in the Kingdom. With its heavy emphasis on war and the financing of war, in fact, government policy in Naples, as in Castile, came to compete with enterprise and to shunt wealth into unproductive endeavors.

Actually, as we shall see in greater detail in the next chapter, in the troubled

---

[8] Cf. also Appendix II.   [9] For the sums sent to Milan, AGS. *Estado*, leg. 3261, f. 149.

Government expense, 1550–1638

1550

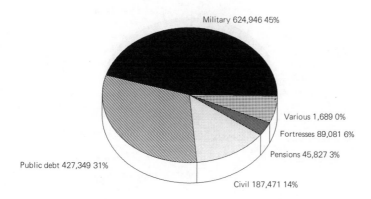

Military 624,946 45%

Various 1,689 0%

Fortresses 89,081 6%

Pensions 45,827 3%

Public debt 427,349 31%

Civil 187,471 14%

Total expenditures: 1,376,363 ducats

1563

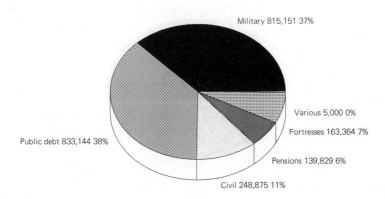

Military 815,151 37%

Various 5,000 0%

Fortresses 163,364 7%

Pensions 139,829 6%

Public debt 833,144 38%

Civil 248,875 11%

Total expenditures: 2,205,363 ducats

Figure 4.6 The structure of government expenses, 1550–1626

83

1574

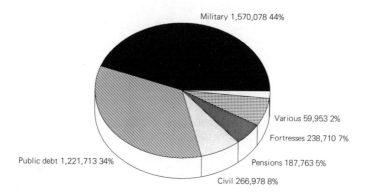

Military 1,570,078 44%

Various 59,953 2%

Fortresses 238,710 7%

Pensions 187,763 5%

Public debt 1,221,713 34%

Civil 266,978 8%

Total expenditures: 3,545,195 ducats

1583

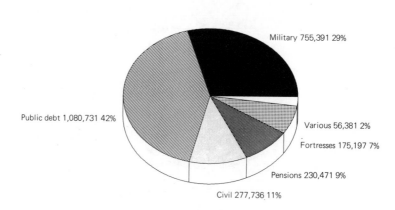

Military 755,391 29%

Public debt 1,080,731 42%

Various 56,381 2%

Fortresses 175,197 7%

Pensions 230,471 9%

Civil 277,736 11%

Total expenditures: 2,575,907 ducats

Government expense, 1550–1638

1600

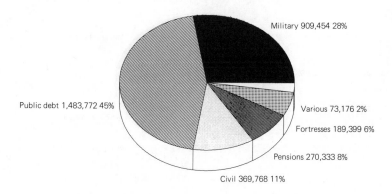

Military 909,454 28%

Various 73,176 2%

Fortresses 189,399 6%

Pensions 270,333 8%

Civil 369,768 11%

Public debt 1,483,772 45%

Total expenditures: 3,295,902 ducats

1605

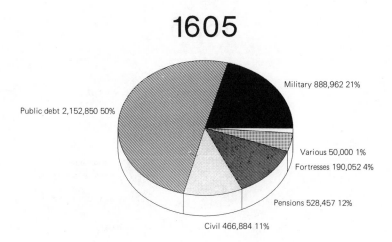

Military 888,962 21%

Various 50,000 1%

Fortresses 190,052 4%

Pensions 528,457 12%

Civil 466,884 11%

Public debt 2,152,850 50%

Total expenditures: 4,277,205 ducats

1616

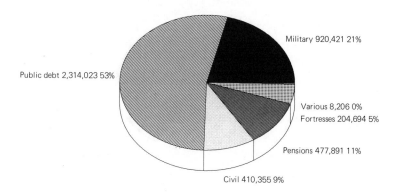

Military 920,421 21%

Public debt 2,314,023 53%

Various 8,206 0%
Fortresses 204,694 5%

Pensions 477,891 11%

Civil 410,355 9%

Total expenditures: 4,335,590 ducats

1626

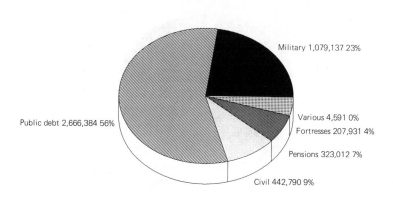

Military 1,079,137 23%

Public debt 2,666,384 56%

Various 4,591 0%
Fortresses 207,931 4%

Pensions 323,012 7%

Civil 442,790 9%

Total expenditures: 4,720,845 ducats

economic climate present in the Kingdom from the 1580s, investment in the public debt was a most rational course of action for capital holders. But one of the effects of such investments, and thus of the massive diversion of capital into government securities, such as occurred in Naples and in other parts of Europe at the same time, was to shunt wealth upwards from the lower segments of society.[10] By itself, of course, that development was not cataclysmic. It was, however, yet another element of crisis in the Kingdom in the late sixteenth and early seventeenth centuries. The necessary consequence of that crisis, and the logical outcome of the type of change which government policy stimulated, was the misery and suffering of countless people in Southern Italy, as in so much of Europe, and the great anti-fiscal revolts which shook Europe from one corner to the other in the 1630s and the 1640s.

In order to trace the course of those developments, it is necessary to examine each category of expense more closely. Because of the important role Naples played in Spanish strategy in the sixteenth and seventeenth centuries, and the heavy mortgage that war and commitments for war brought upon the Kingdom in that period, it might be best to start with military expenses.

In nominal terms, military outlays rose about one and a half times, from nearly 625,000 ducats in 1550 to a little over 1,000,000 ducats in 1638. In real terms, however, as Figure 4.7 shows, that growth stayed well below the price curve for the overwhelming majority of the years from 1550 to 1626.[11] Only in 1574 did military expenses rise above inflation, and markedly so.[12] That, of course, was due to the great struggle against Turkish power in the Mediterranean, which had placed Naples in a front-line position in the war effort and which had required a massive military buildup in the Kingdom, especially in the fleet.[13] In 1560, for example, the galley fleet was made up of six "ordinary," that is, royal, and ten private ships, contracted by Genoese like Andrea Doria, Stefano De Mari and Bendinello Sauli. At the disaster of Djerba (May, 1560), six Neapolitan galleys were lost, but they were quickly replaced, and additional ships were built.[14] In 1574, half a million ducats were budgeted for fifty galleys ordered to be made ready in the Kingdom.[15] As the Turkish danger was felt to recede, and as Spain's strategic focus shifted more decidedly to Northern Europe, however, demobilization from those efforts

---

[10] Jean-Claude Waquet, "Who Profited from the Alienation of Public Revenues in Ancien Régime Societies? Some Reflection on the Examples of France, Piedmont and Naples in the xviith and xviiith Centuries," *Journal of European Economic History*, 1982, pp. 665–73.

[11] The 1638 budget, unfortunately, does not allow expenses to be broken down as do the other texts, or as it does for income. On this question, cf. Appendix II.

[12] Military expenses for 1574, in fact, were the highest in the series (1,570,078 ducats), about a half million ducats higher than even the next amount, for 1626 (1,079,137 ducats).

[13] From 1550 to 1563 and 1574, in fact, expenses for the fleet rose much faster than for landed forces, though they started from a lower base (cf. Figure 4.8 and Appendix I).

[14] Braudel, vol. 2, p. 315, and AGS. *Estado*, leg. 1053, f. 126.

[15] AGS. *Estado*, leg. 1064, f. 146, c. 36v.

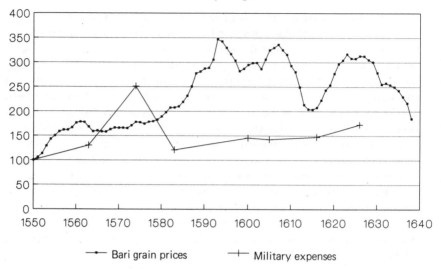

—•— Bari grain prices   —+— Military expenses

Indices of growth

Figure 4.7 Prices and military expenses, 1550–1626

followed, and the Neapolitan fleet became smaller and more localized in its scope.[16]

What was true for the fleet was true for the Neapolitan military as a whole. Starting in the early 1580s expenses for both the army and the navy remained below the price curve, and though expenditures for landed forces always made up the larger part of military outlays, the lag was greater for landed than for naval forces.[17] Such a state of affairs reflected the changing role of the Kingdom within the Empire and the shift in Spain's focus away from the Mediterranean: after the 1570s, in fact, Naples was not to be a front line again, though naturally it remained a supply base, a

---

[16] The number of galleys in it fell to thirty-three by 1583, to twenty-four by 1600 and to twenty-two by 1621. Cf. AGS. *Visitas de Italia*, leg. 25–1, f. 24v (1583: twenty-nine royal galleys and four private ones); ASN. *Sommaria. Dipendenze*, F. 25, f. 226v (1600: twenty-two royal galleys, though six more were to be commissioned, and two private ones); *ibid.*, F. 25, f. 308r (1603: as in 1600); AGS. *Estado*, leg. 1103, f. 214 (1605: twenty-six galleys) and leg. 1884, f. 105, c. 23r (1621: twenty-six galleys, including two which had been taken over by the Court at the beginning of the year, after the death of Andrea Sauli; 272,000 ducats). In 1626, the fleet numbered fifteen galleys, at a cost of 245,660 ducats (Galasso, "Contributo," p. 93); in 1633, it was made up of seventeen ships, all of which were fit only for short trips, as from Naples to Messina or Genoa (AGS. *Secretarías Provinciales*, libro 69, ff. 271–29v).

[17] That lag can be graphed as in Figure 4.8. The amounts added to the budget figures as adjustments (for parliamentary aids in 1550, 1563, 1574, 1626 and for the proceeds from the 4 *grana* per hearth tax in 1626) have been divided equally between land and naval forces. On the question of adjustments to budget totals, cf. Appendix II; for the figures in these and other graphs, cf. Appendix I.

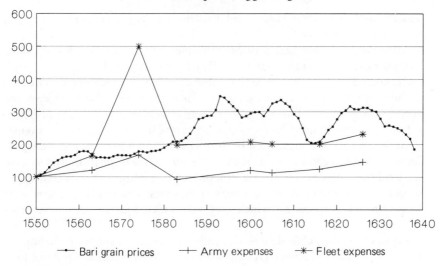

Indices of growth

Figure 4.8 The army, the navy and inflation, 1550–1626

source of soldiers, and a transit station for Spanish troops to and from the front lines.

But the Kingdom was and remained an integral part of the Spanish military system in other ways as well, which were perhaps even more important than direct military ones. Even when it was no longer the beachhead for Spanish action in the Mediterranean, in fact, Naples continued paying, in direct financial terms, for the support of Spanish policy elsewhere in Italy and in Europe.

That role, of course, was not new for the Kingdom. From 1541 to 1560, over 6.75 million ducats had been "assigned for payment" on Naples or "sent to Rome, Genoa, Milan and other places outside the Kingdom," to finance Imperial efforts in Italy, North Africa and Northern Europe.[18] From 1560 to April, 1592, nearly 1,300,000 ducats were sent from Naples to Milan alone.[19] In the course of the Thirty Years' War, very great sums indeed found their way out of the Kingdom to support Spanish arms and to pay for the defense of Northern Italy, the burden of which fell on Naples rather than Milan.[20] From 1631 to 1643 alone, in fact, the Kingdom sent

[18] AGS. *Visitas de Italia*, leg. 346, "Sumario de los dineros, ["Notamento delli dinari che sono stati tratti a pagare"]. Cf. For an analysis of those loans, cf. Mantelli, *Burocrazia e finanze pubbliche*, pp. 333–66 and Calabria, "Finanzieri genovesi.".

[19] ASN. *Sommaria. Consulte*, vol. 14, ff. 147r–168v and ff. 169r–204v.

[20] Villari, *La rivolta, passim*, and Sella, *Crisis and Continuity*, pp. 64–66.

about 11 million ducats to Milan – and that sum takes into account only money, not men, arms and supplies.[21]

More often than not, such financial contributions did not figure directly in the budgets or reports "on the state of the Royal patrimony."[22] But they did appear under other guises, as expenses for the public debt. Those expenditures, as we have already seen, witnessed a tremendous growth in the course of the sixteenth and seventeenth centuries. That was largely because in raising the funds to be sent to other areas of the Empire there was little alternative to mortgaging future revenue. That the exchequer generally did by floating securities backed by predictable tax income. Public debt expenses, then, were quite clearly financial transactions incurred to support Spanish policy. But they ought perhaps to be understood at a deeper level than that, as political–military expenses. Those, after all, were most frequently the purposes for which they were raised and the goals which they served.[23]

Payments on the public debt in sixteenth- and seventeenth-century Naples, we have seen, took up an increasingly large share of the expense budget. They rose from about 425,000 ducats in 1550 to perhaps more than 4,000,000 ducats in 1638. As Figure 4.9 shows, they more than kept up with inflation throughout that time. The graph plots the proceeds from the sale of securities, that is, the consolidated public debt, which accounted for the largest part of such expenditures, and all the other outlays that made up the debt, that is, fiscal concessions and, for some years, part of the revenue from parliamentary aids.[24] There is little doubt that the graph reflects the actual course of indebtedness in the Kingdom. But it might be useful to factor

[21] From 1631 to 1636 alone, the Kingdom provided Milan with 48,000 soldiers, 5,500 horses and 3,500,000 ducats (Galasso, "Le riforme del conte di Lemos," p. 213 and note 11). A Sommaria *consulta* from 1643, which details the monetary contributions to Milan from 1631 to 1643 (ASN. *Sommaria. Consulte*, vol. 47, ff. 107r–126r [also, in Spanish, in AGS. *Estado*, leg. 3267, f. 255]), suggests that the total for 1631–36 might have amounted to 2,282,997.30 ducats. Cf. also Coniglio, *Il Viceregno*, part III, *passim*.

[22] An exception is the budget for 1605, which enters 22,000 ducats ordered sent from Naples to Milan. That sum figures among military expenses in the tables and graphs in this chapter.

[23] The sources available for analysis do not always specify in detail the purposes served by the revenue from the growth of the funded debt in the Kingdom. But it is clear that a good part at least of that revenue served to buttress, and help pay for, Spanish policy in its various theaters of operation.

[24] Fiscal concessions were sums that "certain barons and other persons retain from said ordinary fiscal payments [that is, the hearth base tax] because of past perpetual and feudal concessions. . .and sales by the most serene Kings of this Kingdom" (ASN. *Sommaria. Consulte*, vol. 4, f. 178r). Those sums, then, could be outright grants to the recipients from tax levies or they could consist of the interest from sales of government securities backed by direct taxes, or, in some cases, by gabelles. Thus they straddled the public debt and pensions and stipends (on the latter, cf. below). Though fiscal concessions cannot be separated from other public debt expenses in the budgets for 1550 and 1638, they can be easily identified in all the other budgets. They amounted to 182,096 ducats in 1563; 151,334 ducats in 1574; 113,581 ducats in 1583; 104,359 ducats in 1600; 101,594 ducats in 1605; 115,450 ducats in 1616 and 115,950 ducats in 1626. For an analysis of fiscal concessions in 1575, cf. Calabria, *State Finance*, pp. 243–47 and the Sommaria *consulta* cited above, ff. 178r–185v.

The other components of the public debt figures cited so far in the text and the charts consist of the sums from parliamentary aids in 1550, 1563, 1574 and 1626, which have been added as adjustments to the expense totals in this analysis. For them cf. Appendix II.

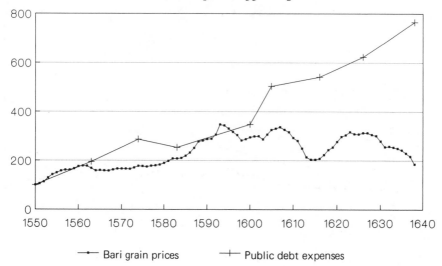

Government expense, 1550–1638

——•—— Bari grain prices   ——+—— Public debt expenses

Indices of growth

Figure 4.9 Prices and public debt expenditures, 1550–1638

out fiscal concessions and parliamentary aids and so plot the growth of the funded debt, which reflected the sale of government securities in the Kingdom, as in Figure 4.10, which points clearly to three major phases in the growth of the consolidated debt in the Kingdom.

The first phase saw funded indebtedness almost quadruple over the last thirty-seven years of the sixteenth century, rising steadily from about 400,000 to about 1,400,000 ducats a year. That growth was impressive in its own right, and it easily outdistanced the price curve. But it paled in comparison to the truly phenomenal increase which took place in the second phase, between 1600 and 1605. In only five years, in fact, funded indebtedness in the Kingdom rose by about 50 percent, going from about 1,400,000 ducats to over 2,000,000 ducats. That was the highest percentage increase, both relatively and absolutely, in the entire period.[25] In the third phase, from 1605 to 1638, the debt grew by about 65 percent, rising to about 4,100,000 ducats.[26]

[25] This obtained despite the fact that between 1600 and 1605 expenditures for the public debt went from 53 percent to 50 percent of total outlay.
[26] The phases in the growth of the debt coincided with some of the great periods of Spanish involvement in the Mediterranean and Europe. The first phase, from 1550 to 1600, witnessed the last period of Emperor Charles V's activity in Germany and all the heavy involvements of Philip II's reign, from the Mediterranean to the Netherlands. The second phase showed the greatest increase in the rhythm of indebtedness in the Kingdom, which can most likely be ascribed to the warfare in the Netherlands. The last phase, from 1605 to 1638, saw the continuation of war in the Low Countries (to the truce of 1609 and the resumption of hostilities in 1621) and the deepening involvement in the Thirty Years' War.

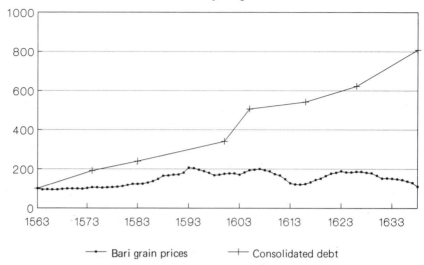

Indices of growth; 1563 = 404,798 ducats

Figure 4.10 Prices and the consolidated debt, 1563–1638
Note: Since it is not possible without doubt to distinguish fiscal concessions from the consolidated debt in 1550, the graph must use 1563 as the base year for both Bari grain prices and public debt expenditure.

It seems safe to suggest from the calculations and interpolations that can legitimately be made that the funded debt in 1550 (without fiscal concessions) stood at something like 1,250,000 ducats.

The exchequer in Naples was able to attract such large amounts of capital and to lure a growing number of investors onto the securities market throughout the sixteenth century by providing investors with a higher return for their money than did other parts of the Monarchy.[27] Redeemable bonds in Naples, for example, paid about 10 percent in the 1540s and 1550s, and though their rate of return declined over time, they still paid more than 7 percent at the end of the century.[28] But on occasion, to stimulate investment, the exchequer would offer lifeterm securities bearing much higher rates of return than even redeemable ones – 20 percent in 1554 and 12–13 percent from the 1580s on.

Thanks to such inducements, capital invested in lifeterm securities grew nearly sixfold between 1583 and 1600, from about 457,000 to over 2,700,000 ducats.[29] The

---

[27] Cf. below, chapter 5.

[28] Redeemable securities paid a mean 9.2 percent in 1563, 8.9 percent in 1572, and 7.7 percent in 1596. See Table 7 in Appendix 1 for interest rates on securities from 1541 to 1598.

[29] Calculations based on AGS. *Visitas de Italia*, leg. 25/1, ff. 1r–30v (the 1583 budget) and ASN. *Sommaria. Dipendenze*, F. 25, ff. 222r–233r (the 1600 budget).

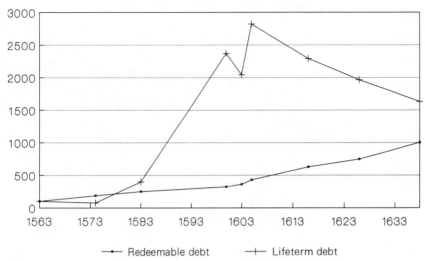

Figure 4.11 Redeemable and lifeterm debt, 1563–1638

high point in the sale of lifeterm securities in the Kingdom seems to have come between 1603 and 1605, when capital indebtedness on those bonds rose from about 2,300,000 to nearly 3,200,000 ducats.[30] Afterwards, as Fig. 4.11 shows, indebtedness incurred through lifeterm securities was gradually reduced, while the redeemable debt, which had stood at about 4,000,000 ducats in 1560 and 13,000,000 ducats in 1600, soared from about 18,000,000 ducats in 1605 to over 41,000,000 ducats in 1638.[31]

As this discussion has shown, it was relatively easy for the Crown, at least in the sixteenth century, to raise capital for its use. But that was an advantage only in the short run, or only from the point of view of financially hard-pressed administrators. The reduction of interest on redeemable securities did reflect an attempt at some measure of fiscal prudence. That attempt, however, was negated by simultaneous issues of lifeterm securities which paid nearly twice the return of redeemable bonds! Those high interest rates attest not so much to financial dynamism as to the scarcity of capital and the poor business climate in the Kingdom. Furthermore, by syphoning funds into the government's coffers, those rates helped decrease what capital was available for enterprise and productive endeavors generally. Thus while in the Netherlands the "financial revolution" heralded by the introduction of deficit

[30] The 1603 figures are in ASN. *Sommaria. Dipendenze*, F. 25, ff. 306r–310r.
[31] These figures are estimates, because the two seventeenth-century texts do not provide a breakdown of indebtedness by rate. But they are conservative estimates: cf. Galasso, "Contributo," pp. 85–86 and note v (1).

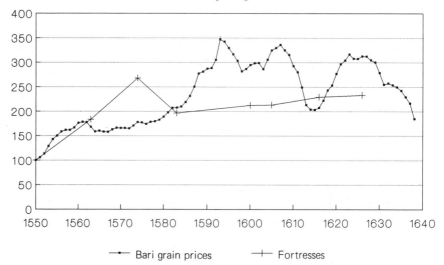

Indices of growth

Figure 4.12 Prices and fortresses, roads and watchtowers, 1550–1626
Note: For the sake of accuracy, here too, as in Figure 4.10, the 1563 figures serve as base 100 (cf. note to Figure 4.10).

financing proved to be a source of strength, and an important factor in the success of the revolt against Spain, in Naples those same expedients had quite different results. High interest rates, the dynamic market in securities and the impressive growth of the funded debt accentuated the effects of an adverse economic conjuncture, served to stifle productive energies, and placed a heavy mortgage on future development in the Kingdom.

Payments on the public debt, then, tied the Kingdom into the system of Spanish strategy in Italy and Europe, while military expenditures paid for the defense of the Kingdom and gave support to Spanish policy in all theaters. Expenses for fortresses, by contrast, provided for the Kingdom's own immediate interests, that is for the construction, manning and upkeep of its network of roads, fortresses and watch-towers.[32] Those expenses were closely related to military outlays in purpose and function, but they were vastly inferior to them: at their highest point, they took up no more than 7 percent of the yearly expense budget. Figure 4.12 plots the relationship between them and inflation.

As the figure shows, expenses for fortresses, roads and towers rose above the price curve only at two points in time, that is between 1550 and 1574 and in 1616. Such a

---

[32] Galasso, "Le riforme del conte di Lemos," p. 221.

development in 1616 was largely fortuitous, because it depended much less on an increase in funding than on the downswing that affected prices after 1608.[33] The considerable rise of these outlays above the price curve between 1550 and 1574, on the other hand, was due to two reasons: first, the building program of the mid-sixteenth century, which witnessed the construction of a defense and communications network and the introduction of the apposite road and watchtower taxes, and, second, the increase in such expenditures, especially for fortresses, as a result of the confrontation with Turkish power on the Mediterranean.

But by 1583, as the Turkish danger had become less insistent, funding for fortresses, roads and towers had been sharply reduced. With the sole exception of 1616, it stagnated for the rest of the period under consideration. Given the dynamism of prices over the same time, that meant that funding was effectively cut.[34] To make matters worse, the sums budgeted were often diverted to other, more pressing concerns. In its report on the state of finances for 1626, the Sommaria described that development, especially as it affected the allocation for the construction and upkeep of watchtowers along the coasts, noting:

The Royal Court has used a great deal of money from said tax for several of its needs, and it continues to do so, for which reason many watchtowers have not been built in places where they are necessary for the defense of this Kingdom. And that has brought about and continues to bring about most notable damage to sea traffic, because enemy corsairs prey on it.[35]

Thus the Kingdom came to witness a situation that was clearly paradoxical, albeit, given the logic of empire and reason of state, not at all uncommon, and not merely in early modern Europe. It contributed enormous sums for the defense of Northern Italy, and it provided money, men and supplies for the pursuit of military and political goals farther afield from its border than even Lombardy. But it did so at the expense of needs that were more properly its own.

A somewhat analogous situation to that of expenses for fortresses, roads and watchtowers obtained with civil expenses. Among these are included all outlays for the bureaucracy in the Kingdom – for the salaries of officials, from the Viceroy's to the provincial counselors', and for the operation of magistracies and councils, like the Sommaria or the Treasury General. Included among civil expenses are also the monies allocated for the administration of justice, the remittances to Spanish embassies in other Italian cities, as well as various other public outlays, such as those for the postal service and the royal stables, for the alms given religious institutions and for the symbolic feudal homage paid yearly to the Pope.

As Figure 4.13 shows, civil expenses rose above the price curve only in 1616; as with expenses for fortresses, roads and towers in the same year, that was due to the

---

[33] For the behavior of prices, see chapters 1 and 3 above. In 1605, expenses for fortresses, roads and towers amounted to 190,052 ducats; in 1616, to 204,694 ducats.

[34] Most sharply for fortresses, less for roads and least for watchtowers.

[35] Quoted in Galasso, "Contributo," p. 89; "Le riforme del conte di Lemos," p. 221.

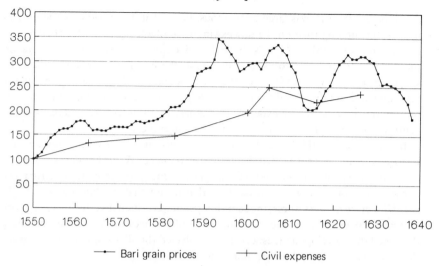

Indices of growth

Figure 4.13 Prices and civil expenses, 1550–1626

behavior of prices, not to the allocation of funds, which had declined from the previous year in the series.

Since civil expenses were made up in large part of the salaries paid to officials and bureaucrats, the fact that they trailed as they did behind prices could not help having important consequences. A royal letter of 16 April 1582 is especially suggestive in this regard.[36] The letter decreed that the salaries of officials in charge of the administration of justice at the provincial level no longer be paid from the proceeds of fines imposed for the settlement of crimes. It lamely stated that "since not as many crimes are punished as in the past," the proceeds from those fines had decreased, thus implying a whole world of collusion and of underhand settlements in criminal cases.

Given the circumstances, however, that was only to be expected, and not simply from judicial officials. Thirty years earlier, in a petition that their salaries be doubled to 300 ducats a year, the Sommaria staff accountants had pointed out that "after the [Sommaria] Lieutenant's and Presidents', [the accountants' offices] are the most worthy, delicate and important. . .in this Royal Chamber to His Majesty's service and the running of this Tribunal. . ."[37] and that, accordingly, "it is not worthwhile at this time to keep them with as little provision as seemed fit at the time they were

---

[36] ASN. *Sommaria. Carte Reali*, vol. 1, ff. 182r–v.
[37] ASN. *Sommaria Consulte*, vol. 2, f. 2r (30 June 1562).

created."[38] One hundred and fifty ducats then, the impassioned request continued, were worth more than 300 now, and with them it was possible to live comfortably, because of the abundance and low cost of all goods in the Kingdom and in the city of Naples. But from the time of the French invasion of the Kingdom, about thirty-four years earlier (1528), "all things that pertain to human sustenance have gone up in price in this city of Naples to almost double what they were before," so that

it is clear that with said provisions said accountants cannot support themselves in His Majesty's service with the authority that befits their office or with the ease and help that they need for the sustenance of their homes and families.[39]

The accountants' condition was not atypical, and like the irregularities suggested by the royal order of 16 April 1582, it was no doubt heavily influenced by the disparity between essentially fixed incomes and spiraling prices.

The last major category of expense to consider is that for pensions, which consisted of a great variety of grants given to royal stipendholders. Those grants ranged from *ad hoc* or lifetime stipends for notables and dignitaries to bonus pay and annuities for military personnel to payments for retainees and pensions for old and disabled veterans.

In the context of the yearly budget, the total outlay for pensions and stipends was not exorbitant. In its own way, though, this category of expense is instructive about early modern fiscality in the Kingdom and about the choices that underlay it. It highlights the very nature of the fiscal system in early modern Naples: lopsided and ponderous, riddled by the givens of inequality and privilege.

For one thing, outlays for pensions and stipends at times matched and even surpassed civil expenses. They posed a sharp contrast to civil expenses in that, as Fig. 4.14 shows, they rose dramatically and stayed well above the price curve throughout the later sixteenth and early seventeenth centuries.[40]

The bulk of allocations for pensions was earmarked for stipends and retainments: together, those outlays amounted to no less than 90 percent of allocation throughout the late sixteenth and early seventeenth centuries. Figure 4.15 details the structure of pensions for three years in the available series, 1563, 1600 and 1626. As the figure makes clear, military pensions of all types (exclusive of the retainees' stipends) were an almost insignificant part of yearly pension expenses. In fact they only took up anywhere from 6 to 9 percent of yearly allocation for pensions. With the usual nearsightedness of governments, however, it was precisely on them that the Council of Italy and Philip II, on Ferrante Fornaro's suggestion, focused in 1593–94 as they sought to reduce expenses in the Kingdom![41] Military annuities to veterans (*piazze morte*), the Council wrote the Viceroy, amounted to 11,522 ducats a year. As they

[38] *Ibid.*, f. 2v.   [39] *Ibid.*, f. 3r.

[40] In the 1550 budget, expenses for pensions are listed as 45,827 ducats. Since that may be a partial figure, the 1563 total, 139,829 ducats, is used as the base period in Fig. 4.13.

[41] AGS. *Secretarías Provinciales*, leg. 6, unfoliated, n.d. ("A la consulta que se hizo").

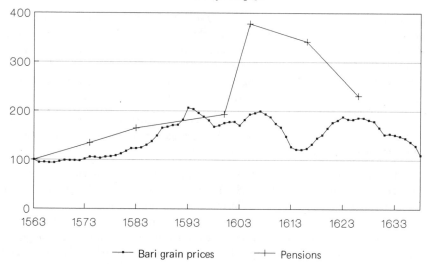

Indices of growth; 1563 = 139,829 ducats

Figure 4.14 Prices and pensions, 1563–1626

expired, they should not be allowed to exceed 4,000 ducats, and they should be the object of royal, not Viceroyal, provision, at Court, not in Naples.[42]

That suggestion seemed shortsighted even to as toughminded a Viceroy as the Count of Miranda, who pointedly wrote the King:

In this matter, I can only represent to Your Majesty two things, the first pertaining to the great need and poverty of the many people who live on these grants, the second with regard to changing these grants to Your Majesty's provision. It seems to me that it would be very inconvenient for those who can lay claim to them to have to go there [to Court] to ask for them. I don't know how that could possibly be done by men as wretched as these usually are – old, crippled, and half-dead with hunger. . .[43]

By contrast to the 1,200-odd ducats due to holders of veterans' pensions in 1600, or the 3,000-odd ducats due to eighty-five disabled men-at-arms and one old halberdier in the same year, or the near 5,000 ducats payable to the Greek refugees from Coron in 1560, Joan of Austria in 1600 received 7,000 ducats for "expenses, food and other necessary things," and the Duke of Urbino, in 1560, more than 29,000 ducats.[44]

The last category of outlay, for "Various" expenses, includes such diverse and

---

[42] *Ibid.*, and AGS. *Estado*, leg. 1094, f. 17.   [43] AGS. *Estado*, leg. 1094, f. 17.
[44] The references are: for 1560, AGS. *Estado*, leg. 1046, f. 203 (4,950 ducats for the Greek refugees and 29,251.20 ducats for the Duke of Urbino); for 1600, ASN. *Sommaria. Dipendenze*, F. 25, f. 229r.

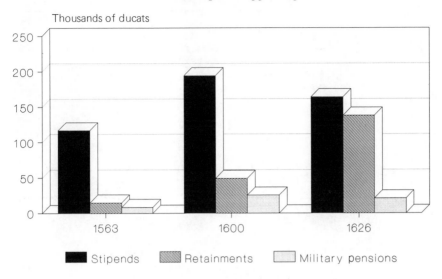

Figure 4.15 The structure of pensions, 1563–1626

discontinuous items as the analogous category for income in the preceding chapter. Rather than elaborate on the essentially contingent nature of those expenses, it is best to note instead that they are not indicative of any meaningful trend in state expense in this period.[45]

This analysis of government expense in the Kingdom of Naples in the late sixteenth and early seventeenth centuries started with a look at Ferrante Fornaro's Short Budget for 1595. It sketched the parlous state of the Neapolitan exchequer, as it emerged from that account, and suggested that it might well be emblematic of the trend in government finances in the entire period. It then focused on the fiscal and financial crisis in the Kingdom in the late sixteenth and early seventeenth centuries, and traced its origins, its course and its reasons. Now, by way of conclusion, it might not be amiss to turn once again to the statements of those contemporaries who dealt on a day-to-day basis with the vexing problems of Imperial finance in the Kingdom.

Contemporaries like the Duke of Alcalá, Viceroy from 1558 to 1571, who wrote the King on 7 February 1566:

Here we have to provide for many essential things. . .and we only have what is in the Treasury now, with no prospect of more coming in during September, all of which means an expected deficit of 542,400 ducats. . .[46]

Or like the Count of Miranda, who addressed a typically blunt, nine-line despatch to Philip II on 18 January 1592. "Your Majesty ordered last month that I send 5,000

---

[45] See Figure 4.16.   [46] AGS. *Estado*, leg. 1055, f. 29.

Indices of growth (thousands of percent)

Figure 4.16 Prices and various expenses, 1550–1626

ducats to the Duke of Sessa, and that was done, as ordered." But, the Viceroy went on,

> . . .I remind Your Majesty that this Royal Court is in no condition to bear such obligations, because it is so weakened that it cannot meet even its ordinary and predictable expenses, as I have represented to Your Majesty on other occasions. . .[47]

Or, to conclude a series that could be as long and repetitive as it could be diverse, contemporaries like the Duke of Medina de las Torres, who in 1639 wrote the Count-Duke of Olivares about

> . . .the state of the Royal Patrimony in this Kingdom, which can[not] supply the contributions which the King our Lord orders for Germany and the State of Milan, or even meet the normal obligations and expenses of this Kingdom. . .[48]

Count-Dukes and Kings, of course, were aware of the financial difficulties of their chief Italian dominion. But their demands on it were dictated by a strategic vision and by strategic needs which no doubt seemed to them wider than could be grasped from Naples. To modern observers, that vision and those needs might amount to nothing less than a disastrous policy of war and grandeur, born in part of Spain's insistence on being the gendarme of Europe. To sixteenth- and seventeenth-century

---

[47] *Ibid.*, leg. 1093, f. 1.   [48] *Ibid.*, leg. 3261, f. 149.

rulers, however, they were nothing less than a duty to provide for what Philip II had called "the defense and security of my kingdoms and states."[49] Like Philip II in 1571, successive kings might be aware "of how much that Kingdom is burdened," and perhaps even offhandedly add that "it would be good to relieve it however we can," yet go on to say with him "but the needs are so great in all parts [of the Monarchy] that it is essential that one help the other as much as possible. . ."[50]

As we have seen, that policy and that obligation to "help" laid heavy burdens on the Kingdom, and they were reflected in the staggering expenses which did so much to unravel the policy of statebuilding, economic reconstruction and social peace nurtured ever since the mid-fifteenth century by a different Iberian dynasty in the Kingdom. Those expenditures and their consequences came to be detailed with growing starkness in the budgets and financial reports drawn up to assess the state of the Royal Patrimony.

At the conclusion of his painstaking "Summary of Income and Expense," Gioann'Antonio Merlo, in 1564, had struck a not altogether pessimistic note:

Thus we can see that the said revenues amount each year to about 1,700,000 ducats. . .and deducting about 100,000 ducats which is what exemptions can amount to, they come to 1,600,000 ducats net, and of these, 1 million are spent outside the Treasury, and the remaining 600,000 come into the Treasurer's hands, and are spent by him, so that after both ordinary expenses and extraordinary ones, which cannot be estimated with certainty, little or nothing is left over. . .[51]

At the end of their "Report on the State of His Majesty's Royal Patrimony in the Kingdom of Naples by the Council of State" for 1600, the Sommaria Presidents painted a much darker picture of finances in the Kingdom than Merlo thirty-six years earlier. They reported to the Viceroy a yearly deficit of 350,000 ducats and noted that 2,400,000 ducats had been assigned for payment on the future proceeds from parliamentary aids and from the Sheep Customhouse, until 1610. Those debts had been incurred to make up previous yearly deficits and to meet expenses that had been due to

the regiments (*terzi*) of Italian infantry which His Majesty ordered to be drafted in this Kingdom and which were sent in past years in the service of His Royal Crown, just as Your Excellency [the Viceroy] sent two of them last year, on which 123,722 ducats and 15 *grana* were spent. . .and also for the price of supplies sent to His Majesty in Spain, and other expenses and extraordinary payments which came up. . .[52]

The interest on the money borrowed, at 9 percent, would amount to about 240,000 ducats a year. Of course, the Presidents added, should the capital be paid when due, upon receipt of each instalment from parliamentary aids, and should no new debts be incurred, the interest payments in future years could be reduced.

---

[49] *Ibid.*, leg. 1069, f. 18.   [50] *Ibid.*, leg. 1059, f. 145.   [51] *Ibid.*, leg. 1046, f. 203.
[52] ASN. *Sommaria. Dipendenze*, F. 25, f. 230v.

But [they went on] we are calculating the entire sum because it is clear that there will continue to be deficits and that money will have to be borrowed at interest in order to meet fixed and necessary expenses, and we think that things will continue this way in future years. . .[53]

So a regular deficit of over half a million ducats a year could be forecast, and, in a vicious circle, it would have to be made up from other loans to be contracted in the future. Even worse, the Presidents continued, the proceeds from direct taxes for future years, including those generated by the increase in the hearth census of 1595, had all been mortgaged. Likewise, little of the revenue to come from the Sheep Customs or the gabelles was uncommitted,

so that we find the Royal Patrimony seriously depleted and overburdened, and even more so if we consider other sets of debts which we have not discussed so as not to get too involved in details. . .but they are many and of great quantity. . .and so we find no source of revenue from which Your Excellency can obtain any substantial sum of money. . .for the preservation and safekeeping of the Kingdom. . .[54]

Thirty-seven years later, the tones used by the then Sommaria Presidents to describe the state of finances in the Kingdom were decidedly more ominous.[55] Government finances lay in shambles. The Military Treasury, which had been set up in 1612 by the reforming Viceroy Count of Lemos so as to guarantee that set expenses would be met, ran a deficit of over 530,000 ducats a year. Of that sum, about 130,000 ducats had been granted as collateral to merchant bankers while they awaited assignment for their loans,[56] and about 55,000 ducats were due a contractor for sums advanced in the galleys' service. But the greater part of that deficit, nearly 350,000 ducats, or more than a fifth of the Treasury's original endowment, had been sold off to secure loans needed in the past. Not only that, but the source of the endowment itself had changed. When the Treasury had been set up, about three-quarters of its revenue had been made up of direct taxes from "the best [that is, solvent] lands." The majority of those sources of revenue, however, had had to be given out to creditors, so that in 1637 most of the Treasury's endowment, or about 616,000 ducats, was assigned instead on direct taxes "in the worst lands, the majority of which are destitute, so that almost no money can be collected from them."[57] As a consequence, that sum

is not enough. . .to pay punctually even the yearly 426,960.67 ducats which, according to the report of the Military Treasury's officials, are the ordinary and fixed expenses in said provinces, that is, for fortresses, watchtowers, the administration of justice and the pursuit of bandits, the provisions of saltpeter and powder, the fixed garrisons, the iron works at Stilo, munitions, aid to the Spanish infantry in the city of Naples and in the Tuscan garrisons, and other matters, for none of which can payment be delayed. . .[58]

A similar situation obtained with that part of the Treasury's endowment which came from the Sheep Customs, the gabelles and other sources of revenue. Money

---

[53] *Ibid.*, f. 231v.   [54] *Ibid.*, ff. 232v–233r.   [55] ASN. *Sommaria. Consulte*, vol. 41, ff. 33r–39v.
[56] i.e. in *fiscali di risguardo.*   [57] *Ibid.*, f. 37r.   [58] *Ibid.*, ff. 37v–38r.

simply could not be collected from the contractors and other court debtors, the Presidents went on, with an eye to the economic crisis in the Kingdom,

primarily because of such pernicious times as these, which are causing the gabelle leases to decline day by day, and were it not for this Tribunal's great diligence in these matters, we would reach a point whereby we would either not find a contractor to lease them, or by necessity they would have to be run by officials in the name of said Royal Court, or else they would have to be let at such a low price that most notable damage would come to the revenues of His Majesty's Royal Patrimony in this Kingdom.[59]

Six years later, in 1643, as they reported to the Viceroy on the impressive burdens Naples had shouldered for the defense of Milan, which had amounted to about 11 million ducats in thirteen years, the Sommaria Presidents could not help noting:

We represent also to Your Excellency that this Kingdom is reduced to its extremity precisely because it has helped Milan. . .with so many gabelles and levies which Your Excellency has been forced to impose in order to do business with the bankers, lest they stop advancing the sums destined for the relief of Milan. . .[60]

Thus, the Sommaria went on, the Viceroy had been forced to

mortgage for this very same reason much of what the Lord our King used to have in this Kingdom – lands, demanial towns, revenues, and even the bulk of the monies that used to make up the endowment of the Military Treasury, at the expense of the fixed obligations and the preservation of this very Kingdom, whose government His Majesty had principally entrusted to Your Excellency. . .[61]

And so, the Sommaria concluded (in an aside that can serve as a fitting epitaph to the story of government finance in Naples in the period we have examined),

neither the Lord Count of Sirvela [Milan's governor] nor the state of Milan can have any reason whatsoever to complain about Your Excellency or about this Kingdom, seeing that, with the heavy and continued sums sent with so much care, Your Excellency in a certain sense has shown to care much more for the relief of that state than for meeting the fixed expenses of this Kingdom.[62]

[59] *Ibid.*, ff. 38v–39r.
[60] *Ibid.*, vol. 47, ff. 107r–126r (f. 125v; for a Spanish translation of this document, cf. AGS. *Estado*, leg. 3267, f. 255).   [61] *Ibid.*, f. 125v.   [62] *Ibid.*, ff. 125v–126r.

5

The creation of a securities market in the later sixteenth century

The preceding two chapters have brought to light the difficult condition of the exchequer in Naples in the later sixteenth and seventeenth centuries. Even before the 1550s government receipts had lagged behind expenditures, and over time the gap between them had widened and become a fixture of fiscal and financial life.[1] Expenses for the military and for the public debt loomed large in that process, for they outstripped other categories of expense and exerted a heavy weight on the Kingdom's finances. In those circumstances, only the spectacular growth of the funded debt had allowed the Kingdom to meet what obligations it did.

In its recourse to indebtedness, Naples was very much in tune with the times, for deficit financing, even in the proportions it assumed in the Kingdom, was one of the great innovations of sixteenth-century government; the term "financial revolution" used by some historians to describe it is only a slight exaggeration. At its best, deficit financing could be a powerful weapon in the arsenals of governments, for it could enable them to mobilize huge amounts of cash and thus greatly to expand their roles and their functions. For better or for worse, "the novel expedients" helped bring states into greater contact with subjects by influencing economic and financial markets, by attracting and, in however lopsided a fashion, redistributing wealth in society.[2] Above all, they made possible the massive military outlays of the Spanish Empire, as well as the resolute defense against the Empire by the United Provinces.

The growth of the funded debt in Naples was assured by the same mechanisms at work in other parts of the Empire, such as Castile or the Netherlands. The Crown would float securities (*juros*) guaranteed by the several sources of fiscal revenue, that is, direct taxes, gabelles and duties and, in the Kingdom, the revenues from the Foggia Sheep Customs. It would receive from the purchasers of those securities a lump sum of money, a capital investment, which would earn the investors yearly interest at a specified rate. That interest would be paid from the future proceeds of the tax source guaranteeing the securities.

Again, as in Castile and the Netherlands, in Naples the Crown came to float different types of securities. Lifeterm rentes paid a higher rate of return than redeemable ones, and they generally expired at the death of their holders. Redeemable instruments, on the other hand, could be passed on as inheritance from

---

[1] For a sense of developments before 1550, cf. Coniglio, *Il Regno, passim.*
[2] Cf. Waquet and the papers in *La fiscalité et ses implications sociales.*

one generation to another, or they could be sold on the market like any other form of property. The government could retire the redeemable debt by refunding its creditors the original sums they had invested. In case of renewed financial need, it could float new securities, perhaps at a lower rate of return. Or else, to reduce its costs, it could carry out a forced conversion of the debt, that is, it could lower the interest on securities from the original rate to a lesser one. If the investors refused the new conditions, they would be refunded their capital, and their securities could be offered to others at the new rate.

Though the system thus summarily described was the common one throughout the Habsburg lands, local conditions and local exigencies made for diversity and variety. In the Netherlands, to cite the most successful example of deficit financing in the Habsburg lands, both the central and the provincial organs of fiscal administration followed the pattern of retiring the debt, even if only to reissue securities at lower rates of return.[3] In Naples, by contrast, the debt was not retired, though the interest payable on funded indebtedness was revised downward on several occasions in the sixteenth and seventeenth centuries. In the Netherlands, again, a favorable economic climate, the States' ability periodically to retire the debt and, eventually, control of fiscal policy by heavy investors in the public debt made deficit financing a positive, even beneficial, tool for government and society. In Naples, on the other hand, the economic reversals of the later sixteenth century and the exchequer's constant need to expand indebtedness had different, though no less important effects.

Securities backed by the yield of tax income were sold in Naples in the very first decade of Spanish rule.[4] But financing through the sale of securities did not come into its own, as a system, until the middle decades of the sixteenth century. Up to that time, other expedients, such as the sale of lands, were more important than the sale of revenues in supplementing the proceeds from taxation. Between 1523 and 1530, for example, the sale of securities yielded only a little over 114,000 ducats. In the same period, the sale of lands from the royal domain netted instead over 235,000 ducats.[5]

By the 1540s, though, and even more clearly by the 1550s, even those measures could not meet the growing need for funds. The number of properties available for sale dwindled, and parliamentary aids could not keep pace with need, even after they were set at 1,200,000 ducats every two years in 1566. Necessity thus provided the

---

[3] Tracy, pp. 95–97, 134. On the general question of the state debt in Castile, cf. the informative recent study by Pilar Toboso Sánchez, *La deuda pública castellana durante el Antiguo Régimen (Juros)* (Madrid, 1987).

[4] Cf. AGS. *Estado*, leg. 1004, f. 69 (1514–15), particularly c. 6v (payments to lessees from the proceeds of the wine gabelle in the city of Naples). For some evidence for the 1520s, cf. AGS. *Visitas de Italia*, leg. 349/1, unfol. (securities sold in 1520 on the Naples Customs) and ASN. *Sommaria. Diversi*, Prima Numerazione, F. 23 (instruments for sales over various years, including 1522 and 1523).

[5] AGS. *Estado*, leg. 1005, f. 27; leg. 1027, f. 71.

motive for the "financial revolution" of the 1540s and 1550s. The Kingdom's demographic growth and its expansive economy offered the opportunity by widening the tax base and by permitting the wave of "new imposts." Between 1542 and 1561 the Kingdom witnessed an increase of 135,194 hearths, and a corresponding rise in the base tax levied on the hearths of 205,466 ducats.[6] While that sum was not trivial by itself, it could generate a much more significant amount of money, over 2 million ducats, through the "multiplier effect" of the *juros* system. Analogous increases in funds could be produced after the 1550s, thanks to the new duties on production, consumption and export and to the steeper tolls levied on the Foggia Customhouse.

Those changes, however, depended upon the creation of a veritable market for government securities, and to assure that, the Crown had to attract investors and earn their confidence. To start, both the Crown and potential investors had to view *juros* more clearly as investments than as what they had also often been in the past – pensions, concessions, remuneration, or compensation, in lieu of cash, for goods or services. In truth, the *juros* never quite lost that older, "patrimonial" aspect, but the Crown was successful in effecting what must have been an important mental change.[7] More directly, though, the Crown provided a whole constellation of inducements to lure capital and reassure investors.

Probably the most important of those inducements was the most difficult to provide initially – a guarantee of the reliability and safety of government securities. As we shall see, the Crown's record on that score in the sixteenth century was quite good, and investors must have been convinced of that even early on. Nothing else can explain the fact that the public debt in the Kingdom rose to something like 1.25 million ducats in 1550, and that it then more than tripled, to over 4 million ducats in 1563.[8]

Very persuasive as well, and immediately tangible, was the high rate of return investors were offered in the securities market. Redeemable securities in Naples, as we have seen, yielded about 10 percent in the 1540s and 1550s.[9] Over the next 50 years, those rates were to decline, but they were still very high in comparison with other areas. In the Netherlands, for example, the "traditional" rate for much of the sixteenth century was 6.25 percent, though exceptionally securities could pay more than that.[10] But Naples was a different story from the Netherlands, and its rates reflected local financial and investment realities.

But at critical junctures the Crown could give actual windfalls to stimulate

---

[6] Calculations based on AGS. *Estado*, leg. 1030, f. 180 (1541–42) and the census data for 1561 listed in chapter 1, n. 83.
[7] That the securities continued having their older function as well is amply demonstrated by the presence on the bond market in Naples of "investors" like Margaret of Parma, who held bonds worth 159,000 ducats, or like Mary of Austria, with securities worth more than 400,000 ducats.
[8] See chapter 4.   [9] See the interest rates in Appendix 1.
[10] Tracy, pp. 60, 93, 207. From 1621 to about 1643, the rate was 5 percent (*ibid.*, pp. 204–05). For Castile, see the very interesting Table XVII in Ulloa, pp. 828–29.

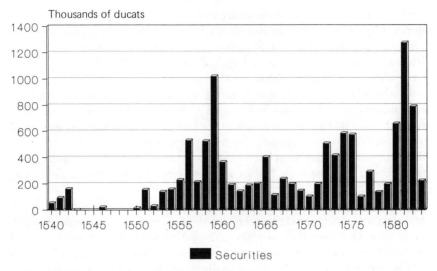

Thousands of ducats

1544-45, 1547-49 missing

Securities

Figure 5.1 Securities sold in Naples, 1540–1583

investment, as it did in 1554. That year it sold 124,000-odd ducats in lifeterm securities guaranteed by direct taxes and bearing no less than 20 percent interest. Twenty-one years later, in 1575, sixty-three of the original 116 investors were still receiving the yearly interest of 20 percent on their capital.[11] As late as 1600, in fact, 4,000 ducats a year, representing 20,000 ducats in capital, remained as an obligation in the year's budget.[12] The lure of high interest rates worked to attract capital into lifeterm securities in 1554, and to give a powerful stimulus to the development of the securities market in the years immediately thereafter.

To judge from the results, those efforts were eminently successful. Figure 5.1 details the sales of securities in the Kingdom from 1540 to 1583.[13] From 1540 to 1583, securities for over 11,500,000 ducats were sold in Naples. As the figure makes clear, the market was sluggish through the 1540s and early 1550s, despite peaks of

[11] ASN. *Sommaria. Consulte*, vol. 4, ff. 186r–188v.
[12] ASN. *Sommaria. Dipendenze*, F. 25, ff. 222r–233r (the 1600 State of the Royal Patrimony [cf. Appendix II, note 14]).
[13] Figure 5.1 uses data from two sources, AGS. *Visitas de Italia*, leg. 20/8 (1540–59) and *ibid.*, leg. 25/1 (1554–83). For the sake of greater reliability and completeness, however, it uses data for the years 1540–58 from the first source and for the years 1559–83 from the second. The first document was probably compiled in 1559, and the data in it for that year do not include all transactions. It lists, in fact, only 949,952.31 ducats as the proceeds for the sale of revenues, whereas the second document lists those proceeds as 1,019,130.62 ducats. For a more detailed discussion of the sources used in this and all other figures and tables in this chapter, cf. Appendix II.

sorts in 1542 and 1551, when the securities sold amounted to 159,000 and 151,000 ducats, respectively.[14] But the pace of those sales quickened in 1553 and 1554, and, probably because of the issue of 20 percent lifetime bonds, it reached unprecedented levels afterwards. In both 1556 and 1558, about half a million ducats in securities were sold, and in 1559 more than 1 million ducats.

By the mid-1550s, then, thanks to the policies which served to attract and reassure investors, the Crown had created a viable securities market which truly revolutionized its finances. Throughout the later sixteenth century, it was able to watch the bond market assume even greater proportions without having to offer lifeterm securities again for at least twenty-five years. Only after 1581, in fact, were new lifeterm bonds issued in Naples, and then generally at 13 percent, still a very attractive rate, but a lower one than that of 1554.[15]

As Figure 5.1 makes clear, then, government securities came to represent a very appealing investment throughout the later sixteenth century. And understandably so, because the interest they bore was paid regularly and in full. In the seventeenth century, by contrast, investors were to see the return on their securities taxed, partly retained or even simply suspended with distressing and increasing frequency. But all that was in the future, not in the sixteenth century.

In addition, securities in the funded debt were not affected by Philip II's "bankruptcies," which targeted instead the short-term loans made by bankers to the Crown. In the course of a "bankruptcy," those loans, or *asientos*, were, essentially, converted into *juros*.[16] Such a royal maneuver, like the one of 1575, might possibly affect investor confidence generally, and perhaps slow down the purchase of securities, but if so, only for a short time. In 1576, in fact, possibly in response to the 1575 suspension of payments, the level of securities purchased in Naples dropped substantially from the previous year's, or even from the previous five years', to about 100,000 ducats.[17] That level, however, had not been unknown in years not marked

---

[14] Note that in this, as in other figures illustrating the sale of securities, the amounts include the sale of securities floated for the first time as well as the resale of older securities which had reverted to the state for various reasons, including the transfer from one investor to another.

[15] See the discussion of the public debt in chapter 4.

[16] For some of the literature on this complex question, cf. the works cited in chapter 2, n. 73.

[17] The effects of the 1575 suspension of payments in the Kingdom need to be studied. Ironically, the Genoese financiers who were the main target of that decree were actually able to profit from it through manipulations made possible by the *juros de resguardo* (cf. A.W. Lovett, "The Castilian Bankruptcy of 1575," esp. pp. 905–06. Cf. also Castillo Pintado, "Los juros de Castilla," and Ruiz Martín, *Lettres marchandes, passim*). Largely because of those manipulations and because of financiers' "greed" and "cruelty," in Genoa it seems to have been small investors – "most of them orphans, widows and other poor people," as a Genoese source called them – who bore the brunt of that decree (AGS. *Estado*, leg. 1412, f. 159).

For the order of suspension of payments in Naples, cf. AGS. *Estado*, leg. 1410, f. 2; for *juros de resguardo* there, cf. AGS. *Secretarías Provinciales*, leg. 2, f. 106 (June 1572): an assignment on the parliamentary aids of 1574 and 1575 to David Imperiale, for a loan 100,000 (Castilian) ducats of 11 *reales* he had made the Court in Spain. *Juros de resguardo* were "a very new thing, not used in that Kingdom," and Viceroy Cardinal Granvelle was to see to it that the assignment "be made with all possible secrecy": *ibid.*, f. 106. Cf. also ff. 263 and 265. In August 1572, the Council of Italy

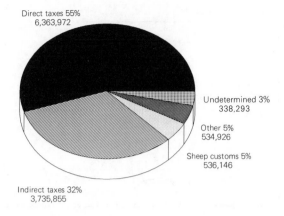

Direct taxes 55%
6,363,972

Undetermined 3%
338,293

Other 5%
534,926

Sheep customs 5%
536,146

Indirect taxes 32%
3,735,855

Total: 11,559,192 d.; 1544-5, 47-9 missing

Figure 5.2 Sources of revenue backing securities, 1540-1583

by bankruptcy (like 1570, with about 100,000 ducats, or 1566, with about 113,000 ducats). But, in any case, the market recovered very quickly. Nearly 300,000 ducats in securities were sold in 1577, about 200,000 in 1579, almost 1,300,000 ducats in 1581.[18]

Figure 5.2 rounds out the picture of the bond market through the early 1580s by showing the sources of revenue which served as backing for the securities sold between 1540 and 1583. As one might expect and as the figure shows, direct taxes were the most important source of tax revenue backing bonds issued through the early 1580s. They guaranteed about 55 percent of the securities floated, or over 6,360,000 ducats. Indirect taxes came to back about a third of the securities, and the proceeds from the Foggia Sheep Customhouse about 5 percent.

Figures 3 and 4, below, complement these statements and offer a different perspective on the same data. By plotting the quantity of securities backed every year by direct taxes and by gabelles, respectively, they help show what changes took place in those sources of funding over time.

Clearly, direct taxes remained a most important source of funding for securities issued in the Kingdom throughout the 1580s. They backed a mean amount of about 172,000 ducats every year, and they peaked in 1559, when they provided funding for

complained that since the grant to Imperiale *juros de resguardo* had been assigned on the same source of revenue to Luciano Centurione (for a loan of 56,000 Castilian ducats) and to Costantino Gentile (for a loan of 67,000 Castilian ducats). For a later reference, cf. *ibid.*, libro 514, ff. 83r–84v, 18 July 1590: a loan of 2.5 million *escudos* for Flanders contracted with the Spinolas on 28 February 1590.

[18] It has not been possible for this work to distinguish between securities *offered* and securities actually *sold* each year.

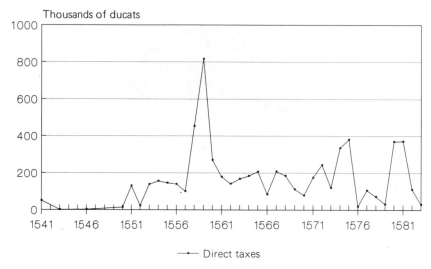

Thousands of ducats

1544-45, 1547-49 missing

Figure 5.3 Bonds backed by direct taxes, 1541–1583
Note: The source of tax revenue guaranteeing securities in 1540 is not specified.

about 816,000 ducats. They backed about 335,000 ducats in 1574 and over 380,000 ducats in 1575, only to fall to slightly more than 18,000 ducats in 1576, no doubt as a result of investor anxiety in the wake of the suspension of payments of 1575. By 1580, however, the crisis seems to have passed. Direct taxes backed nearly 370,000 ducats in bonds sold that year and over 370,000 the next.

Indirect taxes, on the other hand, began playing a significant role in funding securities only in the mid-1550s, thanks no doubt to the "new imposts" of those years. Even so, however, it was not until the 1570s that they backed more than 200,000 ducats in securities floated in a single year. Still, by the end of the series, for three years in the early 1580s, they outstripped direct taxes as a source of funding securities.

This is not at all to say that gabelles replaced direct taxes as the major source of funding for the securities floated in the Kingdom. As we have seen, changes did take place in that funding between the 1540s and the 1580s, particularly in the growing significance that indirect taxes acquired in the 1550s, and especially in the 1570s and 1580s. But direct taxation remained most important throughout the later sixteenth century. That, of course, reflected the fiscal situation and the structure of income in the Kingdom from the 1550s to the 1580s.[19]

---

[19] See chapter 4 for the relative importance of the various sources of revenue in yearly income.

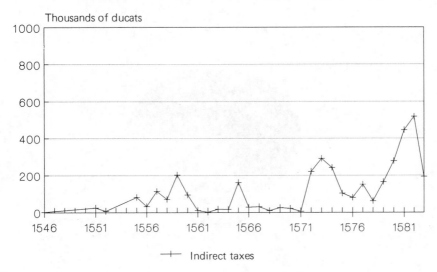

Thousands of ducats

1547-49 missing

+— Indirect taxes

Figure 5.4 Bonds backed by gabelles, 1546–1583
Note: Before 1546 (that is, for the years 1540, 1541, 1542, and 1543) gabelles are not specified among the tax revenues guaranteeing securities. Those revenues are either direct taxes or they are unspecified.

These observations are brought home by Fig. 5.5, which shows the structure of funding for the public debt in the Kingdom at three points in time in the later sixteenth century – 1563, 1572 and 1596.[20] As the figure clearly shows, direct taxes played a preeminent role in funding the consolidated debt throughout the later sixteenth century. In 1563, they accounted for 69 percent of funding; in 1572, for 74 percent and in 1596 for a lower but still substantial 60 percent. Indirect taxes, on the other hand, remained almost static, at about 20 percent, in 1563 and 1572, but they rose to 29 percent by 1596. The revenue from the Foggia Sheep Customs, which accounted for 11 percent of funding in 1563, dipped to 7 percent in 1572 and then returned to 11 percent in 1596.

The figure calls attention also to another critical feature of the consolidated debt in the Kingdom in the later sixteenth century, which the preceding chapter has

---

[20] Figures 5.1–5.4 are based on AGS. *Visitas de Italia*, leg. 20/8 and leg. 25/1, which present data for the sale of revenue in a dynamic form (i.e. at daily or biannual intervals). The other figures in this chapter, on the other hand, are based on the "static" data files for 1563, 1572 and 1596, and they discuss the situation as of a particular year. Note also that, unless otherwise indicated, all statements about securities refer to redeemable instruments. For a fuller discussion of the different types of sources used in this chapter, cf. Appendix II.

1563

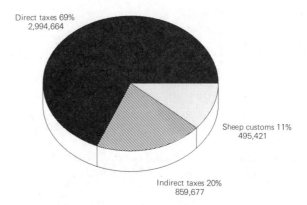

Direct taxes 69%
2,994,664

Sheep customs 11%
495,421

Indirect taxes 20%
859,677

Total: 4,349,762 ducats

1572

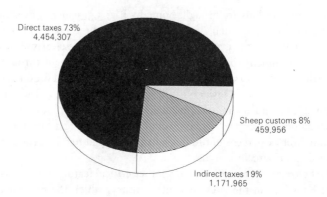

Direct taxes 73%
4,454,307

Sheep customs 8%
459,956

Indirect taxes 19%
1,171,965

Total: 6,086,228 ducats

Figure 5.5 The structure of funding for the public debt

1596

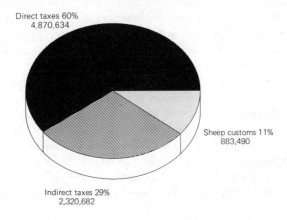

Total: 8,074,806 ducats

already sketched out: its impressive growth in the years to the end of the century.[21] The debt in the Kingdom, in fact, rose from about 4,350,000 ducats in 1563 to about 6,100,000 ducats in 1572 and about 8,100,000 ducats in 1596.[22]

Among other things, of course, that increase was a measure of the government's continued need for capital and of its success in securing it. The increase of the debt thus reflected the success of the "financial revolution" in the Kingdom of Naples. It also reflected one of the key elements of that success, the fact that the funded debt in Naples provided a very good investment indeed for people with capital. This is a basic fact, and it accounts for the dynamic influx of investors in the securities market throughout the later sixteenth century. It helps account also for the fact that not one of the sales of securities effected between 1540 and 1596 represented a forced loan. The government bond market in Naples, in fact, was indeed a free market. By contrast, in the Netherlands wealthy peasants and institutions at times had to be coerced into buying securities.[23]

In addition, investors and their descendants remained in the securities market in the kingdom. That market, in fact, exhibited a substantial genealogical stability,

---

[21] See chapter 4.

[22] The figures are 4,349,762 ducats in 1563; 6,086,228 ducats in 1572 and 8,074,806 ducats in 1596. Note that this represents capital indebtedness for redeemable securities only. By 1600, lifeterm securities amounted to 2,711,197.80 ducats (Calabria, *State Finance*, p. 197).

[23] Tracy, pp. 125, 132.

even though, as we shall see, it also exhibited a great deal of dynamism and change in many of its features. A quite simple comparison of investor last names at each point in the static file series (and so for 1563, 1572 and 1596) shows that at no point did the number of identical last names drop below 51 percent. Between 1563 and 1572, that figure was over 78 percent, no doubt because many investors present in 1563 had not yet died by 1572. Between 1563 and 1596, the beginning and the end point of the series, that figure was over 61 percent.

Reliability and safety, then, served to make government securities very appealing indeed. The case was clinched by the return on those securities, that is, the interest the Crown paid on them. As we have seen, that interest was very high for redeemable securities and even higher for lifeterm bonds, which gave investors an actual windfall. At no point after 1554 did the Crown in Naples offer 20 percent interest on lifeterm bonds, as it had that year. The rates it did pay on the lifeterm securities it subsequently sold, however, were still very attractive, and they help explain the extraordinary influx of investors into lifeterm securities in Naples, especially from the 1580s to the end of the century.[24]

The fact that interest rates on redeemable and lifeterm securities alike show a clear declining trend and that investors crowded into the government bond market is further proof – if any were needed – of the great appeal of those securities in Naples. Because of that appeal and because of the influx of capital onto the securities market, the Monarchy could wield considerable power on the market itself, securing capital without having to resort to forced loans and carrying out forced conversions of the redeemable debt without fear that its securities would find no buyers.

One of the more interesting and significant aspects of the bond market in Naples in the later sixteenth century concerns the social make-up of the debt, that is, the identity of the investors in state securities. Though the sources generally provide very little information beyond the investors' names and gender, it is nonetheless possible to group the people active in the market according to some important ascriptive, professional and geographical categories. Figure 5.6 groups the investors in the funded debt in the Kingdom for 1563, 1572 and 1596 according to whether they were noble or non-noble, institutions or persons, Genoese or not, and it links them to the securities they held in each of the three years.[25]

What is clear from the start is that the debt in sixteenth-century Naples was held predominantly by persons, not institutions. In the seventeenth century, the quite numerous religious institutions in the capital and the Kingdom – the monasteries and convents, the churches, hospitals and confraternities – came to acquire a heavy presence in the funded debt in Naples.[26] In the sixteenth century, however, they did not figure prominently among the investors, and they held only a tiny share of the debt. In 1563, they amounted to nearly 2 percent of the investors, and they held

---

[24] Cf. the discussion of lifeterm revenues in the preceding chapter.
[25] For the sources, cf. Appendix II, pp. 165–66.   [26] Cf. De Rosa, *Studi sugli arrendamenti.*

Investors
1563

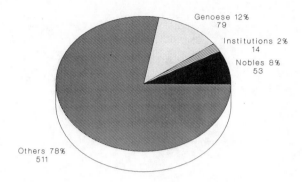

Genoese 12%
79

Institutions 2%
14

Nobles 8%
53

Others 78%
511

Total: 657

Securities
1563

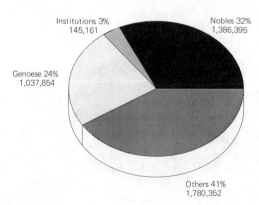

Institutions 3%
145,161

Nobles 32%
1,386,395

Genoese 24%
1,037,854

Others 41%
1,780,352

Total: 4,349,762 ducats

Figure 5.6 Investors and investments in the public debt

115

Investors
1572

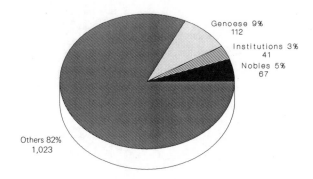

Genoese 9%
112

Institutions 3%
41

Nobles 5%
67

Others 82%
1,023

Total: 1,243

Securities
1572

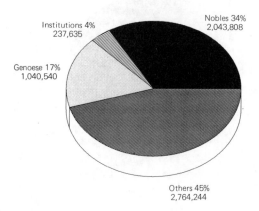

Institutions 4%
237,635

Genoese 17%
1,040,540

Nobles 34%
2,043,808

Others 45%
2,764,244

Total: 6,086,227 ducats

Investors
1596

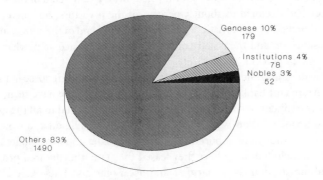

Genoese 10%
179

Institutions 4%
78

Nobles 3%
52

Others 83%
1490

Total: 1,799

Securities
1596

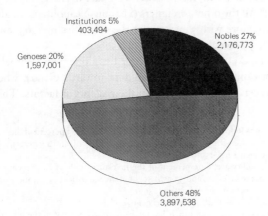

Institutions 5%
403,494

Genoese 20%
1,597,001

Nobles 27%
2,176,773

Others 48%
3,897,538

Total: 8,074,806 ducats

slightly more than 3 percent of the securities. In 1572, they were slightly more than 3 percent of the investors, with nearly 4 percent of the debt, and in 1596 they made up about 4 percent of the investors, with about 5 percent of the investments.[27]

The presence of the titled nobility in the debt, on the other hand, was quite substantial in terms of wealth if not numbers. Nobles, in fact, made up only about 8 percent of the investors in 1563, but they held nearly 32 percent of the securities. In 1572, they had declined to about 5 percent of the investors, but their share of the bonds had inched up to more than 33 percent. At the end of the series, in 1596, both their presence in, and their share of, the debt had declined somewhat, to about 3 percent and 27 percent, respectively.[28]

Also sizable and almost constant was the presence of the Genoese in the securities market. Merchant bankers from the Republic of Genoa, we have seen, were by far the most prominent businessmen in the Kingdom, involved in all the aspects of its trade and finance.[29] They were the most active grain, silk, oil and wine merchants and exporters; they were important shipping magnates and provisioners to the state fleet, which included the galleys they leased the state; they figured prominently in public administration, as tax farmers and fiscal officials. They were also the most important financiers in the Kingdom, and they supplied the lion's share of the loans raised by the Crown in sixteenth-century Naples. In short, the Genoese held a position in sixteenth-century Naples analogous to the one they captured in sixteenth-century Castile.

It is not surprising, therefore, to see that they held a good portion of the state securities and that their presence in the bond market was noteworthy throughout the century. In 1563, in fact, they made up about 12 percent of the investors, with nearly 24 percent of the securities. In 1572, they had shrunk to about 9 percent of the investors, with about 17 percent of the securities. In 1596, on the other hand, they were about 10 percent of the investors, and their share of the securities had risen to nearly 20 percent.[30] All the other foreigners (i.e. non-Neapolitans) made up instead 1 percent of the investors with 3 percent of the securities in 1563, and about 2.5 percent, with about 5 percent of the bonds in 1596.

Genoese investors, even in redeemable securities alone, represent what might be termed a "flight of capital" out of the Kingdom towards Genoa, where many of them resided and received their rentes from their agents or factors. That exodus of

---

[27] The precise figures are as follows: 2.1 percent of the investors, with 3.3 percent of the securities (1563); 3.3 percent of the investors, with 3.9 percent of the securities (1572), and 4.3 percent of the investors, with 5 percent of the securities (1596).

[28] The figures for the nobility are: 8.05 percent of the investors, with 31.87 percent of the securities (1563); 5.39 percent of the investors and 33.57 percent of the securities (1572); and 2.92 percent of the investors with 26.97 percent of the securities (1596).

[29] Cf. chapters 1 and 2, and Calabria, "Finanzieri genovesi".

[30] The figures for Genoese investors and their holdings are: 12.02 percent of the investors, with 23.86 percent of the securities (1563); 9.01 percent of the investors and 17.10 percent of the investments (1572); and 9.95 percent of the investors, with 19.78 percent of the bonds (1596).

capital towards the North highlighted the mediation of foreign merchant bankers in the Neapolitan economy, and it symbolized the South's dependent position *vis-à-vis* the Northern Italian economy.[31]

If the securities held by the Genoese, institutions and nobles were added up, it would be clear that non-noble, non-foreign, non-institutional investments – a cumbersome rendition of what many historians call "bourgeois" wealth – ranged throughout the sixteenth century from 41 to 48 percent of total capital invested in securities. But that may not be a very meaningful statistic, because nobles, foreigners and institutions alike could and indeed did invest in agriculture and business.[32] In addition, the category of "bourgeois" capital includes the city nobility of the capital, so that the figures for it ought to be revised even further downward. But even such rough and ready estimates serve to underline the relative weakness of local middle-class elements in the Kingdom.

An important category of investors is absent from Fig. 5.6, though it is certainly a basic one, for it concerns the grouping by gender. As one might expect, men dominated the securities market, and though their presence declined slightly from 1563 to 1596, they held more than two-thirds of the securities at the lowest point, 1563, and about three-quarters in 1596.[33] Men's gain was, so to speak, women's loss. In the same period, in fact, women increased their presence on the market by about 38 percent, but their share of the securities decreased by about 22 percent.[34] This change amounted to a transfer of capital from noblewomen to noblemen.[35] It is due

---

[31] The fact that a good part of the Neapolitan debt was held by foreigners represented, in the long run, a drain on the Kingdom's resources. The effect of an external debt was compounded by the fact that large amounts of Neapolitan revenues, from both taxes and loans, were spent outside the Kingdom (e.g. Milan). I thank Professor Sella for discussing these points with me.

[32] This area of economic and social history in the Kingdom, however, is still largely uncharted.

[33] Men made up 66.06 percent of the investors, with 68.89 percent of the investments in 1563; 63.31 percent of the investors with 69.34 percent of the securities in 1572, and 61.22 percent of the investors, with 73.07 percent of the securities in 1596.

[34] In 1563, in fact, women made up 15.66 percent of the investors, and held 23.29 percent of the securities. In 1572, their presence was only slightly changed (15.61 percent of the investors), but their share of the securities had declined to 20.23 percent. In 1596, they made up 21.61 percent of the investors, but they held only 18.24 percent of the securities.

[35] Women made up 33.9 percent of noble investors in 1563, with 58.4 percent of noble securities (or 809,671 ducats), but their position precipitated very quickly. In 1572, noble women were 28.4 percent of noble investors, and they held 39.2 percent of noble securities (801,713 ducats). In 1596, they were 23.1 percent of noble investors, with only 6.8 percent of noble securities (551,692 ducats). So while their presence had declined by about 30 percent, their share of the securities had fallen by about 88 percent. Noblemen, of course, showed precisely the opposite trend: from 67.3 percent of noble investors, with 38.6 percent of the noble securities (492,859 ducats) in 1563, they went to 71.7 percent of noble investors, with 59.1 percent of noble capital in 1572 (1,157,382 ducats) to 75 percent of noble investors, with 74.3 percent of noble securities (1,617,541 ducats) in 1596.

Genoese women and clerics did not play a role in the change in the position of women. Religious women were insignificant in it, and Genoese women actually showed a dramatic increase both in their presence and their investments, from 6.3 percent of Genoese investors, with 0.95 percent of the Genoese-held securities in 1563, to 7.1 percent of the Genoese investors and 2.6 percent of the Genoese securities in 1572 and 24% of the Genoese investors, with 14.7% of Genoese investments in 1596.

Table 5.1

	Women		Men	
	Investors	Securities	Investors	Securities
1563	15.55	14.89	66.16	76.45
1572	15.62	21.76	63.29	67.01
1596	21.64	19.27	61.23	71.56

to a quirk of inheritance, which by 1572 had transferred to the King of Poland securities worth 430,000 ducats which in 1563 had belonged to his mother, the late Queen of Poland.[36]

Another important aspect of the funded debt in the Kingdom concerns the distribution of investments by rankings of investors. For the sake of convenience, the bands of investors and investments for each year – 1563, 1572, 1596 – can be grouped into three basic categories: a low range, with capital investments worth up to 999 ducats, a broad "middle" range, with securities ranging from 1,000 to 9,999 ducats, and a top bracket, stretching from 10,000 to more than 100,000 ducats. Fig. 5.7 presents the data for the three years in the series. It brings to light a development that had significance for economy and society in the Kingdom and one that can provide a "key" to understanding the later sixteenth century in Naples and perhaps elsewhere as well. For all three years the figure shows a spread of investors that is very narrow at the top and very wide at the bottom, and an inverse correlation between investors and investments. The top bracket of investors always commanded more than three-fifths of the investments; the middle, a third or thereabouts; and the bottom, the one to show the most variation, from about 2 to nearly 4 percent of the securities.

---

[36] The "Polish pension" represented the interest payable on a loan for 430,000 ducats contracted by Charles V with Bona Sforza [cf. chapter 4]. If the "Polish pension" is factored out of the figures for the three years in the series, it becomes clear that between 1563 and 1596 women actually increased their presence in the bond market (by 39.2 percent) *as well as their holdings* (though only by 29.4 percent). Men, on the other hand, saw both their presence and their holdings decrease over the same time (by 7.5 percent and 6.4 percent, respectively). Table 5.1 presents the relevant percentages with the "Polish pension" factored out. The change in relative standing of women does not reflect the offensive unleashed by the Neapolitan nobility in the second half of the century against succession in the female line. In his brilliant book, *Famille et propriété*, Delille has discussed that offensive, and he has shown that the rationale for it was the nobility's determination to prevent the passage of fiefs from one clan to another. To attain its goal, the nobility pulled out all the stops. In the best of circumstances, a daughter in line to a feudal patrimony was forced to marry a cousin or an uncle. In the worst of cases, and increasingly after 1595, she might simply be excluded from her inheritance or she might be made to "sell" her fiefs and make do with a marital or even a monastic dowry. Noble inheritance was to be only patrilineal, no matter its cost in human terms. But at least in 1596 it was not (yet?) so with securities.

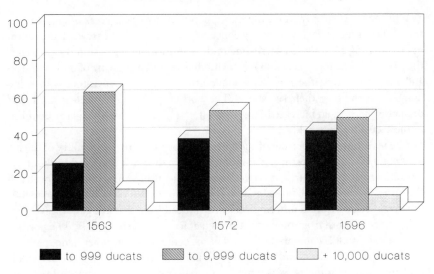

Percentages

Figure 5.7a Investors in the public debt, 1563–1572–1596

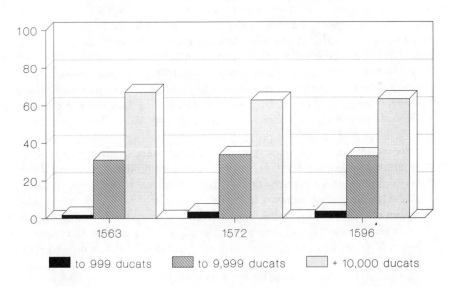

Percentages

Figure 5.7b Investments in the public debt, 1563–1572–1596

Within this basic structure, the figure points also to clear areas of change over time. The market in fact witnessed a concentration of wealth into fewer hands at the upper ranks of the spread, a narrowing middle and a widening base at the bottom of the pyramid. The top bracket, in fact, exhibited a slight narrowing of both investors and their securities; the middle, a moderate narrowing of investors with a less notable widening of their securities. The bottom grouping showed instead very dramatic changes, an increase in investors of nearly 70 percent and a near doubling in the securities they held.

The investors at the bottom of the spread, of course, were the small fry of the lot, with median capital investments amounting to 500 ducats in 1563 and to about 372 ducats in 1596. Those sums, it is true, were not inconsiderable. What was probably the lowest occupation of a freedman in the Kingdom, that of volunteer oarsman in the royal fleet, a position differing very little indeed from that of a galley slave, paid two ducats a month from the 1550s through at least the early 1570s.[37] The position of Sommaria staff accountant at the end of the century, on the other hand, paid 300 ducats a year in salary and 100 in emoluments.[38] Still, 400–500 ducats would probably not amount to a significant capital investment in sixteenth-century Naples, though, of course, in a favorable business climate, several of the lesser investors might have pooled their resources and placed them in agriculture or in business ventures, much as had been done in Italy's medieval past.

But in the later sixteenth century, meaningful capital investment would most likely have come only from the investors in the middle brackets of the spread. Here a comparison of some of the data in Figure 5.7 with some prices for agricultural properties is instructive. A ten-*moia*, or 3.3-hectare, cash crop farm (*massaria*) in Capodimonte cost Anello Bonadies, a contraband official, 1,206 ducats in 1579.[39] That amount of land, 3.3 hectares, was just about what a peasant could farm by himself, without the assistance of oxen or other animals.[40] Some no better defined "farms for agriculture" in Salerno cost Michel Francesco Alfonso 1,900 ducats in 1580, while a "territory" in Caserta cost Alexandro delli Monti about 3,000 ducats in 1582.[41]

This, of course, is not to suggest that the investors in state securities, by themselves or in cooperative ventures with others, could have (or worse, should have) become capitalist farmers, or that they could have reversed the regressive trends in the Neapolitan economy in the later sixteenth century. Indeed, given the uncertain economic climate of the late-sixteenth century, it seems that by entering the state securities market, all the investors, small, middling or large, were showing excellent business sense, or economic rationality, even if they were only trying to

---

[37] For 1550, cf. AGS. *Visitas de Italia*, leg. 348/18; for the 1570s, ASN. *Sommaria. Consulte*, vol. 3, ff. 169v–170r.   [38] AGS. *Visitas de Italia*, libro 44, f. 5v.   [39] *Ibid.*, leg. 25/1, f. 544r.
[40] According to Delille's calculations. Cf. his *Agricoltura e demografia*.
[41] AGS. *Visitas de Italia*, leg. 25/1, ff. 556v and 575v, respectively.

diversify their portfolios and even if the small fry were only imitating their betters and aspiring to become *bourgeois gentilshommes*.[42]

The data from the securities market, however, reflect, if they do not even partially explain, some of the deep changes in the Kingdom in the later sixteenth century. One telling example can give a sense of some of those changes. In 1588, the Prince of Melfi, Gian Andrea Doria, owner of vast feudal estates in Basilicata, liquidated a farming venture in his domains. He sold the cash-crop farm that had grown grain for the market, because the year's profit from the venture had amounted to a mere 6.3 percent of capital investment – and that only because Doria had not had to borrow money to finance his operations.[43] In 1596, on the other hand, Doria held securities in the public debt worth more than 77,000 ducats and paying an easy 8 percent a year.[44] It was a very different story for the Kingdom's cash-crop farmers. They could obtain credit only under the harsh *alla voce* system. In the 1580s and 1590s, as Silvio Zotta has shown, most of them were being driven into bankruptcy or peonage-like indebtedness by high interest rates and by non-existent profits, and land was being taken from cultivation and given over to grazing.

This is not at all to suggest that the growth of the government securities market and its dramatic changes in the sixteenth century were the root cause of the terrible mishaps suffered by Neapolitan agriculture and by the Neapolitan economy generally starting with the 1580s. But the evidence from the securities market shows clearly that sixteenth-century Naples, like sixteenth-century Castile, witnessed what John Elliott pointed out in a classic piece, that is, "the development of a highly elaborate credit system. . .[that tended] to lure money away from risky enterprises into safer channels, of no benefit to economic development."[45]

What might perhaps be called the "demographics" of the bond market bear this point out quite well. As we saw earlier, the investment pyramid witnessed some remarkable changes in the later sixteenth century. The base of that pyramid widened considerably, as small investors gravitated to the securities market in growing numbers already by the 1570s and even more by the end of the century. People with capital investment of less than 1,000 ducats made up about 25 percent of the investors in 1563; about 38 percent in 1572, and about 42 percent in 1596.[46] As Figure 5.8 points out, their ranks grew much more steeply than those of the others,

---

[42] To approach the whole question of capital investment in sixteenth-century Naples we need more information than we have at this point. The obvious question: "What other investments, if any, did the bondholders have?" simply cannot be answered, because we know precious little about investments in early modern Naples, by bondholders, or, for that matter, by anyone else.

[43] Zotta, p. 773.   [44] AGS. *Visitas de Italia*, libro 70, ff. 81v, 82v.

[45] J.H. Elliott, "The Decline of Spain" in Trevor Aston, ed. *Crisis in Europe 1560–1660* (London, 1965), pp. 185–86. The eighteenth-century reformer Giuseppe Maria Galanti analyzed the situation in Naples in very similar terms. Cf. A.M. Rao, *L' 'amaro della feudalità,' La devoluzione di Arnone e la questione feudale a Napoli alla fine del '700* (Naples, 1984), p. 112, n. 192.

[46] The precise figures are as shown in Table 5.2.

Table 5.2

	1563	1572	1596
Investors			
to 999 d.	25.3	38.3	42.4
to 9,999 d.	63.2	53.2	49.4
+ 10,000 d.	11.6	8.5	8.2
Securities			
to 999 d.	1.9	3.4	3.7
to 9,999 d.	31.0	33.8	32.9
+ 10,000 d.	67.1	62.8	63.3

more than quadrupling between 1563 and 1596. As one might expect, the median investment in the market declined, going from 2,000 ducats in 1563 to 1,357 ducats in 1572 and 1,124 ducats in 1596. The steepest decline, not surprisingly, was registered by the investors at the base of the pyramid, whose median investment was 500 ducats in 1563, 444 ducats in 1572 and 368 ducats in 1596. The lowest investment in 1563 amounted to 60 ducats; by 1596, it had fallen to less than two-fifths of a ducat (0.375 ducat).

Men and women, furthermore, increased their presence in the market very unevenly. As Figure 5.9 shows, while men nearly doubled their presence, women nearly quadrupled theirs between 1563 and 1596.

In 1563, 434 men and 103 women were active on the securities market in Naples. In 1572, those numbers had risen to 787 and 194, respectively, and in 1596, to 1,102 and 389.[47] Both men and women, however, decreased their presence in the middle and top brackets of the investment pyramid, and, as Figures 5.10 and 5.11 show, greatly increased it at the base.

All the changes discussed so far are indeed remarkable, and they are first and foremost a measure of the great success achieved by the Crown in its attempts at fashioning an active and dynamic securities market in the Kingdom. They are a reflection also of the proven safety and the more than competitive return guaranteed by that market already in the 1560s and 1570s, and even more clearly at the end of the century. They are, finally, a reflection of the troubled economic times, which lured more investors, and disproportionately greater numbers of the smaller and more vulnerable ones, onto the securities market. Thus those changes are a

[47] The numbers of men and women do not add up to the number of total investors because of the presence of institutions and, even more, because of a number of investors of undertermined gender (entered in the sources as "the heirs," "the creditors," or "the children" of a particular investor). This question, and the problems it presents, will be examined in a forthcoming monograph on the securities market in sixteenth-century Naples.

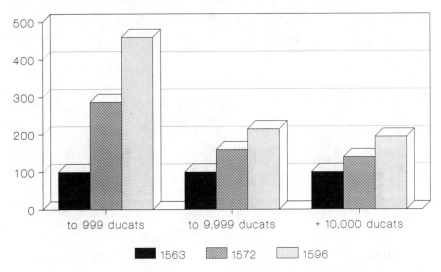

Indices of growth; 1563 = 100

Figure 5.8 Relative growth of investors in the public debt by investment brackets, 1563–1572–1596

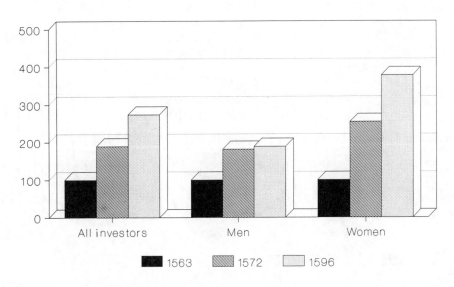

Indices of growth; 1563=100

Figure 5.9 Relative growth of investors in the public debt by gender, 1563–1572–1596

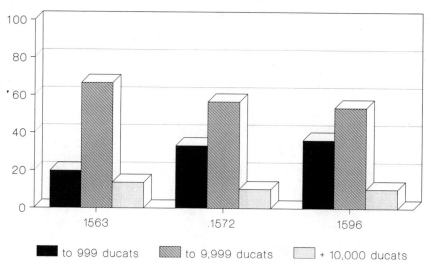

Percentages

Figure 5.10a Male investors, 1563–1572–1596

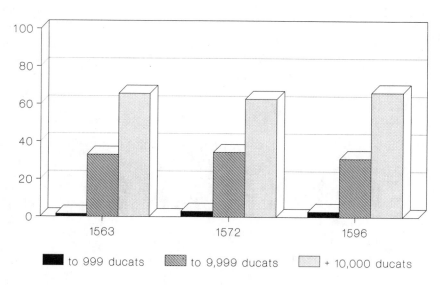

Percentages

Figure 5.10b Men's investments, 1563–1572–1596

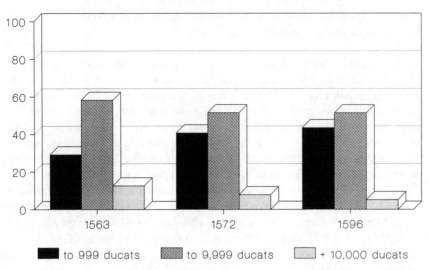

Percentages

Figure 5.11a Women investors, 1563–1572–1596

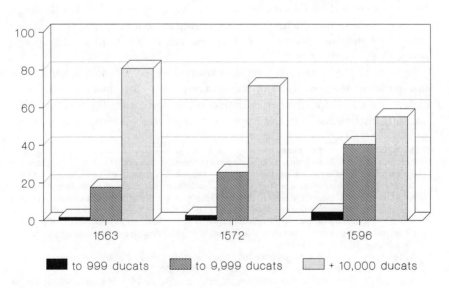

Percentages

Figure 5.11b Women's investments, 1563–1572–1596

commentary on the search for security which was a hallmark of economic and social life at the end of the sixteenth century.

In the sixteenth century, as we have seen, the Crown was able to create and greatly expand an active securities market in the Kingdom of Naples. As we have also seen, many factors helped the exchequer in Naples in its task. The relatively high rate of return it paid on its securities, of course, could only help matters, and for a long time it must have made investment in Neapolitan securities an attractive prospect indeed. But a critical element in that success was without doubt the reputation that the exchequer earned over the course of the sixteenth century as a good debtor. This is not to say that investors in the Neapolitan funded debt did not occasionally grumble, and for a variety of reasons, chief among which were the periodic forced conversions of the debt, which reduced the rate of return on securities.[48] But the seventeenth century was to bring vast changes to the world of investors and investments in the public debt in Naples, just as it brought vast changes to so many other areas of life there.[49]

From 1622 to 1626, the Crown retained a quarter of foreigners' revenues from public debt securities.[50] In 1625, it withheld one third of the revenues belonging to investors with more than 45 ducats' rent a year.[51] In 1630, it did not pay the interest instalment due on all securities in April, that is, a third of the yearly revenues belonging to state creditors. Instead, it assigned those funds on tax revenue at 7 percent a year.[52] Thus, instead of receiving the 749,814.97 ducats due them, investors were to look forward to 52,487.05 ducats' interest that their holdings would earn them over the next year. Such practices continued over the next five years, with defaults ranging from one-twentieth to one third of the interest payments due to investors.[53]

In 1636, and again in 1638, foreigners saw their rentes for the year reduced by two-thirds; in 1639, withheld in their entirety.[54] In 1640, investors who were citizens of the Kingdom received no payment on their securities for two of the three quarterly instalments, April and August; foreigners received no payment in April,

---

[48] An important one was that ordered by Philip II in the Kingdom in 1593 and entrusted to the Genoese merchant banker Antonio Belmosto. Belmosto was to reduce the interest on redeemable securities in the Kingdom to 7 percent. He was provided with 1,000,000 (Castilian) ducats, which was to assist in "repurchasing" the securities of investors who refused the lower rate. In other words, Belmosto was to return to those investors the capital they had originally invested, only to float new securities guaranteed by the same tax revenue, but at the lower rate of 7 percent or below. On 19 October 1598, in a long and detailed *consulta*, the Sommaria reported to the King on Belmosto's activities in the Kingdom over the previous two years. That document is one of the major sources used in this chapter (for the 1596 data; cf. also Appendix 1).

[49] As yet, there is no study of the public debt in seventeenth-century Naples. For some suggestive comments, cf. Villari, *La rivolta*, pp. 141–52.   [50] BNN. Ms. XI–B–39, f. 187r.

[51] *Ibid.*, f. 187v. The entry is unclear in the text; though it is unlikely, it may refer to *capital* investments below 45 ducats.   [52] *Ibid.*, ff. 190v–191v.

[53] *Ibid.*, ff. 192r–v, 193v–194v, 196v–197r. Only the money retained in 1634 and 1635 was assigned on sources of revenue, as had been the case in 1630 (but at 8 percent).

[54] *Ibid.*, ff. 197v–199r, 201r–202v.

August or December.[55] In 1641, only those investors who were citizens of the city of Naples received any payment; in 1642, no one did.[56]

The pressures of the new century thus wreaked havoc with the bond market, and the policies which in the sixteenth century had worked to attract capital and investors into Neapolitan securities were abandoned. As the demands of war in Central Europe reached a crescendo, the Crown in Naples again and again reneged on its obligations, and many of those who had trusted it with their savings reaped a harvest of bitterness and despair.[57]

[55] *Ibid.*, ff. 205r–206r.
[56] *Ibid.*, ff. 208v–209r, 212r (incomplete figures). The text refers to a retention of interest also for 1643 (f. 214v), but it does not state its import because fiscal officials and contractors had not yet presented their accounts (the document refers to 1644 as "the present year" [f. 214v]).
[57] This is no mere rhetorical flourish: cf. Villari, *La rivolta*, pp. 141–52.

Conclusion

This work has attempted to account for economic, social and fiscal change in the Kingdom of Naples from about 1450 to about 1630. It has shown that from the late sixteenth century onwards, economic, social and political forces worked together to undermine the achievements of fifteenth-century kings. By way of conclusion, it might not be amiss briefly to summarize the major themes in this work and to offer some remarks which the story of Naples in the "long sixteenth century" suggests.

As this work has shown, fiscal pressure came to serve as a powerful destabilizing force in the Kingdom. It diverted large amounts of capital into economically unproductive ventures, into shoring up Imperial power, literally from one end of Europe to the other. But it did so at certain critical points, not at all times in the period of Spanish rule. For most of the sixteenth century, in fact, government receipts in the Kingdom (and no doubt also in much of Europe) struggled barely to keep up with the price movement.

Not only that, but given the geographical imperatives of Italian history and the geo-political context of the Mediterranean in the sixteenth century,[1] there is little question that any administration in Southern Italy – Castilian, Aragonese, Italian, or even, for the sake of argument, Turkish – would have had to devote a substantial amount of resources to war and defense. The fact of the matter was that after the changes begun with, and symbolized by, the invasions of 1494, Italy was a frontier area, as it had been so often in the past, before the Spanish Empire, and as it was to be at other times in the future. That fact imposed constraints that no ruling power could avoid.

In addition, many of the items in the Kingdom's budget through at least the 1550s, or even the 1560s, served useful and constructive goals. The road policy and the construction of fortresses and watchtowers, for example, expanded or created a communications and defense network that served the Kingdom's authentic and immediate needs as it helped the cause of Monarchy.

Fiscal pressure came progressively to erode the basis of Habsburg (and Aragonese) achievements in the Kingdom only toward the end of the sixteenth century, and then most clearly and definitely in the decades through the Thirty

[1] On that context, see Braudel's *La Méditerranée*, Part III.

Years' War. As the various chapters of this work have shown, the new phase in fiscal pressure was most intense, and it came at the worst possible time. It fell upon the Kingdom precisely when the Southern Italian economy, which had been faltering ever since the 1580s, had embarked on a progressive and long-lasting downturn.

The relationship of the economy to the political process in Southern Italy in the time of Spanish domination – as one might expect, and as we saw in the course of this work – was most important. It was also intricate, and to be properly understood it had to be studied in its concreteness, with all its contradictory and *ad hoc* qualities, not with apodictic assumptions about class, status and power or about the primacy of the economic or, for that matter, of the political moment.

The tragedy of Spanish policy, of course, was precisely that it ignored that relationship between the economy and the political process, that it became much harsher and more demanding at precisely the wrong time, that it was guided so much by short-term, *ad hoc* considerations, so often simply those of bridging the gap between receipts and expenditures. That fact had important consequences for the fate of Naples, as of Castile. It lured money away from productive enterprises, specifically from agriculture, and it encouraged, if it did not help engender, parasitical tendencies in the Kingdom and the capital. It redistributed money upwards in society, sharpening inequities and injustices. In the seventeenth century, it accentuated the impact of economic crisis, and it worsened the disasters Naples endured.

Much has been written about that policy and its failures, and little should be added here, except perhaps to say that, unfortunately for the people concerned, such was and has been the logic of power and the course of empires, long before and long after the sixteenth century. But it should be added that Spanish policy, and the increasingly harsh fiscal pressure which came to represent it, wreaked havoc as well with the work of "modernization" which the "new monarchies" had undertaken in Europe and which the Kingdom of Naples had witnessed since the fifteenth century.

Beyond graphically illustrating the failures in Spanish policy, the Kingdom's experience in the time of Spanish rule serves as an eloquent commentary on the protean character of early modern "absolutism." On the one hand, Spain was able to extract massive amounts of money from the Kingdom. That fact tells of the progress of "modern," "centralized," or "absolutist" states, even though the cost of that process was enormous, and even though it set back or reversed the cause of "modernization" in the Kingdom, as in other peripheralized areas, for a long time to come.

On the other hand, the cause of "absolutism" met with severe limits in the Kingdom, as in Europe at large in the sixteenth and seventeenth centuries, from causes other than the determination to contain Islam or to roll back the tide of Protestantism. In addition to the familiar obstacles provided by geography, by the state of communications, even by the enclaves of corporate privilege, the lack of a responsible civil service undermined the cause of kings and greatly worsened the burden of taxes. Through much of the sixteenth century, Naples, like Castile,[2] was probably taxed beneath its capacity to contribute. But that was no doubt more than made up for by the rapacity and unscrupulousness of His Majesty's officials. The Spanish kings were by no means alone in having disservice done in their name, but they did little to stop it. But that too may be one of the limits to "absolutism" and part of the cost of empire.

[2] This is the intriguing suggestion made by I.A.A. Thompson for Castile in "Taxation, Military Spending and the Domestic Economy in Castile in the Later Sixteenth Century" (paper presented to the International Economic History Congress, Budapest, 1982), which I thank him for showing me.

Appendix 1

The Tables

Table 1 *Government income, 1550–1638*

	1550	1563	1574	1583	1600	1605	1616	1626	1638
Direct taxes	1,061,763	1,486,910	1,628,023	1,615,140	1,756,769	1,747,513	2,321,866	2,484,732	3,168,270
Indirect taxes	122,868	429,375	458,160	715,586	638,414	933,110	1,466,037	1,584,207	1,838,577
Foggia Sheep Customhouse	80,942	199,427	164,364	279,545	404,580	396,153	319,068	351,811	276,097
Various proceeds	64,668	65,694	93,176	86,578	148,475	123,872	192,667	163,694	174,590
Other									351,304
Total	1,330,241	2,181,406	2,343,723	2,696,849	2,948,238	3,200,648	4,299,638	4,584,444	5,808,838
Index	100	163.99	176.19	202.73	221.63	240.61	323.22	344.63	436.68

Table 2 *Direct taxes, 1550–1638*

	1550	1563	1574	1583	1600	1605	1616	1626	1638
Hearth base	642,549	710,496	734,294	723,902	818,140	796,442			
Spanish infantry (a)	204,558	224,913	232,545	229,417	259,832	252,934			
Both above entries							969,739		
Aids (b)	225,000	500,000	600,000	600,000	600,000	600,000	600,000		
Extraordinary aids (c)							300,000	50,000	
Banditry (d)		15,971	18,424	14,288	21,404	21,403	30,564		
Billeting (e)	56,988	60,740	54,888	71,253	74,264	89,580	80,952		
Roads (f)		38,336	43,074	41,465	53,590	47,425	45,290		
Towers (g)			25,348	25,039	33,075	33,075	47,997		
Reclamation (h)		10,692					27,297		
Fixed garrisons (i)							122,160		
Mint (j)							59,812		
Weights and measures (k)							36,118		
Lump entry				11,000				2,304,840	2,312,480
Other (l)							1,937	129,892	855,790
Gross total	1,129,095	1,561,148	1,708,573	1,716,364	1,860,304	1,840,859	2,321,866	2,484,732	3,168,270
Exemptions and deductions (m)	67,332	74,238	80,550	101,224	103,535	93,346			
Total	1,061,763	1,486,910	1,628,023	1,615,140	1,756,769	1,747,513	2,321,866	2,484,732	3,168,270
Index	100	140.04	153.33	152.12	165.46	164.59	218.68	234.02	298.4

Unless otherwise noted, the figures in the tables are as they appear in the sources. For the budget citations, cf. Appendix II, notes 13, 14.

(a) *Spanish infantry tax*: cf. Appendix II.
(b) *Parliamentary aids*: for 1550–54, cf. Appendix II. For 1616, the budget figure is 593,061. That is without doubt the net amount from aids, without the tax collectors' fee (6,939 ducats). The table reports the gross total, and the fee is entered as a "civil" expense in the tables in chapter 4.
(c) *Extraordinary aids*: for 1616, the amount due for the suspension of the hearth census (cf. ch. 3). For 1626, cf. Appendix II.
(d) *Banditry tax*: cf. ch. 3, note 18 and Appendix II.
(e) *Billeting tax*: cf. ch. 3, note 19 and Appendix II.
(f) *Roads tax*: cf. ch. 3, note 18 and Appendix II.
(g) *Towers tax*: *ibid.*
(h) *Reclamation tax*: cf. ch. 3, note 21.

(i) *Fixed garrisons tax*: cf. ch. 3, note 22.

(j) *Mint tax* ("Regia Zecca di Pesi et Misure del Regno"): cf. ch. 3, note 22.

(k) *Weights and measures tax* ("Portulania per terra"): *ibid.*

(l) *Other*: For 1583, the figure represents a tax of 2.5 *grana* and $\frac{4}{7}$ of a *cavallo* (or 0.0252778 ducat) imposed in 1576 ("*disgravio*") to make up for the loss of some hearth base revenue. That loss is reflected in the dip in the hearth base yield between 1574 and 1583. It was reportedly due to the fact that some lands, which in 1560 had been assessed a higher number of hearths than they actually had, were relieved of those hearths in 1576. But to make up for that loss, the *disgravio* tax was imposed on all hearths until 1590 (BNN. Ms. xi–b–39, ff. 6v–7r; ASN. *Archivi Privati. Giudice–Caracciolo*, F. 33, ff. 271v–272r). In effect, then, the sum calculated on the basis of the 1560 census continued to be levied.

For 1616, the budget (f. 1r) reports the entry listed in the table "For the building of the Fortress of Barletta".

(m) *Exemptions and deductions*: As the terms suggest, these were remissions from any direct tax, especially the hearth base tax. They could involve partial or full immunity, for a specific time or indefinitely. They could be granted to individuals or towns, as reward for services rendered or loyalty shown, though often they were motivated by the towns' poverty.

In their small way, exemptions and deductions are both instructive and suggestive: they show that, at least in the sixteenth century, some attention was paid to the towns' inability to shoulder the entire tax burden. But they point as well to the corporate nature of early modern fiscal systems, with their keen regard for privilege and particularism.

In 1574, for example, fifty-two localities in nine provinces, for a total of 27,336 hearths, enjoyed perpetual immunity, amounting to 41,306.42 ducats, from "said ordinary fiscal payments [the hearth base tax] in virtue of their privileges, confirmed by the Most Serene Kings of the House of Aragon and by the Imperial Majesty of blessed memory" (ASN. *Sommaria. Consulte*, vol. 4, f. 175v). In the same year, thirty-four localities in five provinces, for a total of 11,434 hearths, enjoyed perpetual exemptions from the 48 grana tax, amounting to 5,488.12 ducats, "by virtue of their privileges, and because some are church or garrison lands, which always have billets, and others are islands in the sea, and they are poor" (*ibid.*, f. 189v). Five localities in two provinces, for a total of 2,286 hearths, instead, enjoyed exemptions from the same tax, amounting to 1,097.28 ducats, for a specific time only. Trani, in Terra di Bari, for example, had been granted a fifteen-year exemption, which was renewed in 1571, because of "the poverty of said city, and the disasters it has suffered in past years." Civitella del Tronto and three other localities, on the other hand, were exempt for forty years beginning in 1557 because of their "fealty and services rendered at the time of the invasion of the Kingdom by the French in 1557" (*ibid.*, f. 191r).

As the table shows, exemptions and deductions involve six of the budgets and fiscal reports used in this work, that is, all except those for 1616, 1626 and 1638. In the sixteenth-century budgets, those proceeds appear in the totals column for income, and they are listed among the expenses on the direct tax in question. The texts for 1616, 1626 and 1638 make no mention of exemptions and deductions; they presumably enter net figures for all direct taxes. The 1600 budget reflects a further twist on these accounting procedures: it enters as income from the various direct taxes only net figures, but on the income side of the ledger, it has a special sub-total column that reports gross figures and subtracts exemptions. So as to have comparable totals for all budgets, exemptions and deductions are not entered as income in chapter 3 and they are not considered among expenses in chapter 4 of this work.

Table 3 *Indirect taxes, 1550–1638*

	1550	1563	1574	1583	1600	1605	1616	1626	1638
Naples customs (a)	34,814	63,400	81,628	115,025	102,500	130,000	226,300	250,000	
5 percent duty (b)									
Both above entries								108,862	289,180
Other 5 percent duty (c)									18,950
Puglia customs (d)	12,976	50,233	67,000	97,000	105,450	138,833	131,000	82,411	151,250
Silk and saffron (e)	22,675	86,070	99,333	148,013	137,500	296,000	285,050	335,220	429,182
Oil and soap (f)		82,538	68,046	104,200	76,000	112,000	125,000	132,600	114,000
Naples retail wine (g)	9,803	23,403	37,300	97,013	99,000	132,561	143,062	190,750	220,000
New wine impost		17,480	12,115	7,000	11,706	9,120			
Iron, steel, pitch (h)	16,600	26,443	34,272	64,936	39,050	42,350	43,000	46,100	43,210
Censali (i)		18,728	21,141	27,238	25,283	23,866	26,886	25,342	23,049
Playing cards (j)				4,000	11,510	14,000	16,734	15,500	11,620
Piazza Maggiore		1,080	5,553	9,390	10,280	12,585	17,750	17,555	15,657
Eggs and goats (k)			1,600	2,500	2,721	3,140	4,224	5,150	4,990
Manna forzata			354	700	911	1,200	1,354	1,421	1,270
Horses (l)			324	571					
Powder							20,250	10,773	5,058
Tuscan garrisons (m)	26,000	14,000	12,000	13,000	13,555	15,405	17,000	14,050	13,900
Export licenses (n)		46,000	15,643	25,000			102,139	49,840	51,181
Jus salmarum (o)			1,851		2,948	2,050	1,788	1,683	4,453
Salt							304,500	296,949	361,627
Other (p)									80,000
Total	122,868	429,375	458,160	715,586	638,414	933,110	1,466,037	1,584,207	1,838,577
Index	100	349.46	372.89	582.4	519.59	759.44	1193.18	1289.36	1496.38

Unless otherwise noted, the figures appear in the tables as they do in the texts; for the budget citations, cf. Appendix II, notes 13, 14. For the special problems presented by the budgets for 1550 and 1563, and the solutions adopted in this work, see Appendix II.

(a) *Naples customs*: The 1550 figure includes the amount for the lease of Naples Customs, 34,676 ducats, and the revenue from the Customhouse of Pisciotta, 138 ducats, which came to be considered with Naples Customs (BNN. Ms xi–b–39, f. 83r). The 1574 figure, similarly, includes the amount reported in the text for the Naples Customs lease, 80,853 ducats, and the revenue from the customhouses of Agropoli, Pisciotta, Santo Nicola, Agnone, Casalicchio and Policastro, or 675 ducats (c. 7v). For 1563, cf. BNN. Ms. Branc. vi–b–8, f. 25r.

(b) *5 percent duty:* for this tax, introduced in 1625, cf. BNN. Ms. XI–B–39, f. 81v and Galasso, "Contributo," pp. 59–60.

(c) *Other 5 percent duty:* for 1638, for the provinces of Calabria and Abruzzo (f. 81v).

(d) *Puglia customs:* for 1563, AGS. *Visitas de Italia,* leg. 4/5, #7.

(e) *Silk and saffron:* for 1550, cf. Appendix II, n. 33; for 1563, ASN. *Sommaria. Consulte,* vol. 2, f. 80v. The figure for 1605 is the total from the usual silk gabelle (for 15 *grana per libbra* in Calabria and 2 *reales* in the other provinces [161,400 ducats]) and for the newly imposed duty of 15 additional *grana per libbra* in the other provinces of the Kingdom, which Bianchini (p. 215) dates as starting in 1607. The figure for 1638 is the sum of the entries for the regular silk gabelle (375,182 ducats) and of the Bisignano silk gabelle.

(f) *Oil and soap:* for 1563, the budget itself (81,937.50 ducats for oil; 600 ducats for soap). The figure for oil is reported as 81,437.50 ducats in ASN. *Sommaria. Consulte,* vol. 2, f. 80r.

(g) *Naples retail wine:* for 1563 (the 1562–66 lease), BNN. Ms. Branc. VI–B–8, f. 28r; AGS. *Visitas de Italia,* leg. 349/1.

(h) *Iron, steel, pitch:* for 1563, the budget figure. That amount is reported as 25,279.66 in a fiscal report drafted in 1564. To that figure should be added 400 ducats for the iron contract for the city of Matera, which the Court redeemed from the Duke of Gravina (ASN. *Sommaria. Consulte,* vol. 2, f. 79v).

(i) *Censali:* for 1563, BNN. Ms XI–B–39, f. 163r; ASN. *Sommaria. Consulte,* vol. 2, f. 80v.

(j) *Playing cards:* this gabelle had a most disastrous history from its introduction in 1577 until 1600. It was first leased to Orazio Migliaccio from 1578 to 1580 for 15,310 ducats a year, but Migliaccio was given a discount of 10,233 ducats for his tenure. It was then leased to Donato Castiglia for four more years, for 20,500 ducats a year, but Castiglia went bankrupt and died. The third time, the gabelle was leased to Alfonso Cappuccio, from 1581 to 1585, for 14,500 ducats a year. But Cappuccio too went bankrupt; he died in jail, and the gabelle was administered by the Court ("in demanio") (AGS. *Visitas de Italia,* leg. 25/1, f. 12v).

(k) *Eggs and goats:* for 1563, ASN. *Sommaria. Consulte,* vol. 2, f. 79v. The gabelle had belonged to Gio: Bernardino Bonifacio, Marquis of Oyra, but it was taken over by the Court when the Marquis, fearing exposure for his "Lutheran heresy," had fled "to be with his peers in Geneva, where, unhappy and old, he finished his days." For this quote, and the history of the gabelle, cf. BNN. Ms XI–B–39, ff. 150r–151r; cf. also, ASN. *Sommaria. Consulte,* vol. 2, ff. 103v–104v.

(l) *Horses:* cf. BNN. Ms. XI–B–39, f. 164r; Bianchini, p. 220; Mantelli, *Burocrazia e finanze pubbliche,* pp. 239–40.

(m) *Tuscan garrisons:* for 1563, the text reports 10,000 ducats, but a different hand from Merlo's wrote "d. 14,000" in the margin. That figure is 13,500 ducats in the 1564 financial report (AGS. *Estado,* leg. 1053, f. 126).

(n) *Export licenses:* The 1550 budget enters 18,000 ducats (AGS. *Visitas de Italia,* leg. 22, leg. 348/18). The figure adopted here adds to that sum the amount entered in the alternate budget drawn up by Sommaria President Andrea Stinca (AGS. *Visitas de Italia,* leg. 23/1). To that amount, 24,000 ducats, is also added the amount from the export of saltpeter, 2,000 ducats. Export licenses were granted at the Viceroy's discretion, according to harvest yields, but the figures reported in the budgets and fiscal reports are not reliable guides to production, supply or demand because they are generally estimates.

(o) *Jus salmarum:* This was a duty on "victuals that are exported by sea from place to place and which are imported into the Kingdom" (ASN. *Sommaria. Dipendenze.* F. 25, "Relatione del Stato del Real Patrimonio di Sua Maestà del Regno di Napoli per il Consiglio di Stato" [the 1600 budget], f. 224v. The figure for 1574 includes, for the sake of convenience, the proceeds from the export of sulfur, 193 ducats (c. 17r).

(p) *Other:* for 1638, the entry is for the extraordinary tax on flour (cf. ch. 3, notes 38–39 and Appendix II, note 30).

Table 4 *Sheep customhouse tolls, 1550–1638*

	1550	1563	1574	1583	1600	1605	1616	1626	1638
Foggia customs	103,700	167,464	131,067						
Abruzzi customs	1,426	2,128	2,814						
Subtotal I	105,126	169,591	133,881	3,400	661,855				
Rental of lands (a)		57,723	47,927		107,672				
Rental of Monteserico (b)		10,113	5,780						
All other entries				642,944		686,044	342,068	375,732	503,946
Subtotal II		67,836	53,707	642,944	107,672	686,044	342,068	375,732	503,946
Total	105,126	239,427	187,588	646,344	769,527	686,044	342,068	375,732	503,946
Extraordinary				343,290	364,947				204,510
Unusual fodder	24,184	40,000							
Other fodder			23,224	23,509			23,000	23,921	23,339
Unspecified fodder						289,891			
Net total	80,942	199,427	164,364	279,545	404,580	396,153	319,068	351,811	276,097
Index	100	246.38	203.06	345.36	499.84	489.43	394.19	434.65	341.1

The figures appear in the table as they do in the texts.

(a) *Rental of lands ("terre salde")*: for information on these, cf. ASN. *Sommaria. Consulte*, vol. 1, ff. 244v–250v; vol. 2, ff. 12v–15v, 60v–66v, 223v–224v; vol. 9, ff. 61r–62r; vol. 10, ff. 57r–58r; vol. 13/1, ff. 145r–150v, 158v–169r.

(b) *Rental of Monteserico*: cf. *ibid*, vol. 8, ff. 144v–147r.

Table 5 *Various proceeds, 1550–1638*

	1550	1563	1574	1583	1600	1605	1616	1626	1638
Overdue accounts (a)	10,000	2,000	2,000	9,000	6,339	20,580			
Succession taxes (b)	16,000	10,575	17,816	18,000					
Both above entries							36,375	24,018	19,855
Offices (c)			6,000		17,675	16,700	20,190	40,107	43,001
Administration of justice (d)									
(i) Naples		16,854		18,678	14,223	12,780	25,770	23,842	22,329
(ii) Provinces		13,793		15,000	7,124		10,632	9,107	16,395
(iii) Vicaria jail rental			1,110	2,326	1,600	830	1,341	520	1,005
(iv) Total	25,000	30,647	35,110	36,004	22,947	13,610	37,743	33,469	39,729
Royal stables and lands	4,000	6,816	5,922	8,000	5,377	5,230	11,465	6,302	4,846
Intercepts, contraband (e)	2,000	4,456	2,034	2,000	4,103	5,430	7,087	8,656	16,317
Payment of debts (f)	2,458	8,958	9,322		24,189	11,567			
Various rentals, sales, duties and devolutions (g)	5,210	2,242	14,972	13,574	67,845	50,755	54,280	33,991	31,173
Other (h)							25,527	17,151	19,669
Total	64,668	65,694	93,176	86,578	148,475	123,872	192,667	163,694	174,590
Index	100	101.59	144.08	133.88	229.6	191.55	297.93	253.13	269.98

Unless otherwise noted, the figures appear in the table as they do in the texts. For the budget citations, see Appendix 11, notes 13, 14.

(a) *Overdue accounts* ("*Significatorie*"): For 1550: the Reverter–Sanchez–Monteleone text estimates these proceeds at 3,000 ducats; the Stinca text at 10,000 ducats.

(b) *Succession taxes* ("*Relevii*"): For 1550: 8,000 ducats in the Reverter–Sanchez–Monteleone budget; 10,000 ducats in the Stinca version.

(c) *Offices*: There are no entries for this rubric in the 1550 or 1563 budgets. The figure for 1574 is an estimate of the provision of offices happening to become vacant (c. 30v); the one for 1600, the amount collected from July, 1599 to July [*sic*], 1600 from the sale and grants of offices (f. 225r). For 1605, the figure includes 12,000 ducats from the sale and concession of venal offices, 4,500 for the sale of some offices of royal provision and 200 ducats from "ampliations". The figure for 1616, like that for 1626, is the average of the yield from the previous three years (1616: f. 3r; 1626: pp. 78–79); the one for 1638 is the yield for 1636 (f. 189r).

(d) *Administration of justice:* The yield from this source was spent on the spot, and generally it was allegedly insufficient to cover the cost of administration. In this regard, the 1583 text is instructive. "Tiene V. Md [the budget states] en la gran corte de la Vicaria y Audiencias del Reyno los proventos que se suelen hazer en ellas, assi por compusicion de delitos, como por penas de contumacias, y otras acusaciones de Instrumentos, y pervienen en poder de los officiales para esto deputados, los quales cada año dan cuenta en la Regia Camara de la Sumaria, de lo que han exigido, y pagado dellos. Pero de lo que rentan cada año/los dichos proventos no se puede dezir cosa ni regla cierta, mas de que a la regia corte no le queda cosa ninguna. Porque quanto à los proventos de las Audiencias, no bastan para gasto de las espesas menudas dellas, y para el pagamento de los salarios de los officiales que en ellas sirven por cumplimiento de las quales quedan cerca de quinze mill ducados cada año que se cumplen de dineros de la Thesoreria, y quanto a los proventos que se hazen en la Vicaria, suelen importar cada año cerca de Veinte mill ducados" (ff. 20r–v). The figure for 1550 is an estimate (cf. Appendix II, note 34); the one for 1583 includes the 15,000 ducats contributed by the Treasury General to this fund (cf. Appendix II, note 31). The 1563 figure is the average of yield from 1557 to 1560; the one for 1574 a "customary" yield (c. 18v).

(e) *Intercepts, contraband:* the figure for 1550 is an estimate (cf. Appendix II, note 34).

(f) *Payment of debts:* For 1550, 2,458 ducats for Monopoli's demanial redemption. For 1563, 2,958 [*sic*] ducats for said purpose and 6,000 ducats from the levy for rebuilding Aquila's fortress. For 1574, 6,270.19½ ducats for analogous payments and settlements (cc. 19v–20v), and 3,052 ducats due by Calabrian towns on account of arrears on the hearth tax (c. 29r). For 1600, a single entry for monies levied by fiscal officers for Court debtors "for several causes and reasons" (f. 225r). For 1605, similarly, an entry for "debts due the Royal Court by several people for several reasons."

(g) *Various rentals, sales, duties and devolutions:* This rubric includes a multiplicity of entries ranging from the rental fees of baronial revenues for towns like Viesti and Rossano, of mills and minor offices (like *baglive, mastrodattie*), of fields ["*Mazzone*"] and of the emoluments from offices like that of *protomedico* and *mastro portolano*. It also includes the proceeds from devolutions, reintegrations, the sale of jurisdictions, of surplus goods and of "useless [galley] slaves," as well as the revenue from some minor gabelles in the city of Naples which are considered among "various proceeds" rather than "indirect taxes" because they did not tax consumption (such as the one for forbidden games, for *buon denaro* and for *sicurtà*). Some budgets detail the component items minutely (as does the one for 1574, which lists sixty-four entries totaling 14,972 ducats [cc. 20r–29r], while others enter generic explanations, like "several debts, sale of goods and revenues that devolve to the Court," for much larger sums (30,000 ducats for 1605; 50,000 ducats for 1600).

(h) *Other:* This rubric, for the years 1616, 1626 and 1638 consists of an entry identified only as "extraordinary goods" ("beni extraordinarij," or "diversi beni et corpi extraordinarij"), collected in the provinces and in the city of Naples.

Table 6 *Government expenses, 1550–1638*

	1550	1563	1574	1583	1600	1605	1616	1626	1638
Military	624,946	815,151	1,570,078	755,391	909,454	888,962	920,421	1,079,137	
Public debt	427,349	833,144	1,221,713	1,080,731	1,483,772	2,152,850	2,314,023	2,663,384	3,270,894
Fortresses, roads, towers	89,081	163,364	238,710	175,197	189,398	190,052	204,694	207,931	
Civil	187,471	248,875	266,978	277,736	369,768	466,884	410,355	442,790	
Pensions	45,827	139,829	187,763	230,471	270,333	528,457	477,891	323,012	
Various	1,689	5,000	59,953	56,381	73,176	50,000	8,206	4,591	
Total	1,376,363	2,205,363	3,545,195	2,575,907	3,295,901	4,277,205	4,335,590	4,720,845	7,815,932
Index	100	160.23	257.58	187.15	239.46	310.76	315	342.99	567.87

Table 7 *Interest rates on government securities, 1541–1598, by data file*

Year	Cases	Mean	Median	Mode	Std. Dev.
		Lifeterm securities			
1554 (a)	82	20.0	20.0	20.0	—
1572 (b)	86	19.6	20.0	20.0	.021
1581 (c)	6	12.8	13.0	13.0	.004
1582 (d)	1	12.0	12.0	12.0	—
1598 (e)	1	8.0	8.0	8.0	—
		Redeemable securities			
1540 (f)	1	10.0	10.0	10.0	—
1541	14	10.0	10.0	10.0	.000
1542	1	9.6	9.6	9.6	—
1543	1	10.0	10.0	10.0	—
1546	5	10.5	10.5	10.5	.009
1550	5	8.0	8.0	8.0	.000
1551	57	8.2	8.0	8.0	.007
1552	11	9.2	9.0	9.0	.008
1553	3	11.7	10.0	10.0	.029
1554	16	10.0	10.0	10.0	.000
1555	86	10.2	10.0	10.0	.013
1556	53	9.9	10.0	10.0	.003
1557	92	9.4	9.0	9.0	.005
1558	110	9.9	10.0	10.0	.004
1559	102	9.4	9.0	9.0	.005
1563 (g)	867	9.2	9.0	9.0	.006
99/63 (h)	40	9.2	9.0	9.0	.009
1520 (i)	14	10.0	10.0	10.0	.000
1522	1	10.0	10.0	10.0	—
1524	7	9.9	10.0	10.0	.004
1525	2	9.5	9.5	9.0	.007
1527	6	9.0	9.0	8.0	.009
1528	3	9.7	10.0	10.0	.006
1529	3	8.3	9.0	6.0	.021
1530	6	9.7	10.0	10.0	.005
1531	3	10.0	10.0	10.0	.000
1532	4	11.7	12.2	12.5	.012
1533	2	9.1	9.1	8.3	.012
1534	2	11.2	11.2	10.0	.018
1535	4	10.0	10.0	10.0	.000
1536	2	10.0	10.0	10.0	.000
1537	7	9.7	10.0	10.0	.005
1538	4	9.7	10.0	10.0	.005
1540	2	10.0	10.0	10.0	.000
1541	6	9.2	9.5	10.0	.012
1542	5	9.6	10.0	10.0	.005
1543	3	8.7	9.0	7.0	.015
1545	3	9.7	10.0	10.0	.006

Table 7 (*cont.*)

Year	Cases	Mean	Median	Mode	Std. Dev.
1546	21	9.4	10.0	10.0	.007
1547	3	10.0	10.0	10.0	.000
1550	5	8.0	8.0	8.0	.000
1551	50	8.2	8.0	8.0	.007
1552	13	8.8	9.0	9.0	.004
1554	19	9.5	10.0	10.0	.005
1555	67	9.1	9.0	9.0	.005
1556	44	9.3	9.0	9.0	.006
1557	89	9.2	9.0	9.0	.004
1558	115	9.4	9.0	9.0	.005
1559	171	9.1	9.0	9.0	.003
1560	86	9.1	9.0	9.0	.005
1561	15	9.0	9.0	9.0	.005
1562	40	9.0	9.0	9.0	.002
1563	17	9.0	9.0	9.0	.000
1572 (j)	1,366	8.9	9.0	9.0	.005
1596 (k)	2,261	7.7	7.5	7.5	.004
1598 (l)	2,261	6.8	7.0	7.0	.004
1596 (m)	707	7.5	7.5	7.5	.003
1597 (n)	175	7.4	7.5	7.5	.004
1598 (o)	1	8.0	8.0	8.0	—
1596 (p)	707	6.8	7.0	7.0	.003
1597 (q)	175	6.7	7.0	7.0	.004
1554 (r)	6	10.0	10.0	10.0	.000
1555	3	9.7	10.0	10.0	.006
1556	39	9.7	10.0	10.0	.005
1557	103	9.4	9.0	9.0	.006
1558	136	9.9	10.0	10.0	.007
1559	209	9.3	9.0	9.0	.005
1560	109	9.0	9.0	9.0	.004
1561	31	9.2	9.0	9.0	.005
1562	52	9.1	9.0	9.0	.003
1563	60	9.0	9.0	9.0	.005
1564	66	9.0	9.0	9.0	.003
1565	86	9.1	9.0	9.0	.000
1566	40	9.0	9.0	9.0	.003
1567	81	9.1	9.0	9.0	.003
1568	29	9.3	9.0	9.0	.005
1569	48	8.8	8.5	8.5	.005
1570	44	8.8	9.0	9.0	.004
1571	22	9.0	9.0	9.0	.004
1572	171	9.0	9.0	9.0	.011
1573	161	9.0	9.0	9.0	.007
1574	140	9.3	9.0	9.0	.010
1575	135	9.1	9.0	9.0	.009

Year	Cases	Mean	Median	Mode	Std. Dev.
1576	16	8.4	8.4	9.0	.006
1577	123	8.1	8.0	8.0	.006
1578	18	8.4	8.0	8.0	.005
1579	95	8.0	8.0	8.0	.004
1580	129	8.0	8.0	8.0	.001
1581	94	8.0	8.0	8.0	.005
1582	71	8.0	8.0	8.0	.001
1583	26	8.0	8.0	8.0	.002
1584	1	10.0	10.0	10.0	—

The sources for this table, as for the study of the securities market generally, are: AGS. *Visitas de Italia*, leg. 20/8, ff. 66r–67v, 110r–112v, 134r–135v, 143r–144v, 187r–v, 189r–v, 190v (1541–1559); *ibid.*, leg. 349/1, "Carrichi sopra la Dohana de le Pecore," "Le Intrate che so vendute," "Li Pagamenti fiscali che foro venduti;" and leg. 349/3, "Notamento de li Pagamenti fiscali," (1563); *ibid.*, leg. 25/1, ff. 241r–581r (1554–1584); *ibid.*, *Secretarías Provinciales*, libro 70 (1596–98); ADPR. Scaffale 15, 40A (1572).

(a) AGS. *Visitas de Italia*, leg. 20/8, ff. 66r–67v, 110r–112v, 134r–135v, 143r–144v, 187r–v, 189r–v, 190v (1541–1559).

(b) ADPR. Scaffale 15, 40A (1572).

(c) AGS. *Visitas de Italia*, leg. 25/1, ff. 241r–581r (1554–1584).

(d) *Ibid.*

(e) AGS. *Secretarías Provinciales*, libro 70 (1596–98).

(f) AGS. *Visitas de Italia*, leg. 20/8, ff. 66r–67v, 110r–112v, 134r–135v, 143r–144v, 187r–v, 189r–v, 190v (1541–59).

(g) AGS. *Visitas de Italia*, leg. 349/1, "Carrichi sopra la Dohana de le Pecore," "Le Intrate che so vendute," "Li Pagamenti fiscali che foro venduti"; and leg. 349/3, "Notamento de li Pagamenti fiscali," (1563).

(h) *Ibid.* The entries labeled "99" bear no purchase date.

(i) *Ibid.*, for the years 1520–63. The dates indicated are those on which the securities were purchased. The interest rate indicated may be the one operative at the time of the transaction, unless, of course, it had been lowered or otherwise changed between that time and 1563, when the record was compiled.

(j) ADPR. Scaffale 15, 40A.

(k) AGS. *Secretarías Provinciales*, libro 70 (1596–98).

(l) *Ibid.*; the rates here reported are those operative after the conversion of the debt.

(m) *Ibid.*; these are pre-conversion rates for securities converted in 1596.

(n) *Ibid.*; these are pre-conversion rates for securities converted in 1597.

(o) *Ibid.*

(p) *Ibid.*; these are post-conversion rates for securities converted in 1596.

(q) *Ibid.*; these are post-conversion rates for securities converted in 1597.

(r) AGS. *Visitas de Italia*, leg. 25/1, ff. 241r–581r (1554–84).

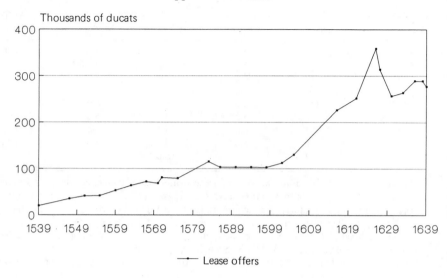

Figure I.I Gabelle lease offers: the Naples customhouse

The data for the graphs are variously drawn from the sources below and from the financial documents used in this work and cited in Appendix II, notes 13 and 14. In the list below, the dates are the earliest and the latest in the document cited; they may thus express the last year of a given lease, though that year may not necessarily be represented in the graphs.

AGS. *Estado*, leg. 1100, f. 18 (1579–1608).
AGS. *Ibid.*, leg. 1884, f. 105 (1620, 1621).
AGS. *Visitas de Italia*, leg. 4/5, n. 7, 13 (1545–65).
AGS. *Ibid.*, leg. 111/4 (1578–1610).
ASN. *Sommaria. Dipendenze*, Ff. 25, 28 (1600, 1602–03, 1616, 1627, 1630, 1633, 1636).
ASN. *Sommaria. Diversi*, Prima Numerazione, F. 51, f. 48v (Naples Customhouse, 1539).
BNN. Ms. XI–B–39, ff. 163r–v (*Censali* before 1564, 1564, 1571).
BNN. Ms. XII–B–46, pp. 915–49 (1639).
BNN. Ms. Branc. VI–B–8, ff. 25r–31v (1562–94).

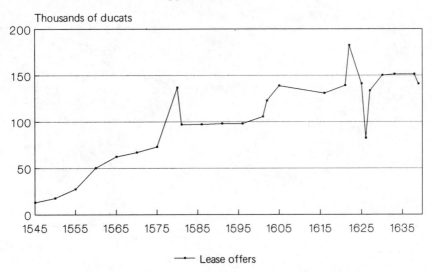

Figure I.2 Gabelle lease offers: the Puglia customhouse

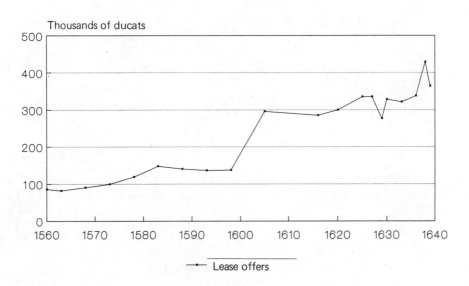

Figure I.3 Gabelle lease offers: the silk and saffron gabelle

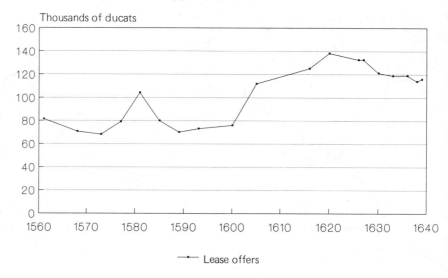

Figure 1.4 Gabelle lease offers: the oil and soap gabelle

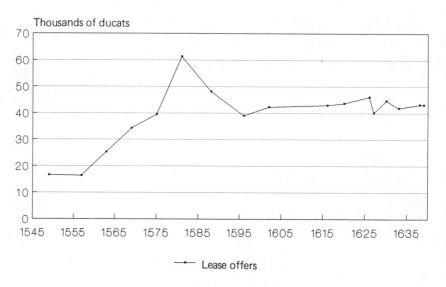

Figure 1.5 Gabelle lease offers: the iron, steel, and pitch gabelle

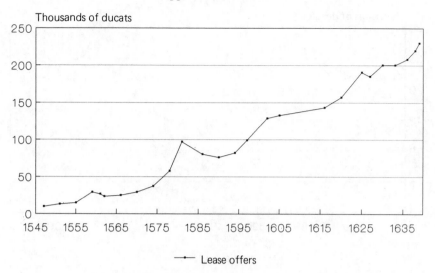

Figure 1.6 Gabelle lease offers: the retail wine gabelle, city of Naples

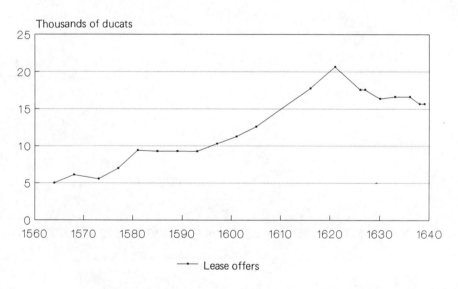

Figure 1.7 Gabelle lease offers: the gabelle of *Piazza Maggiore*

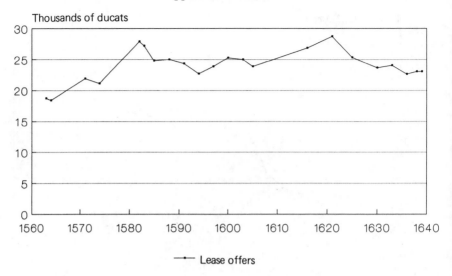

Figure 1.8 Gabelle lease offers: the gabelle of *Censali*

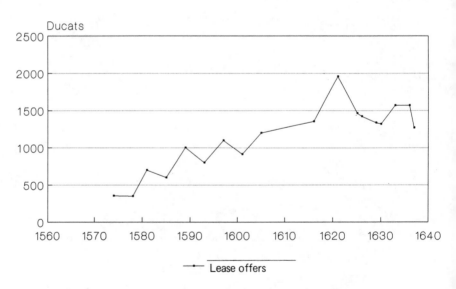

Figure 1.9 Gabelle lease offers: the gabelle of *Manna Forzata*

Appendix I: Tables

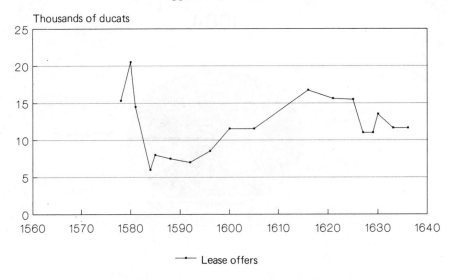

Figure I.10 Gabelle lease offers: the gabelle of playing cards

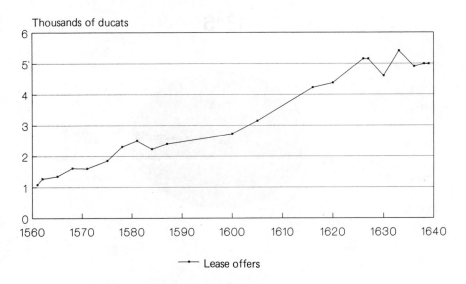

Figure I.11 Gabelle lease offers: the gabelle of eggs and goats

1584

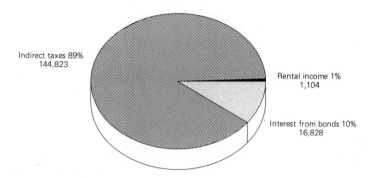

Indirect taxes 89%
144,823

Rental income 1%
1,104

Interest from bonds 10%
16,828

Total expenditures: 152,259 ducats

1616

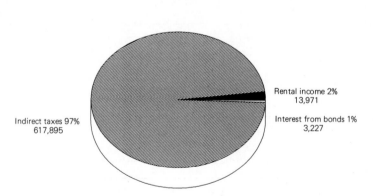

Rental income 2%
13,971

Indirect taxes 97%
617,895

Interest from bonds 1%
3,227

Total revenue: 635,093 ducats

Figure I.12 The finances of the city of Naples, 1584 and 1616: the structure of income

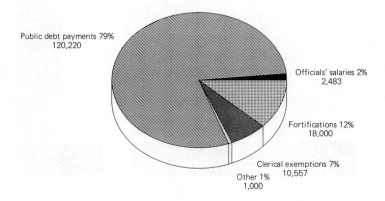

Total revenue: 162,755 ducats

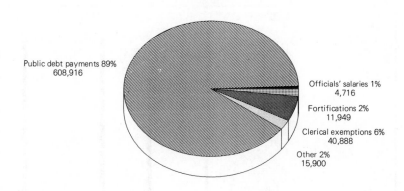

Total expenditures: 682,369 ducats

Figure 1.13 The finances of the city of Naples, 1584 and 1616: the structure of expense

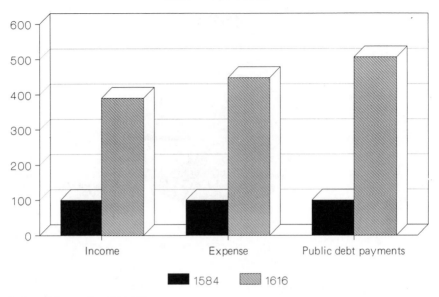

Indices of growth; 1584=100

Figure 1.14 The finances of the city of Naples, 1584 and 1616: income, expenses, and the public debt

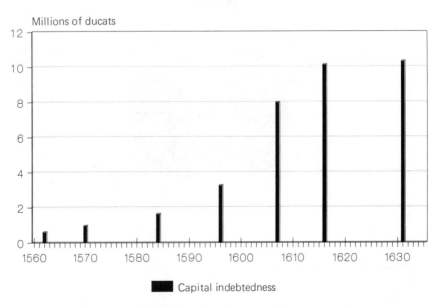

Figure 1.15 The public debt of the city of Naples, 1562–1631

Appendix I: Tables

This note is intended in part to rectify some errors in Francesco Caracciolo's treatment of the finances of the city of Naples in the later sixteenth and early seventeenth century (in *Sud, debiti e gabelle*, esp. pp. 232–41).

Caracciolo argues that between 1596 and 1616 the capital's income did not keep pace with the increase in its public debt, which "rose from more than three million ducats. . .to about. . .10,113,601 ducats" (p. 235). The city's revenues, in fact, allegedly remained more or less static, despite the fact that in the preceding twelve years (1584–96) they had allegedly risen no less than "290 percent, with income amounting to about 635,093 ducats, for the most part from gabelles, and outlay amounting to about 682,369 ducats" (p. 236). Ninety percent of expense, or 614,000 ducats, was allegedly paid to creditors as interest on the public debt. Thus, Caracciolo concludes, "At least in the twenty years after 1596, the increase of the public debt occurred without a corresponding increase in income, which remained just about unchanged" (p. 239).

Caracciolo's argument is untenable. For one thing, the figures do not add up. According to them, one would have to believe that in 1596 the public debt of the city of Naples was capitalized at no less than 20.47 percent (that is, 614,000/3,000,000), even though that same year the mean interest rate paid to state creditors did not exceed 7.7 percent for redeemable securities (cf. this appendix, "Interest Rates on Government Securities, 1541–94, by Data File"). One would also have to believe that in 1596 the city of Naples paid its creditors a higher rate of interest than even the highest ever paid by the Crown to state creditors in the Kingdom in the entire sixteenth century, that is, the 20 percent payable on lifeterm securities floated in 1554 (cf. *ibid.*). One would have to believe that in "1596" an integral part of city revenues was the sum of 80,000 ducats levied from the gabelle on fruit, a tax which, according to Capasso (*Catalogo ragionato*, pp. 52, 74), was first collected in October 1606.

The fact of the matter is that the document which Caracciolo dates "1596" is, in reality, a budget for 1616 (cf. Capasso, pp. 52–53, which admits no doubt of any kind and which does not report any figures for income and expense for 1596).

The budget Caracciolo correctly dates "1616," which is summarized in Giuseppe Coniglio's book, *Il Viceregno* (p. 234), is simply another version of the budget for the same year. The slight variations in the figures reported by Capasso and Coniglio are entirely normal in documents of such type, and should cause no surprise. In any case, it is clear that they have nothing to do, however remotely, with the trend in city finances in Naples at the end of the sixteenth century.

Thus the figures for income and expense which Caracciolo reports for 1596 are actually those for 1616. Ruggiero Romano's *Napoli: dal Viceregno al Regno. Storia economica* (Turin, 1976; the first essay, with the same title as the collection, reprinted from *Storia di Napoli*, vol. 6, pp. 537–606 [Naples, 1970]), p. 37, reports the same error in dating the 1616 text.

For the public debt figures in 1607 and 1631, cf. Capasso, pp. 51 and 53, respectively. Note that the chart detailing the growth of the public debt in the capital enters the amount "600,000 ducats" for 1562. The source for the figures states that the debt stood at "more than 600,000 ducats." The date "1570" in the same table is only approximate. For both of these points, for the actual public debt figure in 1596 and for the citations to archival materials used for all the figures in this section, cf. chapter 1, note 130.

Appendix II The sources

At the end of 1594, a curious incident occurred in the relations between Naples and Madrid. It was emblematic of the difficulties and confusion that some of the most useful sources for the history of state finance can engender, and one worth relating, for it may help illuminate and resolve them.

At that time, three budgets for 1592–93 reached the Spanish Court from Naples.[1] One was a summary document, prepared by Ferrante Fornaro, head of the Sommaria. The others were full-scale budgets drawn up, as was customary, by the Sommaria staff accountants and dated, respectively, October 1592 and April 1594. The documents were examined in the Council of Italy, and on 23 February 1595, a rather stiff royal letter containing fifty-seven headings of "doubts that have arisen. . .in the discussion and auditing of said budgets" was sent to Naples.[2]

The Sommaria's two texts, the royal letter complained, were both forecast records drawn up to estimate the forthcoming year's income and expense (*por arbitrio*). They were late, for they had reached the Court at a time when the actual record (*evacuación*, or *verifica*) for 1592–93, the forecast and actual budgets for 1593–94 and the forecast for 1594–95 should have arrived. Not only that, but the April 1594 budget was superfluous. When it was drawn up, in fact, the royal letter continued, "there was nothing to forecast, the year having passed and the income, charges and expenses being certain and done with for months. . ."[3]

Even more serious than the long delay and the gratuitous nature of that document were the errors and omissions in the other documents, the inconsistencies in their rubrics, and the glaring disparities in their entries. While, for example, the October 1592 budget reported the cash on hand in Treasury General coffers as of 1 September of that year, the April 1594 text nowhere entered that sum. The net proceeds from the Foggia Sheep Customhouse appeared as 230,000 ducats in the October 1592 document but only as 51,564 ducats in the April 1594 budget. The expenses for the maintenance and upkeep of the galley fleet, on the other hand, appeared as 261,486 ducats in the October text, as 245,406 ducats in the April budget and as 216,606 ducats in Fornaro's summary.

Similar discrepancies were to be found for the figures relating to the duty on the export of wine, the taxes on feudal succession, the proceeds from fines on

---

[1] This episode is reconstructed from the Sommaria's *consulta* of 13 October 1595 which is mentioned in the text (ASN. *Sommaria. Dipendenze*, F. 25, ff. 89r–114v).   [2] *Ibid.*, f. 89r.   [3] *Ibid.*, f. 90r.

contraband, and many other items. The October budget, furthermore, listed among its entries the yield from the sale of supplies and surplus goods as well as the profit from the minting of half-*carlini* from a shipment of 200,000 ducats sent to Naples by the Genoese bankers Centurione. The April text, on the other hand, made no mention of those items and of others as well.

The royal letter stopped short of accusing the Sommaria of deception, but it insisted on alleged mistakes and contradictions, and it demanded an item-by-item clarification of "doubts." The Sommaria provided them in a long *consulta* dated 13 October 1595,

but [it countered in its reply] Your Excellency will understand that this budget of 6 April 1594 was not the ordinary budget of income and expense that the Chamber sends each year in advance, as a forecast, to His Majesty, as it did on 22 October 1592. Rather it was intended to inform Your Excellency on the State of the Royal Patrimony in said Indiction year VI, 1593.[4]

It should be no wonder, then, the Sommaria explained, that one budget was not like the other, for they were "different things having different purposes," and no comparison was possible between the one done as a forecast in October, 1592 and the other done as a State of the Royal Patrimony in April, 1594.[5]

The incident between Naples and Madrid allows us a rare glimpse into the by-gone world of early modern accounting and finance. An important aspect of that world was the compilation of the various budgets and financial reports which helped early modern administrators monitor the finances of states. As we have seen, until the early seventeenth century, financial documents drawn up in Naples, were of three different types: forecast (*arbitrio*), actual (*verifica*) and States of the Royal Patrimony. They were indeed "different things having different purposes." The first two concerned themselves with forecasting and auditing, respectively, the movement of Treasury General funds. The third reported on "patrimonial" income and expense.

The basic difference in those records was that between net and gross income. Since a great many expenses, in the Kingdom as in other states, were met directly at the local level by the tax farmers and provincial treasurers themselves, a large part of royal revenues never reached central Treasury organs (in Naples, the Treasury General). What those organs received and administered was a fraction of total income, that is, the amount left over after expenses "assigned" on the different taxes, gabelles and duties had been met. Forecast and actual budgets (*arbitrio* and *verifica*) reported on that residue, that is, only on net income and expenses. In other words, they accounted for expenses handled by the Treasury General, not for those met by fiscal agents at the local level. States of the Royal Patrimony, by contrast, reported on all income and expense, on gross receipts and expenditures, whether handled by local officials or by the Treasury General.

---

[4] *Ibid.*, ff. 91r–v.   [5] *Ibid.*, f. 92v.

An example should suffice to make that distinction clear. From 1590 to 1594, the gabelle of Naples Customs, which included a large number of the Kingdom's customhouses, was farmed out for the substantial sum of 103,000 ducats a year.[6] In the forecast budget for 1592–93, however, no credit was entered for the Treasury General from that sum, since "nothing is left over from it, because of the expenses and assignments made upon it."[7] Because of that, the gabelle was not even mentioned in the actual budget for the same year.[8] Similarly, the expense for saltpeter and gunpowder in the October 1592 forecast was set at 10,000 ducats, since only that amount was paid by the Treasury General. But it figured as 23,200 ducats in the April State of the Patrimony, because in addition to what the Treasury General paid, 13,200 ducats were provided from the proceeds of the Puglia Customs gabelle.[9]

States of the Royal Patrimony, furthermore, generally accounted only for ordinary and extraordinary revenue and expenditures. That is, they dealt only with what was assured and generally predictable, even if variable. By contrast, forecast and actual records accounted for all monies reaching and leaving the Treasury General, regardless of their origin, destination and regularity. Together with the net yield from taxes, they would thus include the proceeds from financial transactions, such as loans, sales of surplus goods, the floating of state securities or the profit accruing from the minting of bullion or specie. Unlike States of the Royal Patrimony, they would account also for any cash on hand from the preceding fiscal year's operations and for other contingent income and expense.[10]

The Spanish auditors in 1594–95, then, had indeed confused "different things

---

[6] AGS. *Visitas de Italia*, leg. 111–4.

[7] ASN. *Sommaria. Dipendenze*, F. 25, ff. 28v–35v; "Consulta per lo bilanzo dell'introijti et exiti per arbitrio dell'anno vie Ind.s 1593," 22 October 1592, f. 29r.

[8] *Ibid.*, F. 25, ff. 79r–89r; "Consulta per la verificatione del bilanzo dell'anno vie Ind.s 1592 et 1593," 31 March 1595.

[9] For the 1592 forecast, cf. the citation in note 7, f. 32r; for the 1594 State of the Royal Patrimony, that in note 1, f. 103v.

[10] Starting in the early seventeenth century, Neapolitan budgets were of two general types, the State of the Royal Patrimony, which served much the same function as in the sixteenth century, and which can be compared, however roughly, to a forecast record, and the "Budget of Collected and Paid" ("Bilancio d'exatto et pagato"), which registered actual income and expenses. That change was traceable to the endowment in 1612 of a new Military Treasury (*Cassa Militare*) entrusted with expenses for defense, public order and other matters (cf. Galasso, "Le riforme del Conte di Lemos," pp. 201–02 for the *Cassa Militare* [which is not to be confused with the preexisting *Tesoreria Generale* or *Scrivania di Ratione*], and esp. pp. 203–06 for a discussion of budget types and the differences between them. Cf. also Muto, pp. 68–75, 91–103).

Such administrative practice was to be enduring, lasting well beyond the period of Spanish rule. Financial reports meant to assess and to forecast the exchequer's needs continued to be drawn up much as before, alongside the two types of budgets. (On Neapolitan finances and budgets in the early eighteenth century, cf. Calabria, "Per la storia della dominazione austriaca," and the archival material there cited. Other States of the Royal Patrimony and forecast reports from that period are in the Viennese archives [HHStA, *It.-Sp. Rat*, *Neapel*, *Collectanea*, vol. 19: forecast report for 1719; vol. 45: forecast report for 1721; vol. 50, "Finanzen": forecast reports for 1717, 1718, 1719, 1720, 1722, 1725; *ibid.*, *Korrespondenzen*, vol. 144: report on the Royal Patrimony for 1727; vol. 171: *consulte* on the state for the Royal Patrimony for 1716 and 1721; vol. 186: report on the state of the patrimony for 1721]).

having different purposes." What led them into confusion is unclear; it might have been the relative infrequency with which States of the Royal Patrimony were drawn up. Whereas by 1595, in fact, forecast and actual records for the movement of Treasury General funds were compiled yearly, States of the Patrimony were drawn up only on the arrival of a new Viceroy, on the accession of a new head to the Sommaria, and on no better specified "other occasions, as the Tribunal [the Sommaria] has deemed it expedient for His Majesty's service."[11]

In order to discuss global income and expense in the Kingdom, the sources should clearly be States of the Royal Patrimony or texts that are analogous to and strictly comparable with them.[12] This is the course adopted in chapters 3 and 4 of this work. The budgets for 1550, 1574, 1583, 1616 and 1626, in fact, are States of the Royal Patrimony.[13] The remaining texts (for 1563, 1600, 1605 and 1638), on the other hand, are comparable summary reports, drawn up by the Sommaria or by fiscal officials in Spain.[14]

---

[11] *Ibid.*, f. 92r. For an earlier, but misleading discussion of budget types, cf. N.F. Faraglia, "Bilancio del Reame di Napoli degli anni 1591 e 1592," *ASPN*, 1876, pp. 211–71, 394–434.

[12] For a fuller discussion of these problems and for the relevance of these cautionary remarks, see Calabria, "Per la storia della dominazione austriaca."

[13] The budget for 1549–50 was drawn up by Sommaria head Francesco Reverter with the assistance of Treasurer General Alonso Sanchez and of the Military Treasurer (*Scrivano di Ratione*), the Duke of Monteleone. (Copies of this document are to be found in AGS. *Visitas de Italia*, leg. 22 and leg. 348–18; it is printed in Coniglio, *Il Viceregno di Don Pietro di Toledo (1532–1553)* [Naples, 1984], vol. 2, pp. 571–612). The 1574 text (AGS. *Estado* 1064, f. 146) was signed by the Sommaria Presidents on 3 November 1574; the one for 1583 is part of Visitor General Guzmán's audit of Neapolitan finances and administration (AGS. *Visitas de Italia*, leg. 25–1, ff. 1r–30v; for the 1580s, cf. also the budgets and fiscal documents in AGS. *Estado*, leg. 1099, f. 70 and BNM. Ms. 2659, ff. 97r–119r [1585], 128r–144v [1586]. For records from the 1570s and 1590s, cf. also BNM. Ms. 2659, ff. 31r–37v [1572] and ff. 49r–93v [1599]). The 1616 text is a "Bilancio di como stà Il Real Patrimonio di questo Regno," ordered by the Viceroy and signed by the Sommaria Presidents on 3 November 1616 (ASN. *Sommaria. Dipendenze*, F. 25). The budget for 1626, a "Bilancio del anno 1626 del stato del real patrimonio per l'intrate et pesi tiene per anno in questo Regno di Napoli" (ASN. *Archivio Farnesiano*, busta 1338, 1) is published as an appendix to Galasso, "Contributo." A budget for 1629 is in BCR, Ms. 2442, ff. 180r–199r.

[14] The 1563 text (AGS. *Estado*, leg. 1046, f. 203) is a minute but succinct report (*relación, relazione*) compiled in Madrid (in Italian) by the fiscal official Gioann'Antonio Merlo and dated 18 October 1564. It is clearly the basis for six other undated and unsigned fiscal documents for the early 1560s (in Spanish; no doubt working drafts for Council meetings [*ibid.*, leg. 1046, ff. 204–6 and 216–17]), and for an undated, unsigned fiscal report in Spanish for 1564 ("Relation del Introito y exito del Patrimonio Real del Reyno de Napoles MDLXIIII" [*ibid.*, leg. 1053, f. 126]).

The document for 1600 (ASN. *Sommaria. Dipendenze*, F. 25, ff. 221v–233r) is a "Relatione del Stato del Real Patrimonio di Sua Maestà del Regno di Napoli per il Consiglio di Stato," a Sommaria *consulta* dated 9 June 1601.

The 1605 report is a "Sumario del Introito y exito de las rentas del Reyno de Napoles con los cargos segun el Bilanzo hecho por el año 3e Indictionis desde lo de 7bre 604 hasta 605, añadido lo que despues han creçido las rentas y los cargos," compiled in Naples by the Sommaria accountant for the Royal Patrimony Paulo di Ruggiero, on 31 October 1606 (AGS. *Estado*, leg. 1103, f. 214).

The document for 1638 is a Sommaria *consulta* informing the Viceroy on the shortfall in the Military Treasury (*Cassa Militare*), which had been set up and endowed in 1612 as part of Viceroy Count of Lemos' reforms (ASN. *Sommaria. Consulte*, vol. 41, ff. 170r–189v; 21 April 1638). A less detailed State of the Royal Patrimony, for 1639, is in BNN. Ms. XII–B–46, pp. 915–49.

Even those texts, however, present some problems, which must be pointed out or, when possible, resolved through adjustments to their figures. In any case, they ought to made clear to the reader. The problems those sources present are twofold. The first set concerns the fact that the 1638 text provides reliable and detailed figures for income, but not for expenses. The document, in fact, was drawn up to report to the Viceroy on the state of the endowment for the Military Treasury which had been set up early in the seventeenth century by the Viceroy Count of Lemos.[15] The document thus comments on the shortfall to endowment allocations established more than twenty-five years before 1638. It is possible to obtain from the text figures for income, for total expenses and for the public debt (the latter, because the sums payable are entered on the various sources of income and they figure in the deficit of each of those sources). But it would be foolhardy to speculate on the allocation of other expenses, even such critical ones as those for the military.

The second set of problems revolves around the fact that even some States of the Patrimony do not account for a number of taxes. That happened for a variety of reasons, generally because the taxes in question were not "ordinary," or because they had their own administration, separate from other funds, or for other reasons. In most cases, the sums in question can be obtained or calculated from contemporary sources; in a few others, they must be estimated. In either case, there is little reason to doubt the accuracy of the figures adopted in this work.

The most important adjustments to the figures in chapters 3 and 4 concern four sets of taxes. First, the levy for the pay of the Spanish infantry (the 48 *grana* per hearth tax), which is mentioned, but not calculated, in the 1550 text. Second, parliamentary aids, which are not entered in the budgets for 1550, 1563 and 1574 and which are not accounted for in full in the budget for 1626. Third, the taxes for the repression of banditry, the billeting of soldiers, the building and repair of roads and the construction and manning of watchtowers along the coasts, which do not figure consistently in the records before 1616.[16] Fourth, the extraordinary taxes levied from the 1620s to the 1640s, which are not accounted for in the texts for 1626 and 1638, precisely because they were "extraordinary."

The case of the tax for the pay of the Spanish infantry in 1550 is perhaps the easiest of all to resolve. The budget states that the proceeds from the 48 *grana* tax were not entered because special accounts of the use of those monies were presented to the Sommaria by the *Scrivania di Ratione*, the then Military Treasury. That, as an auditor suggested, may have been a lame excuse.[17] But the procedure actually conforms to that used for parliamentary aids through 1574 and for other taxes well into the seventeenth century. In any case, the amount of the levy can be easily determined. As the budget itself makes clear, there were 426,162 hearths in the

---

[15] Cf. above, note 10.

[16] The 1600 report is the only one of those texts to list all four entries. The 1583 Visitor's report discusses them at the end, as in an appendix; the budgets for 1550 and 1574 account for none of them, and the one for 1563 enters only partial figures for some of them.   [17] AGS. *Visitas de Italia*, leg. 23/1.

Kingdom in 1549–50. The 48 *grana* tax therefore amounted to 204,557.76 ducats, the figure entered in the tables in chapter 3. The proceeds of that tax, moreover, were used only to pay the Spanish troops stationed in Naples.[18] In the tables for expenditure, in chapter 4, then, the same figure appears in the category of "military expenses" for 1550.

Parliamentary aids involved the most substantial sums of all adjustments necessary, but they, too, are easily determined, as are the purposes they served. Before 1566, when they became a permanent fixture of fiscal administration in the Kingdom, set at 1,200,000 ducats every two years, those aids would be accounted for in special reports.[19] Such documents identify the amounts for 1550 and 1563 as, respectively, 225,000 and 500,000 ducats.[20] For 1574, on the other hand, the total should be the normal (i.e. post-1566) yearly amount, or 600,000 ducats. From the special reports it is clear that the revenues from aids were used for most pressing needs, generally military expenditures and the repayment of debts.[21] That fact is

[18] AGS. *Secretarías Provinciales*, leg. 1, f. 124; Bianchini, p. 206; Mantelli, *Burocrazia e finanze pubbliche*, p. 225.

[19] As, for example, in AGS. *Estado*, leg. 1042, f. 120 (for 1549) and f. 135 (for 1552).

[20] The amount entered for 1550 is the amount due that year from the grant of 600,000 ducats made in August 1549. Those aids were payable in eight instalments (to December 1551). Cf. AGS. *Estado*, leg. 1042, f. 120 (also printed in Coniglio, *Il Viceregno di Don Pietro di Toledo (1532–53)*, vol. 2, pp. 634–41).

    Similarly, the amount entered for 1563 is the amount due that year from the grant of 1,000,000 ducats made in 1562 and payable in two instalments (AGS. *Estado*, leg. 1053, f. 126; for the amount, cf. also Winspeare, p. 189).

[21] The aids for 1549–51 were spent in almost equal amounts for those purposes: 51.05 percent for military expenses and 48.95 percent for payments on the floating public debt (AGS. *Estado*, leg. 1042, f. 120; the document reports on expenses for 566,988 of the 600,000 ducats paid from August 1549 to December 1551).

    The aids for 1562–63 were accounted for as part of the larger sum granted from 1559 to 1563 (AGS. *Estado*, leg. 1053, f. 126: the report lists expenses for 2,244,898.40 ducats on the grant of 2,200,000 ducats [*sic*]. Of that sum, slightly over 53 percent, or almost 1,200,000 ducats, was spent for military purposes, while nearly 35 percent, or about 780,000 ducats, went for various payments on both the floating and the consolidated public debt. About 10 percent of the total, almost 230,000 ducats, was paid for "civil" purposes, but over half that sum, or 150,000 ducats, was taken up by the cost of the 1560 census. Various pensioners received 32,500 ducats, or about 1.5 percent of the total.

    A larger portion of the aids for 1574 seem to have been spent for payments on the public debt than was the case with the other two grants. (The budget does not calculate the levy from parliamentary aids with income, but it lists the expenses met with those proceeds in a brief report at the end. It reports on the allocation of two of the quarterly instalments of the 1574–75 grant). Of the 400,000 ducats to be received in the Christmas 1574 and Easter 1575 instalments, nearly 300,000 ducats were mortgaged as part payment for two loans, one for 100,000 ducats, contracted in Naples, at 13 percent, the other for 125,000 gold ducats, contracted in Spain, at 8 percent, with Luciano Centurione and company. The sums due to merchant bankers for short-term loans and representing, therefore, payments on the floating public debt, totaled about 74 percent of the total levy from the two instalments. They took up 83 percent of the Christmas instalment and about 66 percent of the Easter one.

    In the tables and figures in this work, the amount for aids for 1550, 1563 and 1574 has been distributed equally among military and public debt expenses, after the 1.5 percent deductions to cover the collectors' commissions, which have been added to civil expenses. This has seemed the best course because of the distribution of those aids for 1549–51 and because in 1574 a substantial amount of the sum due to the bankers no doubt represented advances used in military expenses.

reflected in the tables in chapter 4, which report also, for 1626, an extra-budgetary parliamentary grant for 50,000.[22]

The proceeds from taxes for the repression of banditry, the billeting of soldiers, the repair of roads and the building and upkeep of fortresses involved substantially lower sums than parliamentary aids or the 48 *grana* tax. Like aids, they do not appear consistently in sixteenth-century budgets and must be calculated for 1550, 1563 and 1574.[23] The inconsistency in accounting for these taxes was most probably due to the fact that they were administered apart from other monies. The billeting tax, for example, was handled by the Treasury General, where a special account (*cassa degli*

[22] The sum due in 1626 was part of a special grant of 150,000 ducats paid by the baronage from 1 May 1625 to 30 April 1626 (BNN. Ms. xi–b–39, f. 187v). That sum has been allocated in the tables and figures in this work like the proceeds from parliamentary aids in 1550, 1563 and 1574.

[23] For 1583, they are reported in the budget itself, though they appear separately, at the end of the text (AGS. *Visitas de Italia*, leg. 25–1, ff. 29r–30r). Those amounts are reported in the figures and charts for direct taxes in chapter 3 and in the appropriate expense categories in chapter 4 (e.g. "Civil" for the repression of banditry, a police measure; "Military" for the billeting tax; "Fortresses, roads and towers" for the road and tower taxes).

The tax for the repression of banditry appears in the text for 1563 as 15,971 ducats, but not in the one for 1574, when it most likely amounted to 18,424 ducats. That amount is reported in BNN. Ms xi–b–39, f. 21r, and in the figures in chapters 3 and 4. (Since that tax was first imposed in July 1550, it is not reported in the 1550 budget, and no amount for it is added to the amounts for that year.)

The tax for the billeting of soldiers does not appear in the 1550 and the 1574 texts, and an unlikely total is reported in the 1563 text. The proper amounts are: 56,988 for 1550; 60,740 for 1563; and 54,888 for 1574. (The amounts are calculated from ASN. *Sommaria. Consulte*, vol. 5: 126,640 hearths assessed at 45 *grana* per hearth in 1550 [f. 72v] and 176,698 hearths assessed at 31 *grana* and one and one-half *cavallo* per hearth, or 0.31063 ducats per hearth in 1574 [f. 74v]. The amount reported in the 1563 budget is 12,156 ducats, and it is entered as "Per l'allogiamento della gente d'armi per le sei compagnie di lombardia." This is no doubt only a partial sum: the same Sommaria *consulta*, in fact, states that from 1559 to 1567 168,722 of the Kingdom's hearths were subject to the tax, at 36 *grana* per hearth [f. 73v]. The tax thus raised not 12,156, but 60,739.92, ducats. (On the billeting tax generally, in addition to the *consulta* just cited, ff. 71v–76v, cf. BNN. xi–b–39, ff. 10r–19v, and ASN. *Archivi Privati. Giudice–Caracciolo*, F. 33, ff. 299r–300r).

The road tax was introduced in June 1559 and applied initially to six provinces. Shortly thereafter, it was extended to one additional province; in August 1560, to four more, and thereafter to the last remaining province. Assuming that all provinces were assessed for the tax in 1563, the proceeds of the road tax would have amounted to 42,353.01 ducats if the tax applied to the number of hearths reported in the 1563 text, or 470,589. Because a number of hearths were exempted from this tax, as from others, it seems wiser to estimate more conservatively and use a lower figure for hearths, like the total of 425,959 reported by a more detailed budget from the same period (IVdDJ, envio 80/579). That number would set the proceeds of the road tax at 38,336 ducats, the amount used in the figures and graphs in chapters 3 and 4. For 1574, the amount used in this work, 43,074 ducats, is that reported in BNN. Ms. xi–b–39, f. 27v; it is only 790.02 ducats below the total obtained by using the number of hearths listed in the 1574 budget, or 487,378.

A tax for the construction of fortresses and watchtowers was first levied in the Kingdom in 1553; it was revised and updated in 1563, 1567, and 1593 (BNN. Ms xi–b–39, f. 23r). It was not, however, regularly assessed or levied, nor was it very successful in terms of actual yield. (On this point, see the interesting article by Onofrio Pasanisi, "La costruzione generale delle torri maritime ordinata dalla R. Corte di Napoli nel secolo xvi," *Studi di storia napoletana in onore di Michelangelo Schipa* [Naples, 1925], pp. 423–42). Much easier to calculate is the tax for guarding the fortresses and watchtowers, which was introduced in 1566. It is not listed in the 1574 budget, but it can be entered as 25,348 ducats. (BNN. Ms xi–b–39, f. 23v).

allogiamenti) was set up for it.[24] The other three taxes, all yielding relatively smaller sums, were levied and generally paid out in their entirety by local fiscal officials, who kept special records for them and accounted for them yearly to the Sommaria.[25] The separate administration and the special accounting of each of those taxes were no doubt devices intended to guarantee their viability, that is, to provide a set amount for each allocation and to prevent the diversion of funds to other purposes.[26]

The extraordinary taxes imposed between the 1620s and the 1630s must be added to the texts for 1626 and 1638, because they do not appear in them. In the case of the budget for 1626, the sum to be added amounts to 179,892 ducats. It consists of the 50,000 ducats in aids provided by the baronage of the Kingdom, and of 129,892 ducats levied from an extraordinary tax of 4 *grana* per hearth.[27] In the case of the 1638 budget, the sum is much higher, at least 1,287,094 ducats. The adjustment has three major components. The first is the retention of interest on public debt payments, or 351,304 ducats.[28] The second is the proceeds from the levy of another extraordinary tax, for 16 *grana* per hearth per month, or 855,790 ducats.[29] The last is the amount for the flour gabelle imposed on the city of Naples in 1638, which was valued at 80,000 ducats a year.[30]

[24] Actual Treasury General budgets (*verifica*) generally include special sections, sub-budgets, so to speak, to account for the 70,000-odd ducats accruing from it. Cf. ASN. *Sommaria. Dipendenze*, F. 25, f. 127v (report on the movement of funds in the *cassa degli allogiamenti* for 1593–94, in the Treasury General's *verifica* for that year), or *ibid.*, ff. 213r–v, the *verifica* for 1596–97.

[25] The proceeds from the road tax, for example, were sent to a public bank in Naples, not the Treasury General; they were spent by order of a Viceroyal appointee "e sene dava conto in Camara a parte cossi provisto per l'istessa Camara a 27 di Maggio 1562 che li conti di questa impositione si presentassero separatamente" (BNN. Ms XI–B–39, f. 27v). Apparently, no other assignments were made on the monies from these taxes, nor were surpluses available from them.

[26] Another motive, as a Sommaria *consulta* from 1575 makes clear, may also have been that of not having the exchequer pay funds in addition to those raised from the pertinent taxes (ASN. *Sommaria. Consulte*, vol. 5, f. 54r). For an example of the Sommaria's refusal to allow money from the tower tax to be used for other needs, cf. BNN. Ms. XI–B–39, f. 23v: "si discusse [in 1576] se lo danaro di detta Impositione per la Regia Corte per alcun tempo se poteva convertire in altre necessità et dare alle terre Custodia di dette Torri et fu di parere la Camara che non si posseva fare." But this policy no doubt represented an ideal, and it changed under the pressure of need; cf., for 1626, Galasso, "Le riforme del Conte di Lemos," p. 221.

[27] For the extraordinary aids, cf. above, note 21. The entry for the tax of 4 *grana* per hearth (which is not to be confused with the one of 4 *grana* per hearth per month, or "the 48 *grana* tax"), is the amount reported in the sources as both the total for 1627 and the estimate for 1626 (*ibid.*, f. 189r).

[28] *Ibid.*, ff. 201r–v.

[29] *Ibid.*, f. 201v; cf. also ff. 197v, 199v; Coniglio, *Il Viceregno*, pp. 256, 262, 266.

[30] *Ibid.*, f. 202r. This is a problematical entry because, as chapter 3 points out, the government that year sold that gabelle to private parties for 800,000 ducats. It could be argued, therefore, that the adjustment for 1638 should include the entire 800,000 ducats, not simply the estimated yearly yield from that gabelle. The course adopted in chapter 3, that is, the adjustment of 80,000 only for the flour gabelle, probably comes closer to assessing the tax burden on the people of the Kingdom, though of course private collectors would attempt to levy as much as they thought the consumers could bear. In any case, the reader should be aware of this complication and of the fact that the government actually received 800,000 not 80,000 ducats.

A final problem to discuss here concerns some entries in the texts for 1550 and 1563.[31] The 1550 budget, as we have seen, omits from its entries the 48 *grana* tax and the revenue from parliamentary aids and from the billeting tax. Those omissions, and other problems as well, were noticed in an audit, which suggested that an alternate budget, compiled by Andrea Stinca, a Sommaria President, might be "more true."[32]

The most important items in Stinca's version relate to the figures for export licenses, the taxes for feudal succession and the amounts from overdue accounts (*significatorie*). Stinca's alternate amounts are larger than those reported in the Reverter–Sanchez–Monteleone text, and they have been adopted in the tables in chapter 3. In addition, those tables report a larger amount for the silk gabelle, and, unlike the budget, they enter that amount in the calculations.[33] They report as well estimates for the fines on contraband and for the administration of justice.[34]

The 1563 budget, on the other hand, raises some interrelated questions about the figures it reports and the very date it should bear. The budget was drawn up in Madrid in October 1564 to assess income and expenses in the Kingdom in 1560.[35] The figures it reports for several gabelles, however, strongly suggest that it should bear the date 1563, not 1560 or 1564.[36] Furthermore, in order to have a proper

---

[31] A minor problem relating to two entries in the 1583 budget can be dealt with briefly. In that text, the proceeds for export licenses are estimated at 25,000 ducats, but they are not entered in the totals for income because they are not considered "ordinary" income (AGS. *Visitas de Italia*, leg. 25/1, ff. 20r, 28r). The same is true for the proceeds from the administration of justice in Naples (18,677.53 ducats), because they were spent on the spot, and for 15,000 ducats which, the text reports, were provided from Treasury General funds to make up deficits in the expenses for the administration of justice at the provincial level (f. 20v). Those figures are instead calculated as income in chapter 3. The income from the administration of justice at the provincial level is missing from the budget and is not estimated in the figures and graphs for chapter 3.

[32] AGS. *Visitas de Italia*, leg. 23/1. A version of Stinca's text is printed in Coniglio, *Il Viceregno di Don Pietro di Toledo (1532–53)*, vol. 2, pp. 613–23.

[33] The budget estimates the amount as 20,000 ducats, but it does not calculate it among income because it was used to pay for the fortification of Cotrone, Reggio Calabria and Lipari. In chapter 3, the revenue from the silk gabelle is listed as 22,675 ducats, the average of its yield in 1547 and 1548 (ASN. *Sommaria. Arrendamenti*, F. 161/II, ff. 41v–42r (22,718.14 ducats for 1547) and F. 162, ff. 47v–48z (22,632.12 ducats for 1548). In chapter 4, that amount is entered among the expenses for castles, roads and towers.

[34] Those estimates are very conservative, and they affect a category of income that was not critical, "Various proceeds" (cf. chapter 3). For fines on contraband the estimate is for 2,000 ducats, the lowest amount for that entry in the sixteenth-century budgets. For the administration of justice, it is 25,000 ducats, or about 5,000 ducats less than the 1563 total.

[35] This is clear from the date in the budget heading and from one of the Council reports that is based on the budget (AGS. *Estado*, leg. 1046, f. 204: "Relacion de lo que el año de sesenta importaron las rentas y gastos del Reyno de Napoles").

[36] For the Silk and Saffron gabelle, the text enters 86,070 ducats, the lease total for 1560–1563. (In 1564, the lease was for 82,000 ducats). For the Oil and Soap gabelle, it reports 82,537.50 ducats, the lease total for 1559–1563. (In 1564, the Oil and Soap gabelle was administered by the Court [*in demanio*]). In addition, the text does not report an entry for the *Manna Forzata* gabelle, which was introduced in 1564. For the Naples Customs gabelle, it enters 63,400 ducats, the amount of the lease for 1563–67. (The lease from 1559–63 had been 52,450 ducats).

measure of revenues and expenses for that year, some other figures in the text must be adjusted.[37]

Such problems, and the solutions adopted in this work, would not have surprised the author of the 1563 text, Gioann'Antonio Merlo. In the conclusion to his budget, he noted that the totals he had worked out might be different from those in another fiscal report that had been examined at Court. That, he wrote, should be no cause for wonder,

because in such reports, budgets and abstracts there are always variations, even if they are done by the same person. . .especially since here we do not have the Sommaria's accounts to resolve what doubts arise from time to time.[38]

The sources used in chapter 5, on the public debt in the Kingdom in the sixteenth and seventeenth centuries, on the other hand, are a remarkable series of documents which require fewer explanations than do budgets and financial reports. They provide a very great deal of information on the funded debt and on the market in securities in Naples in the course of the later sixteenth century and make possible, for the first time, a detailed analysis of investors and investments on the securities market in the Kingdom. They register nearly 8,000 transactions for the sale of state securities in the Kingdom from 1541 to 1596, thus making for a high degree of reliability.

In addition to listing the amount of interest paid, the source of funding for the security, the rate and often the date on which the security was purchased, the documents identify the investors by their names and surnames. Occasionally, they also specify the investors' occupation or place of origin.

The sources are of two basic types, and they make up what can be called "static" and "running" data files. The static files provide information on investors and investments at three junctures in the later sixteenth century, 1563, 1572, 1596. The two "running" files, on the other hand, register the day-by-day sale of securities from 1540 to 1559 and from 1554 to 1584 respectively.

The record for 1563 consists of a series of lists of state creditors, with their

---

[37] The text reports 79,028.09 ducats for gabelles other than the Naples Customs, and it does not mention the Puglia Customs and the Naples Retail Wine gabelles. It reports 26,443 ducats for Iron, Steel and Pitch; 843 ducats for *Censali* and 300 as the net revenue for Eggs and Goats. (For the amounts adopted in this work, and the sources for them, cf. the appropriate figures and the notes for chapter 3).

In addition, the text enters as income, 43,000 ducats, the amount formerly paid the Queen of Poland as interest for her holdings in the public debt in the Kingdom. That payment, however, had been suspended only temporarily: as the 1564 fiscal report points out, 300,000 ducats in arrears had been paid the then holder of those securities, the King of Poland, from the proceeds of the parliamentary aids granted in 1559 and 1562. (AGS. *Estado*, leg. 1053, f. 126. For some of the vicissitudes of the Polish "pension," which was actually the interest paid on a loan of 430,000 made by Bona Sforza to Charles V and which was plagued by many delays in the course of its long history, cf. ASN. *Sommaria. Consulte*, vol. 1, f. 232v; vol. 4, ff. 28r–v; vol. 7, unfoliated *consulta*, 20 September 1584, and ff. 423r–425r; vol. 9, ff. 3r–12r; vol. 11, ff. 306r–307v). The amount due is not considered as income in this work, and it is included among public debt expenses in chapter 4.

[38] AGS. *Estado*, leg. 1046, f. 203.

holdings.[39] The text for 1572 is a very detailed budget for the Kingdom for that year.[40] Both those sets of documents report on the entirety of the public debt in those years. The document for 1596–98 is a Sommaria *consulta* on Philip II's last forced conversion of the funded debt, which was intended to reduce interest on state securities to 7 percent or below.[41] It provides information on nearly 80 percent of the debt, that is, on that portion of it which paid more than 7 percent. A working assumption for this study is that the structure of the debt reported in 1596–98 reflects the structure of the debt as a whole. This assumption is confirmed by statistical tests run on large sections of the data.[42]

The source for 1554–84 is a list of the day-by-day sales of securities over the course of those years.[43] The one for 1541–59, on the other hand, is a summary of Treasury General records (*cedole*); it lists those sales at biannual intervals, with some gaps for the 1540s.[44]

Since the record for 1596–98 focuses on the redeemable debt, unless otherwise noted, all figures and examples from the bond market cited in chapter 5 refer to redeemable government securities.

---

[39] AGS. *Visitas de Italia*, leg. 349/1, "Carrichi sopra la Dohana de le Pecore," "Le Intrate che so vendute," "Li Pagamenti fiscali che foro venduti;" and leg. 349/3, "Notamento de li Pagamenti fiscali."

[40] ADPR. Scaffale 15, 40A. Mantelli (*Burocrazia e finanze pubbliche*, pp. 301–31) has analyzed the figures for 1563 and 1572 (the latter, on the basis of BNM. Ms. 10292).

[41] AGS., *Secretarías Provinciales*, libro 70.

[42] A discussion of this issue, and of methodological questions generally, will be available in a full-length study of the securities market, which is being prepared for publication.

[43] AGS. *Visitas de Italia*, leg. 25/1, ff. 241r–581r.

[44] AGS. *Visitas de Italia*, leg. 20/8, ff. 66r–67v, 110r–112v, 134r–135v, 143r–144v, 187r–v, 189r–v, 190v. On the Treasury General's *cedole*, now destroyed, cf. the informative paper by Nicola Barone, "Le cedole di Tesoreria nell'Archivio di Stato di Napoli dall'anno 1460 al 1504," *ASPN*, 1884, pp. 1–34, 205–48, 387–424, 601–37; 1885, pp. 5–47.

Bibliography

I ARCHIVAL SOURCES

Archivio di Stato, Naples

Archivi Privati. Giudice–Caracciolo, F. 33.

Sommaria

Arrendamenti, Ff. 161, 161/II; 162, 166, 176, 178/II, 180, 182, 184, 185, 187, 202, 203, 204, 205, 206, 208, 209, 210, 212, 213, 219, 225, 227, 231, 233, 234, 268, 273, 276, 304, 329, 331, 338, 341, 345, 346, 360, 365, 372, 374, 396, 397, 706, 745.

Carte Reali, vol. 1.

Consulte, vols. 1, 2, 3, 4, 5, 7, 8, 9, 10, 11, 13/1, 14, 15, 23, 27, 30, 39, 41, 46, 47, 48.

Dipendenze, Ff. 25, 28.

Diversi, Prima Numerazione, Ff. 23, 51, 54. Seconda Numerazione, Ff. 136 (1584–85), 141 (1586–87).

Archivio Doria Pamphilj, Rome

Scaffale 15, 40A.

Archivo General, Simancas

Estado, legajos 1004; 1005; 1024; 1027; 1030; 1042; 1045; 1046; 1050; 1053; 1055; 1058; 1059; 1063; 1064; 1068; 1069; 1070; 1093; 1094; 1099; 1100; 1103; 1410; 1412; 1882; 1884; 3261; 3267.

Guerra Antigua, legajo 29.

Secretarías Provinciales, legajos 1, 2, 3, 6, 235; libros 69, 70, 428, 429, 478, 479, 514, 516, 634.

Visitas de Italia, legajos 4, 20, 22, 23, 24, 25, 111, 337, 345, 346, 348, 349; libros 44, 70.

Biblioteca Casanatense, Rome
Ms. 2442.

Biblioteca della Società Napoletana di Storia Patria, Naples
Ms. XXVII–C–3.

Biblioteca Nacional, Madrid
Ms. 2659.

Biblioteca Nazionale, Naples
Ms. XI–B–39; XII–B–46.
Ms. Brancacciani II–E–5; VI–B–8.

Bibliothèque Publique et Universitaire, Geneva
Collection Favre, vols. 15, 33, 50, 62.

Haus-, Hof-, und Staatsarchiv, Vienna
It.–Sp. Rat, Neapel, Collectanea, vols. 19, 45, 50; *Korrespondenzen*, vols. 144, 171, 186.

Instituto de Valencia de Don Juan, Madrid
Envío 80/247, 572, 573, 574, 579.

II PRINTED PRIMARY SOURCES

Albèri, Eugenio, ed. *Le relazioni degli ambasciatori veneti al Senato*, series 1, vol. 5 (Florence, 1861); series 2, vol. 5 (Florence, 1858).
   Relazioni degli ambasciatori veneti al Senato, series 1, vol. 1 (Florence, 1839); series 2, vol. 2 (Florence, 1841).
Barozzi, Niccolò and Berchet, Guglielmo, eds. *Le relazioni degli stati europei lette al Senato dagli ambasciatori veneziani nel secolo decimosettimo* (Venice, 1868), vol. 1: *Spagna*.
Ciasca, Raffaele, ed. *Istruzioni e relazioni degli ambasciatori genovesi* (Rome, 1951).
Coniglio, Giuseppe. *Il Viceregno di Don Pietro di Toledo (1532–53)*, vol. 2 (Naples, 1984).
"Corrispondenza tra il Nunzio di Napoli e la Corte di Roma intorno a cose di giurisdizione e di amministrazione economica e civile dall'anno 1592 sino al 1605" (in "Narrazioni e documenti sulla storia del Regno di Napoli dall'anno 1522 al 1667," edited by Francesco Palermo in *ASI*, 1846, pp. 433–69).
"Documenti che riguardano in ispecie la storia economica e finanziera del regno levati dal carteggio degli agenti del Granduca di Urbino in Napoli dall'anno 1522 sino al 1622" (in

Bibliography

"Narrazioni e documenti sulla storia del Regno di Napoli dall'anno 1522 al 1667," edited by Francesco Palermo in *ASI*, 1846, pp. 201–41).

"Documenti sulla storia economica e civile del Regno cavati dal carteggio degli agenti del Granduca di Toscana in Napoli dall'anno 1582 sino al 1648" (in "Narrazioni e documenti sulla storia del Regno di Napoli dall'anno 1522 al 1667," edited by Francesco Palermo in *ASI*, 1846, pp. 243–353).

Pidal and Miraflores, Marquises of, and Don Miguel Salva, eds. *Colección de documentos inéditos para la historia de España*, vol. 47 (Madrid, 1865).

III SECONDARY SOURCES

Abulafia, David. *The Two Italies* (Cambridge, 1977).

Afan de Rivera, Carlo. *Tavole di riduzione dei pesi e delle misure delle Due Sicile* (Naples, 1840).

Aspetti e cause della decadenza economica veneziana nel secolo XVII (Venice, 1961).

Barone, Nicola. "Le cedole di Tesoreria nell'Archivio di Stato di Napoli dall'anno 1460 al 1504," *ASPN*, 1884, pp. 1–34, 205–48, 387–424, 601–37; 1885, pp. 5–47.

Beloch, Karl Julius. "La popolazione d'Italia nei secoli sedicesimo, diciassettesimo e diciottesimo" in *Storia dell'economia italiana. Saggi di storia economica* (Turin, 1959), vol. 1, pp. 449–500.

Bevölkerungsgeschichte Italiens, vol. 1 (Berlin, 1937).

Bianchini, Lodovico. *Storia delle finanze del Regno di Napoli* (Naples, 1859).

Braudel, Fernand. *La Méditerranée et le monde méditerranéen à l'époque de Philippe II*, 2 vols. (Paris, 1966).

Buisseret, David J. "Les budgets de Henri IV," *Annales: Economies, Sociétés, Civilizations*, 1984, pp. 30–34.

Bulgarelli-Lukacs, Alessandra. Review of Caracciolo's *Sud, debiti e gabelle*, *NRS*, 1985, pp. 170–77; reprinted in 1986, pp. 646–52.

Calabria, Antonio. "Finanzieri genovesi nel Regno di Napoli nel Cinquecento," *RSI*, 1989, pp. 578–613.

"Per la storia della dominazione austriaca a Napoli, 1707–1734," *ASI*, 1981, pp. 459–77.

State Finance in the Kingdom of Naples in the Age of Philip II (Ph.D. dissertation, University of California, Berkeley, 1978).

Capasso, Bartolommeo. *Catalogo ragionato dei libri registri e scritture esistenti nella sezione antica o prima serie dell'Archivio Municipale di Napoli* (Naples, 1876).

Caracciolo, Francesco. "In margine ad un recente studio di storia del Mezzogiorno," *Clio*, 1988, pp. 283–306 (Reply to Mantelli).

"A proposito della recensione di A. Bulgarelli-Lukacs al libro di F. Caracciolo *Sud, debiti e gabelle. Gravami, potere e società nel Mezzogiorno in età moderna*," *NRS*, 1985, pp. 668–72; reprinted in 1986, pp. 653–58 (Reply to Bulgarelli-Lukacs).

Sud, debiti e gabelle. Gravami, potere e società nel Mezzogiorno in età moderna (Naples, 1983).

"Fisco e contribuenti in Calabria," *NRS*, 1963, pp. 504–38.

Carande, Ramón. *Otros siete estudios de historia de España* (Barcelona, 1978).

Carlos V y sus banqueros (Madrid, 1945–67).

Carignani, G. "Le rappresentanze e i dritti [sic] dei Parlamenti napoletani. Notizie tratte dai libri detti Praecedentiarum," *ASPN*, 1883, pp. 655–69.

Bibliography

"L'ultimo Parlamento generale del Regno di Napoli nel 1642," *ASPN*, 1883, pp. 34–57.

Castaldo, V. "I vescovi e il viceré Cardinal di Granvela (Dalle lettere esortatorie)," *Studi di storia napoletana in onore di Michelangelo Schipa* (Naples, 1926), pp. 443–57.

Castillo Pintado, Alvaro. "'Decretos' et 'medios generales' dans le système financier de la Castille. La crise de 1596," *Mélanges en l'Honneur de Fernand Braudel* (Toulouse, 1973), vol. 1, pp. 137–44.

"Dette flottante et dette consolidée en Espagne de 1557 à 1600," *Annales. Economies, Sociétes, Civilizations*, 1963, pp. 745–59.

"Los juros de Castilla. Apogeo y fin de un instrumento de crédito," *Hispania*, 1963, pp. 43–70.

Chabod, Federico. "Was There a Renaissance State?" (a translation of "Y a-t-il un état de la Renaissance?" in Heinz Lubasz, ed., *The Development of the Modern State* [New York, 1964], pp. 26–42).

Lo stato di Milano nella prima metà del secolo XVI (Rome, 1955).

Cipolla, Carlo Maria. *Storia dell'economia italiana. Saggi di storia economica* (Turin, 1959), vol. 1.

"Il declino economico dell'Italia" (a revised version of "The Decline of Italy: the case of a fully matured economy," *The Economic History Review*, 1952, pp. 178–87) in *Storia dell'economia italiana*, vol. 1, pp. 605–23.

Colapietra, Raffaele. "Vicende storiche ed ordinamento della Dogana di Foggia fino a Carlo di Borbone," *Rassegna di Politica e di Storia*, 1959, pp. 13–29.

Comparato, Vittor Ivo. *Uffici e società a Napoli (1600–1647). Aspetti dell'ideologia del magistrato nell'età moderna* (Florence, 1974).

Coniglio, Giuseppe. "Note sulla società napoletana ai tempi di Don Pietro di Toledo," *Studi in onore di R. Filangieri*, vol. 2 (Naples, 1959), pp. 345–65.

Il Viceregno di Napoli nel sec. XVII (Rome, 1955).

Il Regno di Napoli al tempo di Carlo V (Naples, 1951).

"La rivoluzione dei prezzi nella città di Napoli nei secoli XVI e XVII," *Società Italiana di Statistica*. Atti della VIII Riunione Scientifica, 1949, pp. 205–40.

"Annona e calmieri a Napoli durante la dominazione spagnuola. Osservazioni e rilievi," *ASPN*, 1940, pp. 105–53.

Croce, Benedetto. *Storia del Regno di Napoli* (Bari, 1925).

La Spagna nella vita italiana durante la Rinascenza (Bari, 1917).

Croce, Elena. "I parlamenti napoletani sotto la dominazione spagnuola," *ASPN*, 1936, pp. 341–79.

D'Agostino, Guido. *Parlamento e società nel Regno di Napoli* (Naples, 1979).

Delille, Gérard. *Famille et propriété dans le Royaume de Naples (XVe–XIX siècle* (Rome, 1985).

Agricoltura e demografia nel regno di Napoli nei secoli XVIII e XIX (Naples, 1978).

Croissance d'une société. Montesarchio et la Vallée Caudine aux XVIIe et XVIIIe siècles (Naples, 1973).

Dell'Erba, L. "La riforma monetaria angioina e il suo sviluppo storico nel Reame di Napoli," *ASPN*, 1932, pp. 195–206; 1933, pp. 5–66; 1934, pp. 39–136; 1935, pp. 46–153.

Del Treppo, Mario. "Il re e il banchiere. Strumenti e processi di razionalizzazione dello stato aragonese a Napoli" in *Spazio, società, potere nell'Italia dei Comuni* (Naples, 1986).

"Aspetti dell'attività bancaria a Napoli nel '400," paper presented to the Convegno di

Bibliography

Studi nel X Anniversario della morte di Federigo Melis (Florence, March 1984).

"Napoli e la Corona d'Aragona: appunti per un bilancio storiografico" in *Fonti e cronache italo-iberiche del basso medioevo. Prospettive di ricerca* (Florence, 1984).

De Maddalena, Aldo. *Dalla città al borgo. Avvio di una metamorfosi economica e sociale nella Lombardia spagnola* (Milan, 1982).

"I bilanci dal 1600 al 1647 di un'azienda fondiaria lombarda" in Cipolla, ed., *Storia dell'economia italiana. Saggi di storia economica* (Turin, 1959), vol. 1, pp. 557–604.

De Rosa, Luigi. *Studi sugli arrendamenti del Regno di Napoli. Aspetti della distribuzione della ricchezza mobiliare nel Mezzogiorno continentale (1649–1806)* (Naples, 1958).

"Un'operazione d'alta finanza alla fine del '500," *ASPN*, 1957, pp. 267–83.

I cambi esteri del Regno di Napoli dal 1591 al 1707 (Naples, 1955).

De Seta, Cesare. *Storia della città di Napoli dalle origini al Settecento* (Bari, 1973).

Dent, Julian. *Crisis in Finance: Crown Financiers and Society in Seventeenth-Century France* (New York, 1973).

Di Giacomo, Salvatore. *La prostituzione a Napoli nei secoli XV, XVI e XVII* (Naples, 1899; reprinted, 1968).

Dietz, Frederick C. *English Public Finance 1558–1641* (London, 1964 [New York, 1932]).

The Receipts and Issues of the Exchequer during the Reigns of James I and Charles I (Northampton, Mass., 1928).

The Exchequer in Elizabeth's Reign (Northampton, Mass., 1923).

English Government Finance 1485–1558 (London, 1964 [Urbana, 1921]).

Finances of Edward VI and Mary (Northampton, Mass., 1918).

Dockès, Pierre. *Medieval Slavery and Liberation* (Chicago, 1982; a translation of *La Libération médiévale*; [Paris, 1979]).

Domínguez Ortiz, Antonio. *Política y Hacienda de Felipe IV* (Madrid, 1960).

Elliott, John. "The Decline of Spain" in T. Aston, ed., *Crisis in Europe 1560–1660* (London, 1965).

The Revolt of the Catalans (Cambridge, 1963).

Faraglia, Nunzio Federico, *Il comune nell'Italia meridionale [1100–1806]* (Naples, 1883).

"Bilancio del Reame di Napoli degli anni 1591 e 1592," *ASPN*, 1876, pp. 211–71, 394–434.

Forster, Robert and Greene, Jack P. *Preconditions of Revolution in Early Modern Europe* (Baltimore, 1970).

Galanti, Giuseppe Maria. *Della descrizione geografica e politica delle Sicilie* (F. Assante and D. De Marco, eds. [Naples, 1969]).

Galasso, Giuseppe. *Intervista sulla storia di Napoli* (edited by Percy Allum; Bari, 1978).

Dal Comune medievale all'Unità. Linee di storia meridionale (Bari, 1971).

Economia e società nella Calabria del Cinquecento (Naples, 1967).

Mezzogiorno medievale e moderno (Turin, 1965).

"Contributo alla storia delle finanze del Regno di Napoli nella prima metà del Seicento," *Annuario dell'Istituto Storico Italiano per l'età moderna e contemporanea*, 1959, pp. 5–106.

Gasparrini, P. "Un ignorato parlamento generale napoletano del 1504 e un altro poco noto del 1507," *ASPN*, 1957, pp. 203–10).

Guéry, Alain. "Les finances de la monarchie française sous l'Ancien Régime," *Annales: Economies, Sociétés, Civilizations*, 1978, pp. 216–39.

Hobsbawm, Eric. *Bandits* (New York, 1969).

Jones, Philip. "Italy," Part II of "Medieval Agrarian Society in its Prime" in *The New Cambridge Economic History of Europe*, vol. I, 1966, pp. 340–431.

Koenigsberger, Helmut. *The Government of Sicily under Philip II of Spain. A Study in the Practice of Empire* (London, 1951).

La fiscalité et ses implications sociales en Italie et en France aux XVIIe et XVIIIe siècles (Rome, 1980).

Lapeyre, Henri. *Simon Ruiz et les "Asientos" de Philippe II* (Paris, 1953).

Lepre, Aurelio. *Storia del Mezzogiorno d'Italia*, vol. I: *La lunga durata e la crisi (1500–1656)* (Naples, 1986).

"La crisi del XVII secolo nel Mezzogiorno d'Italia," *Studi Storici*, 1981, pp. 51–77.

Terra di Lavoro nell'età moderna (Naples, 1978).

Feudi e masserie. Problemi della società meridionale nel Sei e Settecento (Naples, 1973).

Lonchay, H. "Etude sur les emprunts des souverains belges au XVIe et au XVIIe siècle," *Académie Royale de Belgique. Bulletin de la Classe des Lettres et des Sciences Morales et Politiques et de la Classe des Beaux Arts*, 1907, pp. 921–1013.

Lovett, A.W. "The Castilian Bankruptcy of 1575," *The Historical Journal*, 1980, pp. 899–911.

Luzzatto, Gino. *Breve storia economica dell'Italia medievale* (Turin, 1959).

Storia economica. L'età moderna, vol. I (Padua, 1938).

Mantelli, Roberto. "A proposito del dibattito fra Alessandra Bulgarelli e Francesco Caracciolo sul libro di quest'ultimo *Sud, debiti e gabelle. Gravami, potere e società nel Mezzogiorno in età moderna*," *NRS*, 1986, pp. 659–70.

Il pubblico impiego nell'economia del Regno di Napoli: retribuzioni, reclutamento e ricambio sociale nell'epoca spagnuola (secc. XVI–XVII) (Naples, 1986).

Burocrazia e finanze pubbliche nel Regno di Napoli (Naples, 1981).

Marino, John. *Pastoral Economics in the Kingdom of Naples* (Baltimore, 1988).

Marongiu, Antonio. "Pagine dimenticate di storia parlamentare napoletana del Cinquecento," *Studi in onore di R. Filangieri*, vol. 2 (Naples, 1959), pp. 317–27.

Mendella, Michelangelo. *Il moto napoletano del 1585 e il delitto Storace* (Naples, 1967).

Mira, Giuseppe. "Contributo per una storia dei prezzi in alcune province delle Puglie," *Società Italiana di Statistica*. Atti della IV e V Riunione Scientifica, 1942, pp. 153–73.

Musto, Dora. *La regia dogana della mena delle pecore di Puglia* (Rome, 1964).

Muto, Giovanni. *Le finanze pubbliche napoletane tra riforme e restaurazione (1520–1634)* (Naples, 1980).

Palumbo, Lorenzo. *Prezzi e salari in Terra di Bari (1530–1860)* (Bari, 1979).

Pardi, Giuseppe. *Napoli attraverso i secoli. Disegno di storia economica e demografica* (Milan, 1924).

Parker, Geoffrey. *The Army of Flanders and the Spanish Road, 1567–1659: The Logistics of Spanish Victory and Defeat in the Low Countries' War* (Cambridge, 1972).

Parker, Geoffrey and Smith, Lesley M. *The General Crisis of the Seventeenth Century* (London, 1978).

Pasanisi, Onofrio. "La costruzione generale delle torri marittime ordinata dalla R. Corte di Napoli nel secolo XVI," *Studi in onore di Michelangelo Schipa* [Naples, 1925], pp. 423–42.

Bibliography

Pepe, Gabriele. *Il Mezzogiorno d'Italia sotto gli Spagnoli. La tradizione storiografica* (Florence, 1952).

Petraccone, Claudia. *Napoli moderna e contemporanea* (Naples, 1981).

Napoli dal Cinquecento all'Ottocento. Problemi di storia demografica e sociale (Naples, 1974).

Petrocchi, Massimo. *Lo stato di Milano al novembre 1535 ed altre ricerche sulla storia dell'economia e degli ordinamenti degli Stati italiani* (Naples, 1957).

Pontieri, Ernesto. *Nei tempi grigi della storia d'Italia* (Naples, 1966).

Porchnev, Boris. *Les soulèvements populaires en France de 1623 à 1648* (Paris, 1963; a translation of *Narodnie vosstaniya vo Frantsii pered Frondoi, 1623–1648* [Moscow, 1948]).

Pullan, Brian, ed. *Crisis and Change in the Venetian Economy in the Sixteenth and Seventeenth Centuries* (London, 1968).

Rao, Anna Maria. *L' 'amaro della feudalità.' La devoluzione di Arnone e la questione feudale a Napoli alla fine del '700* (Naples, 1984).

Roberts, Michael. *The Military Revolution, 1560–1660* (Belfast, 1956).

Romano, Ruggiero, ed. "Tra XVI e XVII secolo. Una crisi economica: 1618–1622," *RSI*, 1962, pp. 480–531 (available also in the author's *L'Europa tra due crisi* [Turin, 1980], pp. 76–147 and in English translation in Geoffrey Parker and Lesley M. Smith, ed., *The General Crisis of the Seventeenth Century* [London, 1978], pp. 165–225).

Napoli: dal Viceregno al Regno. Storia economica (Turin, 1976).

"La storia economica" in *Storia d'Italia* (Ruggiero Romano and Corrado Vivanti, editors [Turin, 1974]), vol. 2: part 2, pp. 1813–1931.

I prezzi in Europa dal XIII secolo a oggi (Turin, 1967).

Ruiz Martín, Felipe. "Las finanzas españolas durante el reinado de Felipe II," *Hispania. Cuadernos de Historia*, 1968, pp. 109–73.

Lettres marchandes échangées entre Florence et Medina del Campo (Paris, 1965).

"Un expediente financiero entre 1560 y 1575. La hacienda de Felipe II y la Casa de la Contratación de Sevilla," *Moneda y Crédito*, 1965, pp. 3–58.

Ryder, Alan. *The Kingdom of Naples under Alfonso the Magnanimous: The Making of a Modern State* (Oxford, 1976).

Salmon, J.H.M. "Venality of Office and Popular Sedition in Seventeenth-Century France," *Past and Present*, 1967, pp. 21–43.

Salvati, Catello. *Misure e pesi nella documentazione storica dell'Italia del Mezzogiorno* (Naples, 1970).

Sella, Domenico. *Crisis and Continuity: the Economy of Spanish Lombardy in the Seventeenth Century* (Cambridge, Mass., 1979).

Commerci e industrie a Venezia nel secolo XVII (Venice, 1961).

Silvestri, Alfonso. "Sull'attività bancaria napoletana durante il periodo aragonese," *Bollettino dell'Archivio Storico del Banco di Napoli*, 1953, pp. 80–120.

Tenenti, Alberto. *Venezia e i corsari* (Bari, 1961).

Naufrages, corsaires et assurances maritimes à Venise (1592–1609) (Paris, 1959).

Thompson, I.A.A. "Taxation, Military Spending and the Domestic Economy in Castile in the Later Sixteenth Century," paper presented to the International Economic History Congress, Budapest, 1982.

War and Government in Habsburg Spain 1560–1620 (London, 1976).

Bibliography

Toboso Sánchez, Pilar. *La deuda pública castellana durante el Antiguo Régimen (Juros)* (Madrid, 1987).

Tracy, James. *A Financial Revolution in the Habsburg Netherlands* (Berkeley, 1985).

Ulloa, Modesto. *La hacienda real de Castilla en el reinado de Felipe II* (Madrid, 1977).

Urga, Renato. "La privativa del tabacco nel Napoletano durante il Viceregno" *Studi in onore di R. Filangieri* (Naples, 1959), vol. 2, pp. 551–72.

Villari, Rosario. *La rivolta antispagnola a Napoli. Le origini (1585–1647)* (Bari, 1967).
Mezzogiorno e contadini nell'età moderna (Bari, 1961).

Waquet, Jean-Claude. "Who Profited from the Alienation of Public Revenues in Ancien Régime Societies? Some Reflection on the Examples of France, Piedmont and Naples in the xviith and xviiith Centuries," *Journal of European Economic History*, 1982, pp. 665–73.

Winspeare, Davide. *Storia degli abusi feudali* (Naples, 1883; reprinted, Bologna, 1967).

Wolfe, Martin. *The Fiscal System of Renaissance France* (New Haven, 1972).

Zotta, Silvio. "Momenti e problemi di una crisi agraria in uno 'stato' feudale napoletano (1585–1615)," *Mélanges de l'Ecole Française de Rome*, 1978, pp. 715–96.

Zupko, Ronald E. *Italian Weights and Measures from the Middle Ages to the Nineteenth Century* (Philadelphia, 1981).

Index

Index

Cambridge Studies in Early Modern History

The Old World and the New*
J.H. ELLIOTT

The Army of Flanders and the Spanish Road, 1567–1659: The Logistics of
Spanish Victory and Defeat in the Low Countries Wars*
GEOFFREY PARKER

Gunpowder and Galleys: Changing Technology and Mediterranean Warfare at
Sea in the Sixteenth Century
JOHN FRANCIS GUILMARTIN JR

The State, War and Peace: Spanish Political Thought in the Renaissance,
1516–1559
J.A. FERNANDEZ-SANTAMARIA

Calvinist Preaching and Iconoclasm in the Netherlands, 1544–1569
PHYLLIS MACK CREW

The Kingdom of Valencia in the Seventeenth Century
JAMES CASEY

Filippo Strozzi and the Medici: Favor and Finance in Sixteenth-Century
Florence and Rome
MELISSA MERIAM BULLARD

Rouen during the Wars of Religion
PHILIP BENEDICT

Neostoicism and the Early Modern State
GERHARD OESTREICH

The Emperor and his Chancellor: A Study of the Imperial Chancellery under
Gattinara
JOHN M. HEADLEY

The Military Organisation of a Renaissance State: Venice *c.* 1400–1617
M.E. MALLETT and J.R. HALE

Prussian Society and the German Order: An Aristocratic Corporation in Crisis
c. 1410–1466
MICHAEL BURLEIGH